2nd Workshop on Natural Language Processing Techniques for Educational Applications 2015

Co-located with ACL-IJCNLP 2015

Beijing, China
31 July 2015

ISBN: 978-1-5108-0951-2

Printed from e-media with permission by:

Curran Associates, Inc.
57 Morehouse Lane
Red Hook, NY 12571

proceedings.com

Some format issues inherent in the e-media version may also appear in this print version.

Printed by Curran Associates, Inc. (2015)

For permission requests, please contact the Association for Computational Linguistics at the address below.

Association for Computational Linguistics
209 N. Eighth Street
Stroudsburg, Pennsylvania 18360

Phone: 1-570-476-8006
Fax: 1-570-476-0860

acl@aclweb.org

Additional copies of this publication are available from:

Curran Associates, Inc.
57 Morehouse Lane
Red Hook, NY 12571 USA
Phone: 845-758-0400
Fax: 845-758-2634
Email: curran@proceedings.com
Web: www.proceedings.com

ACL-IJCNLP 2015

The 53rd Annual Meeting of the Association for Computational Linguistics and the 7th International Joint Conference on Natural Language Processing

Proceedings of The 2nd Workshop on Natural Language Processing Techniques for Educational Applications

July 31, 2015
Beijing, China

Preface

Welcome to the 2nd Workshop on Natural Language Processing Techniques for Educational Applications (NLP-TEA-2), with a Shared Task on Chinese Grammatical Error Diagnosis (CGED).

The development of Natural Language Processing (NLP) has advanced to a level that affects the research landscape of many academic domains and has practical applications in many industrial sectors. On the other hand, educational environment has also been improved to impact the world society, such as the emergence of MOOCs (Massive Open Online Courses). With these trends, this workshop focuses on the NLP techniques applied to the educational environment. Research issues in this direction have gained more and more attention, examples including the activities like the workshops on Innovative Use of NLP for Building Educational Applications since 2005 and educational data mining conferences since 2008.

This is the second workshop held in the Asian area, with the first one NLP-TEA-1 being held in conjunction with the 22nd International Conference in Computer Education (ICCE 2014) from Nov. 30 to Dec. 4, 2014 in Japan. This year, we continue to promote this research line by holding the workshop in conjunction with the 2015 ACL-IJCNLP conference and also holding the second shared task on Chinese Grammatical Error Diagnosis. During this short period between the first and second workshop, we still receive 14 valid submissions for regular session, each of which was reviewed by three experts, and have 9 teams participating in the shared task, with 6 of them submitting their testing results. In total, there are 6 oral papers and 12 posters accepted. We also organize a keynote speech session from the industrial sector in this workshop.

Overall, we would like to promote this line of research and benefit the participants of the workshop and the shared task.

Workshop Chairs
Hsin-Hsi Chen, National Taiwan University
Yuen-Hsien Tseng, National Taiwan Normal University
Yuji Matsumoto, Nara Institute of Science and Technology
Lung Hsiang Wong, Nanyang Technological University

Organizers

Workshop Organizers:

Hsin-Hsi Chen, National Taiwan University
Yuen-Hsien Tseng, National Taiwan Normal University
Yuji Matsumoto, Nara Institute of Science and Technology
Lung Hsiang Wong, Nanyang Technological University

Shared Task Organizers:

Lung-Hao Lee, National Taiwan Normal University
Liang-Chih Yu, Yuan Ze University
Li-Ping Chang, National Taiwan Normal University

Program Committee:

Yuki Arase, Osaka University
Aoife Cahill, Educational Testing Services
Li-Ping Chang, National Taiwan Normal University
Mariano Felice, Cambridge University
Dongfei Feng, Google Inc.
Trude Heift, Simon Fraser University
Mamoru Komachi, Tokyo Metropolitan University
Lun-Wei Ku, Academia Sicina
Lung-Hao Lee, National Taiwan Normal University
Xiaofei Lu, Pennsylvania State University
Detmar Meurers, University of Tubingen
Ildiko Pilan, University of Gothenburg
Benno Stein, Bauhaus-University Weimar
Yukio Tono, Tokyo University of Foreign Studies
Elena Volodina, University of Gothenburg
Houfeng Wang, Peking University
Jinhua Xiong, Chinese Academy of Science
Jui-Feng Yeh, National Chiayi University
Liang-Chih Yu, Yuan Ze University
Marcos Zampieri, Saarland University
Torsten Zesch, University of Duisburg-Essen
Hui Zhang, Facebook Inc.

Table of Contents

Workshop Program

Friday, July 31, 2015

09:30–09:40 Opening Ceremony

09:40–10:30 Invited Speech

09:40–10:30 *Big Data-Based Automatic Essay Scoring Service — www.pigai.org*
Zhang Yu, Beijing Cikuu Corp.

10:30–11:00 Coffee Break

11:00–12:00 Shared Task Session

11:00–11:20 *Overview of the NLP-TEA 2015 Shared Task for Chinese Grammatical Error Diagnosis*
Lung-Hao Lee, Liang-Chih Yu and Li-Ping Chang

11:20–11:40 *Chinese Grammatical Error Diagnosis by Conditional Random Fields*
Shih-Hung Wu, Po-Lin Chen, Liang-Pu Chen, Ping-Che Yang and Ren-Dar Yang

11:40–12:00 *NTOU Chinese Grammar Checker for CGED Shared Task*
Chuan-Jie Lin and Shao-Heng Chen

12:00–14:00 Lunch

Friday, July 31, 2015 (continued)

14:00–15:30 Regular Paper Session

14:00–14:30 *Collocation Assistant for Learners of Japanese as a Second Language*
Lis Pereira and Yuji Matsumoto

14:30–15:00 *Semi-automatic Generation of Multiple-Choice Tests from Mentions of Semantic Relations*
Renlong Ai, Sebastian Krause, Walter Kasper, Feiyu Xu and Hans Uszkoreit

15:00–15:30 *Interactive Second Language Learning from News Websites*
Tao Chen, Naijia Zheng, Yue Zhao, Muthu Kumar Chandrasekaran and Min-Yen Kan

15:30–16:00 Coffee Break

16:00–17:00 Poster Session

16:00–16:05 *Bilingual Keyword Extraction and its Educational Application*
Chung-Chi Huang, Mei-Hua Chen and Ping-Che Yang

16:05–16:10 *Annotating Entailment Relations for Shortanswer Questions*
Simon Ostermann, Andrea Horbach and Manfred Pinkal

16:10–16:15 *An Automated Scoring Tool for Korean Supply-type Items Based on Semi-Supervised Learning*
Minah Cheon, Hyeong-Won Seo, Jae-Hoon Kim, Eun-Hee Noh, Kyung-Hee Sung and EunYong Lim

16:15–16:20 *A System for Generating Multiple Choice Questions: With a Novel Approach for Sentence Selection*
Mukta Majumder and Sujan Kumar Saha

16:20–16:25 *The "News Web Easy" news service as a resource for teaching and learning Japanese: An assessment of the comprehension difficulty of Japanese sentence-end expressions*
Hideki Tanaka, Tadashi Kumano and Isao Goto

16:25–16:30 *Grammatical Error Correction Considering Multi-word Expressions*
Tomoya Mizumoto, Masato Mita and Yuji Matsumoto

16:30–16:35 *Salinlahi III: An Intelligent Tutoring System for Filipino Heritage Language Learners*
Ralph Vincent Regalado, Michael Louie Boñon, Nadine Chua, Rene Rose Piñera and Shannen Rose Dela Cruz

Friday, July 31, 2015 (continued)

16:35–16:40 *Using Finite State Transducers for Helping Foreign Language Learning*
Hasan Kaya and Gülşen Eryiğit

16:40–16:45 *Chinese Grammatical Error Diagnosis Using Ensemble Learning*
Yang Xiang, Xiaolong Wang, Wenying Han and Qinghua Hong

16:45–16:50 *Condition Random Fields-based Grammatical Error Detection for Chinese as Second Language*
Jui-Feng Yeh, Chan Kun Yeh, Kai-Hsiang Yu, Ya-Ting Li and Wan-Ling Tsai

16:50–16:55 *Improving Chinese Grammatical Error Correction with Corpus Augmentation and Hierarchical Phrase-based Statistical Machine Translation*
Yinchen Zhao, Mamoru Komachi and Hiroshi Ishikawa

16:55–17:00 *Chinese Grammatical Error Diagnosis System Based on Hybrid Model*
Xiupeng Wu, Peijie Huang, Jundong Wang, Qingwen Guo, Yuhong Xu and Chuping Chen

17:00–17:10 Closing Remarks

Overview of the NLP-TEA 2015 Shared Task for Chinese Grammatical Error Diagnosis

Lung-Hao Lee[1], Liang-Chih Yu[2,3], Li-Ping Chang[4]
[1]Information Technology Center, National Taiwan Normal University
[2]Department of Information Management, Yuan Ze University
[3]Innovative Center for Big Data and Digital Convergence, Yuan Ze University
[4]Mandarin Training Center, National Taiwan Normal University
lhlee@ntnu.edu.tw, lcyu@saturn.yzu.edu.tw, lchang@ntnu.edu.tw

Abstract

This paper introduces the NLP-TEA 2015 shared task for Chinese grammatical error diagnosis. We describe the task, data preparation, performance metrics, and evaluation results. The hope is that such an evaluation campaign may produce more advanced Chinese grammatical error diagnosis techniques. All data sets with gold standards and evaluation tools are publicly available for research purposes.

1 Introduction

Human language technologies for English grammatical error correction have attracted more attention in recent years (Ng et al., 2013; 2014). In contrast to the plethora of research related to develop NLP tools for learners of English as a foreign language, relatively few studies have focused on detecting and correcting grammatical errors for use by learners of Chinese as a foreign language (CFL). A classifier has been designed to detect word-ordering errors in Chinese sentences (Yu and Chen, 2012). A ranking SVM-based model has been further explored to suggest corrections for word-ordering errors (Cheng et al., 2014). Relative positioning and parse template language models have been proposed to detect Chinese grammatical errors written by US learners (Wu et al., 2010). A penalized probabilistic first-order inductive learning algorithm has been presented for Chinese grammatical error diagnosis (Chang et al. 2012). A set of linguistic rules with syntactic information was manually crafted to detect CFL grammatical errors (Lee et al., 2013). A sentence judgment system has been further developed to integrate both rule-based linguistic analysis and n-gram statistical learning for grammatical error detection (Lee et al., 2014).

The ICCE-2014 workshop on Natural Language Processing Techniques for Educational Applications (NLP-TEA) organized a shared task on CFL grammatical error diagnosis (Yu et al., 2014). Due to the greater challenge in identifying grammatical errors in CFL leaners' written sentences, the NLP-TEA 2015 shared task features a Chinese Grammatical Error Diagnosis (CGED) task, providing an evaluation platform for the development and implementation of NLP tools for computer-assisted Chinese learning. The developed system should identify whether a given sentence contains grammatical errors, identify the error types, and indicate the range of occurred errors.

This paper gives an overview of this shared task. The rest of this article is organized as follows. Section 2 provides the details of the designed task. Section 3 introduces the developed data sets. Section 4 proposes evaluation metrics. Section 5 presents the results of participant approaches for performance comparison. Section 6 summarizes the findings and offers futures research directions.

2 Task Description

The goal of this shared task is to develop NLP tools for identifying the grammatical errors in sentences written by the CFL learners. Four PADS error types are included in the target modification taxonomy, that is, mis-ordering (Permutation), redundancy (Addition), omission (Deletion), and mis-selection (Substitution). For the sake of simplicity, the input sentence is selected to contain one defined error types. The developed tool is expected to identify the error types and its position at which it occurs in the sentence.

Proceedings of The 2nd Workshop on Natural Language Processing Techniques for Educational Applications, pages 1–6,
Beijing, China, July 31, 2015.

The input instance is given a unique sentence number *sid*. If the inputs contain no grammatical errors, the tool should return "sid, correct". If an input sentence contains a grammatical error, the output format should be a quadruple of "sid, start_off, end_off, error_type", where "start_off" and "end_off" respectively denote the characters at which the grammatical error starts and ends, where each character or punctuation mark occupies 1 space for counting positions. "Error_type" represents one defined error type in terms of "Redundant," "Missing," "Selection," and "Disorder". Examples are shown as follows.

- Example 1

Input: (sid=B2-0080) 他是我的以前的室友
Output: B2-0080, 4, 4, Redundant

- Example 2

Input: (sid=A2-0017) 那電影是機器人的故事
Output: A2-0017, 2, 2, Missing

- Example 3

Input: (sid=A2-0017) 那部電影是機器人的故事
Output: A2-0017, correct

- Example 4

Input: (sid=B1-1193) 吳先生是修理腳踏車的拿手
Output: B1-1193, 11, 12, Selection

- Example 5

Input: (sid=B2-2292) 所 以 我 不 會 讓 失 望 她
Output: B2-2292, 7, 9, Disorder

The character "的" is a redundant character in Ex. 1. There is a missing character between "那" and "電影" in Ex. 2, and a missed character "部" is shown in the correct sentence in Ex. 3. In Ex. 4, "拿手" is a wrong word. One of correct words may be "好手". "失望她" is a word ordering error in Ex. 5. The correct order should be "她失望".

3 Data Preparation

The learner corpus used in our task was collected from the essay section of the computer-based Test of Chinese as a Foreign Language (TOCFL), administered in Taiwan. Native Chinese speakers were trained to manually annotate grammatical errors and provide corrections corresponding to each error. The essays were then split into three sets as follows.

(1) Training Set: This set included 2,205 selected sentences with annotated grammatical errors and their corresponding corrections. Each sentence is represented in SGML format as shown in Fig. 1. Error types were categorized as redundant (430 instances), missing (620), selection (849), and disorder (306). All sentences in this set were collected to use for training the grammatical diagnostic tools.

```
<DOC>
<SENTENCE id="B1-1120">
我的中文進步了非常快
</SENTENCE>
<MISTAKE start_off="7" end_off="7">
<TYPE>
Selection
</TYPE>
<CORRECTION>
我的中文進步得非常快
</CORRECTION>
</MISTAKE>
</DOC>
```

Figure 1. An sentence denoted in SGML format

(2) Dryrun Set: A total of 55 sentences were distributed to participants to allow them familiarize themselves with the final testing process. Each participant was allowed to submit several runs generated using different models with different parameter settings of their developed tools. In addition, to ensure the submitted results could be correctly evaluated, participants were allowed to fine-tune their developed models in the dryrun phase. The purpose of dryrun is to validate the submitted output format only, and no dryrun outcomes were considered in the official evaluation

(3) Test Set: This set consists of 1,000 testing sentences. Half of these sentences contained no grammatical errors, while the other half included a single defined grammatical error: redundant (132 instances), missing (126), selection (110), and disorder (132). The evaluation was conducted as an open test. In addition to the data sets provided, registered research teams were allowed to employ any linguistic and computational resources to identify the grammatical errors.

4 Performance Metrics

Table 1 shows the confusion matrix used for performance evaluation. In the matrix, TP (True Positive) is the number of sentences with grammatical errors that are correctly identified by the developed tool; FP (False Positive) is the number of sentences in which non-existent grammatical errors are identified; TN (True Negative) is the number of sentences without grammatical errors that are correctly identified as such; FN (False Negative) is the number of sentences with grammatical errors for which no errors are identified.

The criteria for judging correctness are determined at three levels as follows.

(1) Detection level: binary classification of a given sentence, that is, correct or incorrect should be completely identical with the gold standard. All error types will be regarded as incorrect.

(2) Identification level: this level could be considered as a multi-class categorization problem. All error types should be clearly identified. A correct case should be completely identical with the gold standard of the given error type.

(3) Position level: in addition to identifying the error types, this level also judges the occurred range of grammatical error. That is to say, the system results should be perfectly identical with the quadruples of gold standard.

The following metrics are measured at all levels with the help of the confusion matrix.

- False Positive Rate (FPR) = FP / (FP+TN)
- Accuracy = (TP+TN) / (TP+FP+TN+FN)
- Precision = TP / (TP+FP)
- Recall = TP / (TP+FN)
- F1= 2 *Precision*Recall/(Precision+Recall)

Confusion Matrix		System Result	
		Positive (Erroneous)	Negative (Correct)
Gold Standard	Positive	**TP**	**FN**
	Negative	**FP**	**TN**

Table 1. Confusion matrix for evaluation.

For example, given 8 testing inputs with gold standards shown as "B1-1138, 7, 10, Disorder", "A2-0087, 12, 13, Missing", "A2-0904, correct", "B1-0990, correct", "A2-0789, 2, 3, Selection", "B1-0295, correct", "B2-0591, 3, 3, Redundant" and "A2-0920, correct", the system may output the result shown as "B1-1138, 7, 8, Disorder", "A2-0087, 12, 13, Missing", "A2-0904, 5, 6, Missing", "B1-0990, correct", "A2-0789, 2, 5, Disorder", "B1-0295, correct", "B2-0591, 3, 3, Redundant" and "A2-0920, 4, 5, Selection". The evaluation tool will yield the following performance.

- False Positive Rate (FPR) = 0.5 (=2/4) Notes: {"A2-0904, 5, 6, Missing", "A2-0920, 4, 5, Selection"} /{"A2-0904, correct", "B1-0090, correct", "B1-0295, correct", "A2-0920, correct"}
- Detection-level
  - Accuracy =0.75 (=6/8)

  Notes: {"B1-1138, Disorder", "A2-0087, Missing", "B1-0990, correct", "A2-0789, Disorder", "B1-0295, correct", "B2-0591, Redundant"} / {"B1-1138, Disorder", "A2-0087, Missing", "A2-0904, Missing", "B1-0990, correct", "A2-0789, Disorder", "B1-0295, correct", "B2-0591, Redundant", "A2-0920, Selection".}

  - Precision = 0.67 (=4/6)

  Notes: {"B1-1138, Disorder", "A2-0087, Missing", "A2-0789, Disorder", "B2-0591, Redundant"} / {"B1-1138, Disorder", "A2-0087, Missing", "A2-0904, Missing", "A2-0789, Disorder", "B2-0591, Redundant", "A2-0920, Selection".}

  - Recall = 1 (=4/4).

  Notes: {"B1-1138, Disorder", "A2-0087, Missing", "A2-0789, Disorder", "B2-0591, Redundant"} / {"B1-1138, Disorder", "A2-0087, Missing", "A2-0789, Selection", "B2-0591, Redundant"}

  - F1=0.8 (=2*0.67*1/(0.67+1))
- Identification-level
  - Accuracy =0.625 (=5/8)

  Notes: {"B1-1138, Disorder", "A2-0087, Missing", "B1-0990, correct", "B1-0295, correct", "B2-0591, Redundant"} / {"B1-1138, Disorder", "A2-0087, Missing", "A2-0904, Missing", "B1-0990, correct", "A2-0789, Disorder", "B1-0295, correct", "B2-0591, Redundant", "A2-0920, Selection"}

  - Precision = 0.5 (=3/6)

  Notes: {"B1-1138, Disorder", "A2-0087, Missing", "B2-0591, Redundant"} / {"B1-1138, Disorder", "A2-0087, Missing", "A2-0904, Missing", "A2-0789, Disorder", "B2-0591, Redundant", "A2-0920, Selection".}

- Recall = 0.75 (=3/4)

Notes: {"B1-1138, Disorder", "A2-0087, Missing", "B2-0591, Redundant"} / {"B1-1138, Disorder", "A2-0087, Missing", "A2-0789, Selection", "B2-0591, Redundant"}

- F1=0.6 (=2*0.5*0.75/(0.5+0.75))

- Position-level

  - Accuracy =0.5 (=4/8)

Notes: {"A2-0087, 12, 13, Missing", "B1-0990, correct", "B1-0295, correct", "B2-0591, 3, 3, Redundant"} / {"B1-1138, 7, 8, Disorder", "A2-0087, 12, 13, Missing", "A2-0904, 5, 6, Missing", "B1-0990, correct", "A2-0789, 2, 5, Disorder", "B1-0295, correct", "B2-0591, 3, 3, Redundant", "A2-0920, 4, 5, Selection"}

  - Precision = 0.33 (=2/6)

Notes: {"A2-0087, 12, 13, Missing", "B2-0591, 3, 3, Redundant"} / {"B1-1138, 7, 8, Disorder", "A2-0087, 12, 13, Missing", "A2-0904, 5, 6, Missing", "A2-0789, 2, 5, Disorder", "B2-0591, 3, 3, Redundant", "A2-0920, 4, 5, Selection"}

  - Recall = 0.5 (=2/4)

Notes: {"A2-0087, 12, 13, Missing", "B2-0591, 3, 3, Redundant"} / {"B1-1138, 7, 10, Disorder", "A2-0087, 12, 13, Missing", "A2-0789, 2, 3, Selection", "B2-0591, 3, 3, Redundant"}

  - F1=0.4 (=2*0.33*0.5/(0.33+0.5))

5 Evaluation Results

Table 2 summarizes the submission statistics for the participating teams. Of 13 registered teams, 6 teams submitted their testing results. In formal testing phase, each participant was allowed to submit at most three runs using different models or parameter settings. In total, we had received 18 runs.

Table 3 shows the task testing results. The CYUT team achieved the lowest false positive rate of 0.082. Detection-level evaluations are designed to detect whether a sentence contains grammatical errors or not. A neutral baseline can be easily achieved by always reporting all testing errors are correct without errors. According to the test data distribution, the baseline system can achieve an accuracy level of 0.5. All systems achieved results slightly better than the baseline. The system result submitted by NCYU achieved the best detection accuracy of 0.607. We used the F1 score to reflect the tradeoff between precision and recall. In the testing results, NTOU provided the best error detection results, providing a high F1 score of 0.6754. For correction-level evaluations, the systems need to identify the error types in the given sentences. The system developed by NCYU provided the highest F1 score of 0.3584 for grammatical error identification. For position-level evaluations, CYUT achieved the best F1 score of 0.1742. Note that it is difficult to perfectly identify the error positions, partly because no word delimiters exist among Chinese words.

Participant (Ordered by abbreviations of names)	**#Runs**
Adam Mickiewicz University on Poznan (**AMU**)	0
University of Cambridge (**CAM**)	0
Chinese Academy of Sciences (**CAS**)	0
Confucius Institute of Rutgers University (**CIRU**)	0
Chaoyang University of Technology (**CYUT**)	3
Harbin Institute of Technology Shenzhen Graduate School (**HITSZ**)	3
Lingage Inc. (**Lingage**)	0
National Chiayi University (**NCYU**)	3
National Taiwan Ocean University (**NTOU**)	3
National Taiwan University (**NTU**)	0
South China Agriculture University (**SCAU**)	3
Tokyo Metropolitan University (**TMU**)	3
University of Leeds (**UL**)	0
Total	**18**

Table 2. Submission statistics for all participants

Submission	False Positive Rate	Detection Level				Identification Level				Position Level			
		Acc.	Pre.	Rec.	F1	Acc.	Pre.	Rec.	F1	Acc.	Pre.	Rec.	F1
CYUT-Run1	0.096	0.584	0.7333	0.264	0.3882	0.522	0.5932	0.14	0.2265	0.504	0.52	0.104	0.1733
CYUT-Run2	**0.082**	0.579	**0.7453**	0.24	0.3631	**0.525**	**0.6168**	0.132	0.2175	**0.505**	**0.5287**	0.092	0.1567
CYUT-Run3	0.132	0.579	0.6872	0.29	0.4079	0.505	0.5182	0.142	0.2229	0.488	0.45	0.108	**0.1742**
HITSZ-Run1	0.956	0.509	0.5047	0.974	0.6648	0.173	0.2401	0.302	0.2675	0.031	0.0185	0.018	0.0182
HITSZ-Run2	0.938	0.505	0.5027	0.948	0.657	0.149	0.201	0.236	0.2171	0.036	0.0105	0.01	0.0103
HITSZ-Run3	0.884	0.51	0.5056	0.904	0.6485	0.188	0.2273	0.26	0.2425	0.068	0.0221	0.02	0.021
NCYU-Run1	0.48	0.53	0.5294	0.54	0.5347	0.354	0.2814	0.188	0.2254	0.274	0.0551	0.028	0.0371
NCYU-Run2	0.396	0.567	0.5724	0.53	0.5504	0.423	0.3793	0.242	0.2955	0.343	0.1715	0.082	0.111
NCYU-Run3	0.374	**0.607**	0.6112	0.588	0.5994	0.463	0.4451	0.3	**0.3584**	0.374	0.246	0.122	0.1631
NTOU-Run1	1	0.5	0.5	**1**	0.6667	0.117	0.1896	0.234	0.2095	0.005	0.0099	0.01	0.01
NTOU-Run2	0.914	0.531	0.5164	0.976	**0.6754**	0.225	0.2848	**0.364**	0.3196	0.123	0.149	**0.16**	0.1543
NTOU-Run3	0.948	0.519	0.5098	0.986	0.6721	0.193	0.2605	0.334	0.2927	0.093	0.1238	0.134	0.1287
SCAU-Run1	0.62	0.505	0.504	0.63	0.56	0.287	0.2383	0.194	0.2139	0.217	0.0801	0.054	0.0645
SCAU-Run2	0.636	0.503	0.5023	0.642	0.5637	0.279	0.2337	0.194	0.212	0.209	0.0783	0.054	0.0639
SCAU-Run3	0.266	0.503	0.5056	0.272	0.3537	0.416	0.2692	0.098	0.1437	0.385	0.1192	0.036	0.0553
TMU-Run1	0.478	0.516	0.5162	0.51	0.5131	0.313	0.1787	0.104	0.1315	0.27	0.0363	0.018	0.0241
TMU-Run2	0.134	0.524	0.5759	0.182	0.2766	0.479	0.4071	0.092	0.1501	0.449	0.1928	0.032	0.0549
TMU-Run3	0.35	0.546	0.5581	0.442	0.4933	0.42	0.3519	0.19	0.2468	0.362	0.1745	0.074	0.1039

Table 3. Testing results of our Chinese grammatical error diagnosis task.

In summary, none of the submitted systems provided superior performance. It is a really difficult task to develop an effective computer-assisted learning tool for grammatical error diagnosis, especially for the CFL uses. In general, this research problem still has long way to go.

6 Conclusions and Future Work

This paper provides an overview of the NLP-TEA 2015 shared task for Chinese grammatical error diagnosis, including task design, data preparation, evaluation metrics, and performance evaluation results. Regardless of actual performance, all submissions contribute to the common effort to produce an effective Chinese grammatical diagnosis tool, and the individual reports in the shared task proceedings provide useful insight into Chinese language processing.

We hope the data sets collected for this shared task can facilitate and expedite the future development of NLP tools for computer-assisted Chinese language learning. Therefore, all data sets with gold standards and evaluation tool are publicly available for research purposes at http://ir.itc.ntnu.edu.tw/lre/nlptea15cged.htm.

We plan to build new language resources to improve existing techniques for computer-aided Chinese language learning. In addition, new data sets with the contextual information of target sentences obtained from CFL learners will be investigated for the future enrichment of this research topic.

Acknowledgments

We thank all the participants for taking part in our task. We would like to thank Bo-Shun Liao for developing the evaluation tool. This research is partially supported by the "Aim for the Top University" and "Center of Learning Technology for Chinese" of National Taiwan Normal University (NTNU), sponsored by the Ministry of Education, Taiwan, ROC and is also sponsored in part by the "International Research-Intensive Center of Excellence Program" of NTNU and Ministry of Science and Technology, Taiwan, ROC under the Grant no. MOST 104-2911-I-003-301, and MOST 102-2221-E-155-029-MY3.

References

Ru-Yng Chang, Chung-Hsien Wu, and Philips Kokoh Prasetyo. 2012. Error diagnosis of Chinese sentences using inductive learning algorithm and decomposition-based testing mechanism. *ACM Transactions on Asian Language Information Processing*, 11(1), article 3.

Shuk-Man Cheng, Chi-Hsin Yu, and Hsin-Hsi Chen. 2014. Chinese word ordering errors detection and correction for non-native Chinese language learners. *Proceedings of the 25th International Conference on Computational Linguistics (COLING-14)*, pages 279-289.

Lung-Hao Lee, Li-Ping Chang, Kuei-Ching Lee, Yuen-Hsien Tseng, and Hsin-Hsi Chen. 2013. Linguistic rules based Chinese error detection for second language learning. *Work-in-Progress Poster Proceedings of the 21st International Conference on Computers in Education (ICCE-13)*, pages 27-29.

Lung-Hao Lee, Liang-Chih Yu, Kuei-Ching Lee, Yuen-Hsien Tseng, Li-Ping Chang, and Hsin-Hsi Chen. 2014. A sentence judgment system for grammatical error detection. *Proceedings of the 25th International Conference on Computational Linguistics (COLING-14)*, pages 67-70.

Hwee Tou Ng, Siew Mei Wu, Ted Briscoe, Christian Hadiwinoto, Raymond Hendy Susanto, and Christopher Bryant. 2014. The CoNLL-2014 shared task on grammatical error correction. *Proceedings of the 18th Conference on Computational Natural Language Learning (CoNLL-14): Shared Task*, pages 1-12.

Hwee Tou Ng, Siew Mei Wu, Yuanbin Wu, Christian Hadiwinoto, and Joel Tetreault. 2013. The CoNLL-2013 shared task on grammatical error correction. *Proceedings of the 17th Conference on Computational Natural Language Learning (CoNLL-13): Shared Task*, pages 1-14.

Chung-Hsien Wu, Chao-Hong Liu, Matthew Harris, and Liang-Chih Yu. 2010. Sentence correction incorporating relative position and parse template language models. IEEE Transactions on Audio, Speech, and Language Processing, 18(6), pages 1170-1181.

Chi-Hsin Yu and Hsin-Hsi Chen. 2012. Detecting word ordering errors in Chinese sentences for learning Chinese as a foreign language. *Proceedings of the 24th International Conference on Computational Linguistics (COLING-12)*, pages 3003-3017.

Liang-Chih Yu, Lung-Hao Lee, and Li-Ping Chang. 2014. Overview of grammatical error diagnosis for learning Chinese as a foreign language. *Proceedings of the 1st Workshop on Natural Language Processing Techniques for Educational Applications (NLPTEA-14)*, pages 42-47.

Chinese Grammatical Error Diagnosis by Conditional Random Fields

Po-Lin Chen, Shih-Hung Wu*
Chaoyang University of Technology/
Wufeng, Taichung, Taiwan, ROC.
streetcatsky@gmail.com,
*contact author: shwu@cyut.edu.tw

Liang-Pu Chen, Ping-Che Yang, Ren-Dar Yang
IDEAS, Institute for Information Industry/
Taipei, Taiwan, ROC.
{eit, maciaclark, rdyang}@iii.org.tw

Abstract

This paper reports how to build a Chinese Grammatical Error Diagnosis system based on the conditional random fields (CRF). The system can find four types of grammatical errors in learners' essays. The four types or errors are redundant words, missing words, bad word selection, and disorder words. Our system presents the best false positive rate in 2015 NLP-TEA-2 CGED shared task, and also the best precision rate in three diagnosis levels.

1 Introduction

Learning Chinese as foreign language is on the rising trend. Since Chinese has its own unique grammar, it is hard for a foreign learner to write a correct sentence. A computer system that can diagnose the grammatical errors will help the learners to learn Chinese fast (Yu et al., 2014; Wu et al., 2010;Yeh et al., 2014;Chang et al., 2014).

In the NLP-TEA-2 CGED shared task data set, there are four types of errors in the leaners' sentences: Redundant, Selection, Disorder, and Missing. The research goal is to build a system that can detect the errors, identify the type of the error, and point out the position of the error in the sentence.

2 Methodology

Our system is based on the conditional random field (CRF) (Lafferty, 2001). CRF has been used in many natural language processing applications, such as named entity recognition, word segmentation, information extraction, and parsing (Wu and Hsieh, 2012). For different task, it requires different feature set and different labeled training data. The CRF can be regarded as a sequential labeling tagger. Given a sequence data X, the CRF can generate the corresponding label sequence Y, based on the trained model. Each label Y is taken from a specific tag set, which needs to be defined in different task. How to define and interpret the label is a task-depended work for the developers.
Mathematically, the model can be defined as:

$$P(Y|X) = \frac{1}{Z(X)}\exp(\sum_k \lambda_k f_k) \qquad (1)$$

where Z(X) is the normalization factor, f_k is a set of features, λ_k is the corresponding weight. In this task, X is the input sentence, and Y is the corresponding error type label. We define the tag set as: {O, R, M, S, D}, corresponding to no error, redundant, missing, selection, and disorder respectively. Figure 1 shows a snapshot of our working file. The first column is the input sentence X, and the third column is the labeled tag sequence Y. Note that the second column is the Part-of-speech (POS) of the word in the first column. The combination of words and the POSs will be the features in our system. The POS set used in our system is listed in
Table 1, which is a simplified POS set provided by CKIP[1].

Figure 2 (at the end of the paper) shows the framework of the proposed system. The system is built based on the CRF++, a linear-chain CRF model software, developed by Kudo[2].

```
可是 C O
有 Vt O
一點 DET O
冷 Vi O
了 T R

你 N O
的 T R
過年 Vi O
呢 T O
```

Figure 1: A snapshot of our CRF sequential labeling working file

[1] http://ckipsvr.iis.sinica.edu.tw/
[2] http://crfpp.sourceforge.net/index.html

Proceedings of The 2nd Workshop on Natural Language Processing Techniques for Educational Applications, pages 7–14,
Beijing, China, July 31, 2015. ©2015 Association for Computational Linguistics and Asian Federation of Natural Language Processing

Simplified CKIP POS	Corresponding CKIP POS
A	非謂形容詞
C	對等連接詞，如：和、跟
	關聯連接詞
POST	連接詞，如：等等
	連接詞，如：的話
	後置數量定詞
	後置詞
ADV	數量副詞
	動詞前程度副詞
	動詞後程度副詞
	句副詞
	副詞
ASP	時態標記
N	普通名詞
	專有名稱
	地方詞
	位置詞
	時間詞
	代名詞
DET	數詞定詞.
	特指定詞
	指代定詞
	數量定詞
M	量詞
Nv	名物化動詞
T	感嘆詞
	語助詞
	的, 之, 得, 地
P	介詞
Vi	動作不及物動詞
	動作類及物動詞
	狀態不及物動詞
	狀態類及物動詞
Vt	動作使動動詞
	動作及物動詞
	動作接地方賓語動詞
	雙賓動詞
	動作句賓動詞
	動作謂賓動詞
	分類動詞
	狀態使動動詞
	狀態及物動詞
	狀態句賓動詞
	狀態謂賓動詞
	有
	是

Table 1: Simplified CKIP POS

2.1 Training phase

In the training phase, a training sentence is first segmented into terms. Each term is labeled with the corresponding POS tag and error type tag. Then our system uses the CRF++ leaning algorithm to train a model. The features used in CRF++ can be expressed by templates. Table 12 (at the end of the paper) shows one sentence in our training set.

Table 13 (at the end of the paper) shows all the templates of the feature set used in our system and the corresponding value for the example. The format of each template is %X[row, col], where row is the number of rows in a sentence and column is the number of column as we shown in Figure 1. The feature templates used in our system are the combination of terms and POS of the input sentences. For example, the first feature template is "Term+POS", if an input sentence contains the same term with the same POS, the feature value will be 1, otherwise the feature value will be 0. The second feature template is "Term+Previous Term", if an input sentence contains the same term bi-gram, the feature value will be 1, otherwise the feature value will be 0.

2.2 Test phase

In the Test phase, our system use the trained model to detect and identify the error of an input sentence. Table 2, Table 3, and Table 4 show the labeling results of examples of sentences with error types Redundant, Selection, Disorder, and Missing respectively.

Word	POS	tag	Predict tag
他	N	O	O
是	Vt	O	O
真.	ADV	R	R
很	ADV	O	O
好	Vi	O	O
的	T	O	O
人	N	O	O

Table 2: A tagging result sample of a sentence with error type Redundant

Term	POS	tag	Predict tag
你	N	O	O
千萬	DET	O	O
不要	ADV	O	O
在意	Vt	O	O
這	DET	O	O
個	M	S	S
事情	N	O	O

Table 3: A tagging result sample of a sentence with error type Selection

r

Term	POS	tag	Predict tag
你	N	O	O
什麼	DET	D	D
要.	ADV	D	D
玩	Vt	D	D

Table 4: A tagging result sample of a sentence with error type Disorder

.

Term	POS	Tag	Predict tag
看	Vt	O	O
電影	N	O	O
時候	N	M	M

Table 5: A tagging result sample of a sentence with error type Missing example

If all the system predict tags in the fourth column are the same as the tags in the third column, then the system labels the sentence correctly. In the formal run, accuracy, precision, recall (Clevereon, 1972), and F-score (Rijsbergen,1979) are considered. The measure metrics are defined as follows. The notation is listed in
Table 6.

		System predict tag	
		A	**B**
Known tag	**A**	tpA	eAB
	B	eBA	tpB

Table 6: The confusion matrix.

$$\text{Precision A} = \frac{tpA}{tpA+eBA}$$

$$\text{Recall A} = \frac{tpA}{tpA+eAB}$$

$$\text{F1-Score A} = 2 \times \frac{\text{Precision } A \times \text{Recall } A}{\text{Precision } A + \text{Recall } A}$$

$$\text{Accuracy} = \frac{tpA+tpB}{All\ Data}$$

3 Experiments

3.1 Data set

Our training data consists of data from NLP-TEA1(Chang et al.,2012)Training Data, Test Data, and the Training Data from NLP-TEA2. Figure 3 (at the end of the paper)shows the format of the data set. Table 7 shows the number of sentences in our training set.

size	NLP-TEA1	NLP-TEA2
Redundant	1830	434
Correct	874	0
Selection	827	849
Disorder	724	306
Missing	225	622

Table 7: Training set size

3.2 Experiments result

In the formal run of NLP-TEA-2 CGED shared task, there are 6 participants and each team submits 3 runs. Table 8 shows the false positive rate. Our system has the lowest false positive rate 0.082, which is much lower than the average.
Table 9, Table 10, and Table 11 show the formal run result of our system compared to the average in Detection level, Identification level, and Position level respectively. Our system achieved the highest precision in all the three levels, but the accuracy of our system is fare. However, the recall of our system is relatively low. The numbers in boldface are the best performance amount 18 runs in the formal run this year.

Submission	False Positive Rate
CYUT-Run1	0.096
CYUT-Run2	**0.082**
CYUT-Run3	0.132
Average of all 18 runs	0.538

Table 8: The false positive rate.

	Detection Level			
	Accuracy	Precision	Recall	F1
CYUT-Run1	0.584	0.7333	0.264	0.3882
CYUT-Run2	0.579	**0.7453**	0.24	0.3631
CYUT-Run3	0.579	0.6872	0.29	0.4079
Average of all 18 runs	0.534	0.560	0.607	0.533

Table 9: Performance evaluation in Detection Level.

	Identification Level			
	Accuracy	Precision	Recall	F1
CYUT-Run1	0.522	0.5932	0.14	0.2265
CYUT-Run2	**0.525**	**0.6168**	0.132	0.2175
CYUT-Run3	0.505	0.5182	0.142	0.2229
Average of all 18 runs	0.335	0.329	0.208	0.233

Table 10: Performance evaluation in Identification Level.

	Position Level			
	Accuracy	Precision	Recall	F1
CYUT-Run1	0.504	0.52	0.104	0.1733
CYUT-Run2	**0.505**	**0.5287**	0.092	0.1567
CYUT-Run3	0.488	0.45	0.108	**0.1742**
Average of all 18 runs	0.263	0.166	0.064	0.085

Table 11: Performance evaluation in Position Level.

4 Error analysis on the official test result

There are 1000 sentences in the official test set of the 2015 CGED shared task. Our system labeled them according to the CRF model that we trained based on the official training set and the available data set from last year.

The number of tag O dominates the number of other tags in the training set for sentences with or without an error. For example, sentence no. B1-0436, a sentence without error:
{上次我坐了 MRT 去了圓山站參觀寺廟了，O(上)，O(次)，O(我)，O(坐)，R(了)，O(MRT)，O(去)，O(了)，O(圓山)，O(站)，O(參觀)，O(寺廟)，O(了)}

And, sentence no. A2-0322, a sentence with an error:
{他們從公車站走路走二十分鐘才到電影院了，O(他們)，O(從)，O(公車站)，O(走路)，O(走)，O(二十)，O(分鐘) ，O(才) ，O(到) ，O(電影院) ，R(了)}

Therefore, our system tends to label words with tag O and it is part of the reason that our system gives the lowest false positive rate this year. Our system also has high accuracy and precision rate, but the Recall rate is lower than other systems. We will analyze the causes and discuss how to improve the fallbacks.

We find that there are 11 major mistake types of our system result.

1. Give two error tags in one sentence.
2. Fail to label the Missing tag
3. Fail to label the Disorder tag
4. Fail to label the Redundant tag
5. Fail to label the Selection tag
6. Label a correct sentence with Missing tag
7. Label a correct sentence with Redundant tag
8. Label a correct sentence with Disorder tag
9. Label a correct sentence with Selection tag
10. Label a Selection type with Redundant tag
11. Label a Disorder type with Missing tag

Analysis of the error cases:

1. Give two error tags in one sentence: In the official training set and test set, a sentence has at most one error type. However, our method might label more than one error tags in one sentence. For example, a system output: {他是很聰明學生，O(他)，R(是)，O(很)，O(聰明)，M(學生)}. Currently, we do not rule out the possibility that a sentence might contain more than one errors. We believe that in the real application, there might be a need for such situation. However, our system might compare the confidence value of each tag and retain only one error tag in one sentence.

2. Fail to label the Missing tag: The missing words might be recovered by rules. For example, a system output: {需要一些東西修理好，O(需要)，**O(一些)**，O(東西)，O(修理好)} should be {需要一些東西修理好，O(需要)，M(一些)，O(東西)，O(修理好)} and the missing word should be ”被” or “把”. A set of rule for ”被” or “把” can be helpful.

3. Fail to label the Disorder tag: The disorder

error is also hard for CRF model, since the named entity (NE) is not recognized first. For example, a system output: {離台北車站淡水不太近，**O(離)，O(台北)，O(車站)，O(淡水)**，O(不)，O(太)，O(近)} should be {離台北車站淡水不太近，D(離)，D(台北)，D(車站)，D(淡水)，O(不)，O(太)，O(近)}. The disorder error can only be recognized once the named entities "台北車站" and "淡水" are recognized and then the grammar rule " NE1+離+NE2+近" can be applied.

4. Fail to label the Redundant tag: Some adjacent words are regarded as redundant due to the semantics. Two adjacent words with almost the same meaning can be reduced to one. For example: a system output: {那公園是在台北北部最近新有的，O(那)，O(公園)，O(是)，O(在)，O(台北)，**O(北部)**，O(最近)，O(新)，O(有的)} fail to recognize the redundant word R(台北) or R(北部). In this case, "新有的" is also bad Chinese, it should be "新建的". However, the word segmentation result makes our system hard to detect the error.

5. Fail to label the Selection tag: We believe that it required more knowledge to recognize the selection error than limited training set. For example, a system output: {這是一個很好的新聞，O(這)，O(是)，O(一)，**O(個)**，O(很)，O(好)，O(的)，O(新聞)} fail to recognize the classifiers (also called measure words) for"新聞" should not be "個", the most common Mandarin classifier. It should be "則". A list of the noun to classifier table is necessary to recognize this kind of errors.

6. Label a correct sentence with Missing tag: This case is relative rare in our system. For example, a system output: {一個小時以前我決定休息一下，**M(一)**，O(個)，O(小時)，O(以前)，M(我) ，O(決定)，O(休息) ，O(一下)} accurately contains no error. However our system regard a single "一" should be a missing error according to the trained model.

7. Label a correct sentence with Redundant tag: There are cases that we think our system perform well. For example, our system output: {平常下了課以後他馬上回家，O(平常)，O(下)，R(了)，O(課)，O(以後) ，O(他)，O(馬上)，O(回家) }. Where "了" can be regarded as redundant in some similar cases.

8. Label a correct sentence with Disorder tag: This is a rare case in our system. For example, a system output: {以後慢慢知道他這種方式其實是很普通的交朋友的方式，D(以後)，D(慢慢)，D(知道)，D(他)，D(這) ，D(種)，O(方式)，O(其實)，O (是) ，O (很)，O (普通)，O (的)，O (交) ，O (朋友)，O (的)，O (方式) }. It is a sentence that cannot be judged alone without enough contexts.

9. Label a correct sentence with Selection tag: In one case, our system output: {今天是個很重要的一天，O(今天)，O(是)，**S(個)**，O(很)，R(重要) ，O(的)，O(一)，O(天) }, where "個" is also not a good measure word.

10. Label a Selection type with Redundant tag: Sometimes there are more than one way to improve a sentence. For example, a system output: {下了課王大衛本來馬上回家，O(下)，**R(了)**，O(課)，O(王大衛)，O(本來) ，O(馬上)，O(回家) }, which is no better than {下了課王大衛本來馬上回家，O(下)，O(了)，O(課)，O(王大衛)，S(本來) ，O(馬上)，O(回家) }. Where "本來" should be "就". However, in a different context, it could be "本來想"+"但是...".

11. Label a Disorder type with Missing tag: Since a Disorder error might involve more than two words, comparing to other types, it is hard to train a good model. For example, a system output: {中國新年到了的時候，O(中國)，O(新年)，O(到)，O(了)，M(的) ，O(時候) } should be {中國新年到了的時候，O(中國)，D(新年)，D(到)，D(了)，O(的) ，O(時候) }, and the correct sentence should be "到了中國新年的時候". A grammar rule such as "到了"+Event+"的時候" might be help.

5 Conclusion and Future work

This paper reports our approach to the NLP-TEA-2 CGED Shared Task evaluation. Based on the CRF model, we built a system that can achieve the lowest false positive rate and the highest precision at the official run. The approach uniformly dealt with the four error types: Redundant, Missing, Selection, and Disorder.

According to our error analysis, the difficult cases suggest that to build a better system requires more features and more training data. The system can be improved by integrating rule based system in the future.

Due to the limitation of time and resource, our system is not tested under different experimental settings. In the future, we will test our system with more feature combination on both POS labeling and sentence parsing.

Acknowledgments

This study is conducted under the "Online and Offline integrated Smart Commerce Platform(2/4)" of the Institute for Information Industry which is subsidized by the Ministry of Economic Affairs of the Republic of China .

Reference

Lafferty, A. McCallum, and F. Pereira. (2001) *Conditional random fields: Probabilistic models for segmenting and labeling sequence data.* In Intl. Conf. on Machine Learning.

C. W. Clevereon, (1972), *On the inverse relationship of recall and precision*, Workshop on Machine Learning for Information Extraction, pp.195-201.

C. van Rijsbergen, (1979),*Information Retrieval*, Butterworths.

Ru-Yng Chang, Chung-Hsien Wu, and Philips Kokoh Prasetyo. (2012). *Error Diagnosis of Chinese Sentences Using Inductive Learning Algorithm and Decomposition-Based Testing Mechanism.* ACM Transactions on Asian Language Information Processing, 11(1), article 3, March.

Chung-Hsien Wu, Chao-Hong Liu, Matthew Harris, and Liang-Chih Yu (2010). *Sentence Correction Incorporating Relative Position and Parse Template Language Models.* IEEE Transactions on Audio, Speech, and Language Processing, 18(6), 1170-1181.

Shih-Hung Wu, Hsien-You Hsieh. (2012). *Sentence Parsing with Double Sequential Labeling in Traditional Chinese Parsing Task.* Second CIPS-SIGHAN Joint Conference on Chinese Language Processing, pages 222–230.

Jui-Feng Yeh, Yun-Yun Lu, Chen-Hsien Lee, Yu-Hsiang Yu, Yong-Ting Chen. (2014). Detecting Grammatical Error in Chinese Sentence for Foreign.

Tao-Hsing Chang, Yao-Ting Sung , Jia-Fei Hong, Jen-I CHANG. (2014). KNGED: a Tool for Grammatical Error Diagnosis of Chinese Sentences.

Yu, L.-C., Lee, L.-H., & Chang, L.-P. (2014). *Overview of grammatical error diagnosis for learning Chinese as a foreign language.* In Proceedings of the 1stWorkshop on Natural Language Processing Techniques for Educational Applications, 42-47.

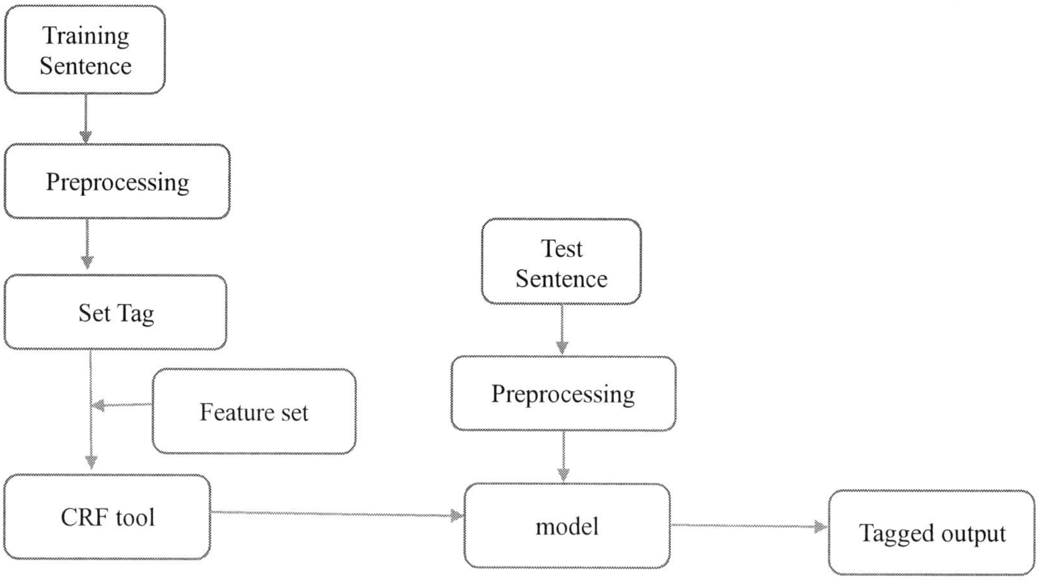

Figure 2: The framework of the proposed system.

```
<root>
<ESSAY title="不能參加朋友
找到工作的慶祝會">
<TEXT>
<SENTENCE id="A2-0003-1">
我以前知道妳又很聰明又用功
</SENTENCE>
</TEXT>
<MISTAKE id="A2-0003-1">
<TYPE>Redundant</TYPE>
<CORRECTION>我以前知道妳又
聰明又用功</CORRECTION>
</MISTAKE>
</ESSAY>
```


Figure 3: An example of the source data.

	col0	**col1**	**col2**
r-2	他	N	O
r-1	是	Vt	O
r0 (目前 Token)	真	ADV	R
r1	很	ADV	O
r2	好	Vi	O
r3	的	T	O
r4	人	N	O

Table 12: A sample training sentence.

Template Meaning	*Template*	*Feature rule*
Term+POS	%x[0,0]/%x[0,1]	真/ADV
Term+Previous Term	%x[0,0]/%x[-1,0]	真/是
Term+Previous POS	%x[0,0]/%x[-1,1]	真/ Vt
POS+Previous Term	%x[0,1]/%x[-1,0]	ADV/是
POS+Previous POS	%x[0,1]/%x[-1,1]	ADV/ Vt
Term+Previous Term+Previous POS	%x[0,0]/%x[-1,0]/%x[-1,1]	真/是/ Vt
POS+Previous Term+Previous POS	%x[0,1]/%x[-1,0]/%x[-1,1]	ADV/是/ Vt
Term+Second Previous Term	%x[0,0]/%x[-2,0]	真/他
Term+Second Previous POS	%x[0,0]/%x[-2,1]	真/N

POS+Second Previous Term	%x[0,1]/%x[-2,0]	ADV/他
POS+Second Previous POS	%x[0,1]/%x[-2,1]	ADV/N
Term+Second Previous Term+Second Previous POS	%x[0,0]/%x[-2,0]/%x[-2,1]	真/他/N
POS+Second Previous Term+Second Previous POS	%x[0,1]/%x[-2,0]/%x[-2,1]	ADV/他/N
Term+Next Term	%x[0,0]/%x[1,0]	真/很
Term+Next POS	%x[0,0]/%x[1,1]	真/ADV
POS+Next Term	%x[0,1]/%x[1,0]	ADV/很
POS+Next POS	%x[0,1]/%x[1,1]	ADV/ADV
Term+Next Term+Next POS	%x[0,0]/%x[1,0]/%x[1,1]	真/很/ADV
POS+Next Term+Next POS	%x[0,1]/%x[1,0]/%x[1,1]	ADV/很/ADV
Term+Second Next Term	%x[0,0]/%x[2,0]	真/好
Term+Second Next POS	%x[0,0]/%x[2,1]	真/ Vi
POS+Second Next Term	%x[0,1]/%x[2,0]	ADV/好
POS+Second Next POS	%x[0,1]/%x[2,1]	ADV/ Vi
Term+Second Next Term+Second Next POS	%x[0,0]/%x[2,0]/%x[2,1]	真/好/Vi
POS+Second Next Term+Second Next POS	%x[0,1]/%x[2,0]/%x[2,1]	ADV/好/ Vi

Table 13: All the templates and the corresponding value for the sample sentence.

NTOU Chinese Grammar Checker for CGED Shared Task

Chuan-Jie Lin and Shao-Heng Chen
Department of Computer Science and Engineering
National Taiwan Ocean University
No 2, Pei-Ning Road, Keelung 202, Taiwan R.O.C.
{cjlin, shchen.cse}@ntou.edu.tw

Abstract

Grammatical error diagnosis is an essential part in a language-learning tutoring system. Participating in the second Chinese grammar error detection task, we proposed a new system which measures the likelihood of sentences generated by deleting, inserting, or exchanging characters or words. Two sentence likelihood functions were proposed based on frequencies of space-removed version of Google n-grams. The best system achieved a precision of 23.4% and a recall of 36.4% in the identification level.

1 Introduction

Although that Chinese grammars are not defined as clearly as English, Chinese native speakers can easily identify grammatical errors in sentences. This is one of the most difficult parts for foreigners to learn Chinese. They are often uncertain about the proper grammars to make sentences. It is an interesting research topic to develop a Chinese grammar checker to give helps in Chinese learning. There have been several researches focused on Chinese (Wu *et al.*, 2010; Chang *et al.*, 2012; Yu and Chen, 2012; Tseng *et al.*, 2014).

In NLPTEA-1 (Yu *et al.*, 2014), the first Chinese grammatical error diagnosis evaluation project, the organizers defined four kinds of grammatical errors: redundant, missing, selection, and disorder. The evaluation was based on detection of error occurrence in a sentence, disregarding its location and correction. We developed an error detection system by machine learning.

However in NLPTEA2-CGED (Lee *et al.*, 2015), it is required to report the location of a detected error. To meet this requirement, two new systems were proposed in this paper. The first one was an adaptation of the classifier developed by machine learning where location information was considered. The second one employed hand-crafted rules to predict the locations of errors.

We also designed two scoring functions to predict the likelihood of a sentence. Totally three runs were submitted to NLPTEA2-CGED task. Evaluation results showed that rule-based systems achieved better performance. More details are described in the rest of this paper.

This paper is organized as follows. Section 2 gives the definition of Chinese grammatical error diagnosis task. Section 3 delivers our newly proposed n-gram statistics-based systems. Section 4 gives a brief description about our SVM classifier. Section 5 shows the evaluation results and Section 6 concludes this paper.

2 Task Definition

The task of Chinese grammatical error diagnosis (CGED) in NLPTEA2 is defined as follows. Given a sentence, a CGED system should first decide if there is any of the four types of errors occur in the sentence: redundant, missing, selection, and disorder. If an error is found, report its beginning and ending locations.

Training data provided by the task organizers contain the error types and corrected sentences. Four types of errors are shortly explained here. All examples are selected from the training set where the locations of errors are measured in Chinese characters.

- Redundant: some unnecessary character appears in a sentence

Proceedings of The 2nd Workshop on Natural Language Processing Techniques for Educational Applications, pages 15–19,
Beijing, China, July 31, 2015. ©2015 Association for Computational Linguistics and Asian Federation of Natural Language Processing

[A2-0598, Redundant, 3, 3]
(X) 他是真很好的人
(He is a *really very good man.)
(O) 他是很好的人
(He is a very good man.)

- Missing: some necessary character is missing in a sentence

[B1-0046, Missing, 4, 4]
(X) 母親節一個禮拜就要到了
(Mother's Day is coming in one week.)
(O) 母親節再一個禮拜就要到了
(Mother's Day is coming in one more week.)

- Selection: a word is misused and should be replaced by another word

[B1-1544, Selection, 1, 2]
(X) 還給原來的地方只花幾秒鐘而已
(It only takes a few seconds to *return it to its original place.)
(O) 放回原來的地方只花幾秒鐘而已
(It only takes a few seconds to put it back to its original place.)

Note that sometimes a SELECTION error looks like a missing character rather than a misused word. It is because there are many one-character words in Chinese. An example is given as follows.

[B1-1546, Selection, 5, 5]
(X) 關於跟你見的事
(About the seeing with you...)
(O) 關於跟你見面的事
(About the meeting with you...)

- Disorder: some words' locations should be exchanged

[B1-2099, Disorder, 4, 6]
(X) 當然我會一定開心
(Of course I will be certainly happy.)
(O) 當然我一定會開心
(Of course I will certainly be happy.)

3 N-gram Statistics-Based System

Besides the classifiers developed in the last CGED task (Yu *et al.*, 2014), we proposed a new method to build a CGED system based on n-gram statistics from the World Wide Web.

Our assumption is: a corrected sentence has a larger probability than an erroneous sentence. I.e. deleting unnecessary characters, adding necessary characters, and exchanging locations of misplaced words will result in a better sentence. Our system will try to delete, insert, or exchange characters or words in a given sentence to see if the newly generated sentence receives a higher score of likelihood. Steps and details are described in this section.

3.1 Sentence Likelihood Scores

Since our method heavily counts on likelihood of a sentence being seen in Chinese, it is important to choose a good scoring function to measure the likelihood. Although n-gram language model is a common choice, a corpus in a very large scale with word-segmentation information is not easy to obtain. An alternation is to use Google N-gram frequency data.

Chinese Web 5-gram[1] is real data released by Google Inc. who collected from all webpages in the World Wide Web which are unigram to 5-grams. Frequencies of these ngrams are also provided. Some examples from the Chinese Web 5-gram dataset are given here:

Unigram:	稀釋劑	17260
Bigram:	蒸發量 超過	69
Trigram:	能量 遠 低於	113
4-gram:	張貼 色情 圖片 或	73
5-gram:	幸好 我們 發現 得 早	155

We have proposed several sentence likelihood scoring functions when dealing with Chinese spelling errors (Lin and Chu, 2015). But in order to avoid interference of word segmentation errors, we further design some likelihood scoring functions which utilize substring frequencies instead of word n-gram frequencies.

By removing space between n-grams in the Chinese Web 5-gram dataset, we constructed a new dataset containing identical substrings with their web frequencies. For instances, n-grams in the previous example will become:

Length=9:	稀釋劑	17260
Length=15:	蒸發量超過	69
Length=15:	能量遠低於	113
Length=18:	張貼色情圖片或	73
Length=24:	幸好我們發現得早	155

Note that if two different n-gram sets become the same after removing the space, their will merge

[1] https://catalog.ldc.upenn.edu/LDC2010T06

into one entry with the summation of their frequencies. Simplified Chinese words were translated into Traditional Chinese in advanced.

Given a sentence S, let $SubStr(S, n)$ be the set of all substrings in S whose lengths are n bytes. We define ***Google String Frequency*** $gsf(u)$ of a string u with length n to be its frequency data provided in the modified Chinese Web 5-gram dataset. If a string does not appear in that dataset, its gsf value is defined to be 0.

Two new sentence likelihood scoring functions are defined as follows. Equation 1 gives the definitions of ***length-weighted string log frequency score*** $SL(S)$ where each substring in S with a length of n contributes a score of the logarithm of its Google string frequency multiplied by n. We think that short strings are not that meaningful, this function only considers strings no shorter than 6 bytes (i.e. a two-character Chinese words or a bigram of one-character Chinese words.)

$$SL(S) = \sum_{n=6}^{len(S)} \left(n \times \sum_{u \in SubStr(S,n)} \log(gsf(u)) \right) \quad (1)$$

Equation 2 gives a macro-averaging version of Equation 1 where scores are averaged within each length before summation over different lengths.

$$SLe(S) = \sum_{n=6}^{len(S)} \left(\frac{n \times \sum_{u \in SubStr(S,n)} \log(gsf(u))}{|SubStr(S,n)|} \right) \quad (2)$$

3.2 Character Deletion (Case of Redundant)

To test if a sentence has a redundant character, a set of new sentences are generated by removing characters in the original sentence one by one. If any of the new sentences has a higher likelihood score than the original sentence, it may be the case of redundant-type error.

Because the experimental data are essays written by Chinese-learning foreign students, some redundant errors are commonly seen across different students. Table 1 shows the most frequent redundant errors in the training data.

Char	Freq	Char	Freq	Char	Freq
了	66	去	15	就	6
的	56	在	13	很	6
是	27	會	8	要	6
有	27	得	7	把	5

Table 1. Frequent Redundant Errors

In order not to generate too many new sentences, we only deleted the characters of the frequent redundant errors which occurred at least three times. There were 23 of them which covered 66% of the redundant errors in the training data. Examples of character deletion are as follows where 很 and 到 are frequent redundant errors.

[B1-0764] org: 我很想到跟你見面
new: 我想到跟你見面
new: 我很想跟你見面

3.3 Character Insertion (Case of Missing)

To test if a sentence has a missing character, a set of new sentences are generated by inserting a character into the original sentence at each position (including the beginning and the end). If any of the new sentences has a higher likelihood score than the original sentence, it may be the case of missing-type error.

Similarly, some missing errors are commonly seen across the essays written by Chinese-learning foreign students. Table 2 shows the most frequent missing errors in the training data.

Char	Freq	Char	Freq	Char	Freq
的	74	有	24	要	13
了	65	會	18	在	12
是	44	就	17	過	12
都	34	很	16	讓	11

Table 2. Frequent Missing Errors

In order not to generate too many new sentences, we only inserted the characters of the frequent redundant errors which occurred at least three times. There were 34 of them which covered 73.7% of the missing errors in the training data. Examples of character deletion are as follows.

[B1-1047] org: 我真很怕
new: 的我真很怕
new: 我的真很怕
......
new: 我真很怕的
new: 了我真很怕
......
new: 我真很怕買

3.4 Word Exchanging (Case of Disorder)

To test if a sentence has a disorder error, the original sentence is word-segmented, and a set of new sentences are generated by exchanging words in the original sentence, each pair at a time. If any of the new sentences has a higher likelihood score than the original sentence, it may be the case of disorder-type error. Examples of word exchange are as follows.

[B1-1047] org: 我 真 很 怕
new: 真 我 很 怕
new: 很 真 我 怕
new: 怕 真 很 我
new: 我 很 真 怕
new: 我 怕 很 真
new: 我 真 怕 很

3.5 Error Decision

All the new sentences, whenever generated by removing characters, inserting characters, or exchanging words, are scored by the sentence likelihood functions. The creation type and the modification location of the top-1 new sentence are reported as the error type and error location. If no new sentence's score is higher than the original's, it is reported as a "Correct" case.

3.6 Selection-Error Detection

If a detected error in Section 3.5 is a redundant case, it may also be a Selection-type error. If the deleted character occurs in a multi-character word in the original sentence, report this error as a Selection-type error.

[B1-0764] Redundant => Selection
org: 我 很 想 到 跟 你 見面
(I really want to to meet you.)
new: 我 很 想 跟 你 見面
(I really want to meet you.)

Similarly, if a detected error in Section 3.5 is a missing case, it may also be a Selection-type error. To make a decision, the new sentence is also word-segmented. If the inserted character occurs in a multi-character word in the original sentence, report this error as a Selection-type error.

[B1-1047] Missing => Selection
[org] 我 真 很 怕
(I am *real scared.)
[new] 我 真的 很 怕
(I am really scared.)

4 Error Detection by Machine Learning

We also modified our previous CGED system participated in NLPTEA-1 to do error detection. It was a SVM classifier where 3 features were used for error detection:

f_{bi}: **number of infrequent word bigrams** appearing in the sentence, where "infrequent bigram" is defined as a bigram whose Google N-gram frequency is less than 100 or not even collected in the Chinese Web 5-gram dataset

f_{stop}: a Boolean feature denoting the **occurrence of a stop POS bigram** which is often seen in a redundant-type error, such as **VH + T** (a stative intransitive verb followed by a particle) or **Cbb + DE** (a correlative conjunction followed by a function word "的")

f_{len}: **length of the original sentence,** because a short sentence usually does not have missing- or disorder-type errors

Since the error detection classifier does not provide location information of an error, its location is decided by heuristic rules as follows.

1. If a stop POS bigram appears in the original sentence, the beginning and ending location of the first word matching this bigram are reported.
2. Or, if an infrequent word bigram appears in the original sentence, the beginning and ending location of the first word matching this bigram are reported.
3. Otherwise, simply report "1" as location.

5 Experiments

Three formal runs from our systems were submitted to NLPTEA2-CGED this year. The first run was created by the SVM classifier. The second run as created by the newly proposed CGED system with the original version of the length-weighted string log frequency function. The third run as created by the newly proposed CGED system with the macro-averaging version of the length-weighted string log frequency function.

	NTOU1	NTOU2	NTOU3
Detection Level			
Precision	50.00	**51.64**	50.98
Recall	**100.00**	97.60	98.60
F-1 Score	66.67	**67.54**	67.21
Identification Level			
Precision	18.96	**23.40**	20.95
Recall	28.48	**36.40**	31.96
F-1 Score	26.05	**33.40**	29.27
Position Level			
Precision	0.99	**1.00**	**1.00**
Recall	14.90	**16.00**	15.43
F-1 Score	12.38	**13.40**	12.87

Table 3. Evaluation Results of NTOU Runs

Table 3 shows the evaluation results of our three formal runs. All results suggest that a system using the length-weighted string log frequency function achieves better performance than a SVM classifier.

6 Conclusion

This is the second Chinese grammatical error diagnosis task. We proposed three systems to do the task. One is a SVM classifier where features are length, numbers of infrequent word bigrams, and occurrence of stop POS bigrams. The other two measure the likelihood of newly generated sentences by deleting, inserting, or exchanging characters or words. Two sentence likelihood functions were proposed based on frequencies of space-removed Google n-grams. The second system performed better than the other two which achieved a precision of 23.4% and a recall of 36.4%.

Although the performance seemed not good enough, our system was ranked at the second place in the identification level and the third in the position level, which means that the task is very hard. More rules and features should be studied in the future.

Reference

Ru-Yng Chang, Chung-Hsien Wu, and Philips Kokoh Prasetyo (2012). "Error Diagnosis of Chinese Sentences Using Inductive Learning Algorithm and Decomposition-Based Testing Mechanism," *ACM Transactions on Asian Language Information Processing*, 11(1), article 3, March 2012.

Lung-Hao Lee, Liang-Chih Yu, Kuei-Ching Lee, Yuen-Hsien Tseng, Li-Ping Chang, and Hsin-Hsi Chen (2014). "A Sentence Judgment System for Grammatical Error Detection," *Proceedings of the 25th International Conference on Computational Linguistics* (*COLING '14*), 67-70.

Lung-Hao Lee, Liang-Chih Yu, and Li-Ping Chang (2015). "Overview of Shared Task on Chinese Grammatical Error Diagnosis," *Proceedings of the 2nd Workshop on Natural Language Processing Techniques for Educational Applications*, to be appeared.

Chuan-Jie Lin and Wei-Cheng Chu (2015). "A Study on Chinese Spelling Check Using Confusion Sets and N-gram Statistics," *International Journal of Computational Linguistics and Chinese Language Processing*, to be appeared.

Chung-Hsien Wu, Chao-Hong Liu, Matthew Harris, and Liang-Chih Yu (2010). "Sentence Correction Incorporating Relative Position and Parse Template Language Models," *IEEE Transactions on Audio, Speech, and Language Processing*, 18(6), 1170-1181.

Chi-Hsin Yu and Hsin-Hsi Chen (2012). "Detecting Word Ordering Errors in Chinese Sentences for Learning Chinese as a Foreign Language," *Proceedings of the 24th International Conference on Computational Linguistics* (*COLING '12*), 3003-3017.

Liang-Chih Yu, Lung-Hao Lee, and Li-Ping Chang (2014). "Overview of Grammatical Error Diagnosis for Learning Chinese as a Foreign Language," *Proceedings of the 1st Workshop on Natural Language Processing Techniques for Educational Applications* (*NLPTEA '14*), 42-47.

Collocational Aid for Learners of Japanese as a Second Language

Lis Pereira and Yuji Matsumoto
Graduate School of Information Science
Nara Institute of Science and Technology
{lis-k, matsu}@is.naist.jp

Abstract

We present Collocation Assistant, a prototype of a collocational aid designed to promote the collocational competence of learners of Japanese as a second language (JSL). Focusing on noun-verb constructions, the tool automatically flags possible collocation errors and suggests better collocations by using corrections extracted from a large annotated Japanese language learner corpus. Each suggestion includes several usage examples to help learners choose the best candidate. In a preliminary user study with JSL learners, Collocation Assistant received positive feedback, and the results indicate that the system is helpful to assist learners in choosing correct word combinations in Japanese.

1 Introduction

Collocational competence is one of the factors which contribute to the differences between native speakers and second language learners (Shei and Pain, 2000). However, studies confirm that the correct use of collocations is challenging, even for advanced second language learners (Liu, 2002; Nesselhauf, 2003; Wible et al., 2003). Since there are no well-defined rules to determine collocation preferences, language learners are prone to produce word combinations that, although they may be grammatically and semantically well formed, may sound "unnatural" to a native speaker. Moreover, the number of tools designed to target language learners' collocation errors is limited or inexistent for many languages, which makes it difficult for learners to detect and correct these errors. Therefore, an application that can detect a learners' collocation errors and suggest the most appropriate "ready-made units" as corrections is an important goal for natural language processing (Leacock et al., 2014).

In this paper, we describe Collocation Assistant, a web-based and corpus-based collocational aid, aiming at helping JSL learners expand their collocational knowledge. Focusing on noun-verb constructions, Collocation Assistant flags possible collocation errors and suggests a ranked list of more conventional expressions. Each suggestion is supported with evidence from authentic texts, showing several usage examples of the expression in context to help learners choose the best candidate. Based on our previous study (Pereira et al., 2013), the system generates corrections to the learners' collocation error tendencies by using noun and verb corrections extracted from a large annotated Japanese learner corpus. For ranking the collocation correction candidates, it uses the Weighted Dice coefficient (Kitamura and Matsumoto, 1997). We add to our previous work by implementing an interface that allows end-users to identify and correct their own collocation errors. In addition, we conducted a preliminary evaluation with JSL learners to gather their feedback on using the tool.

2 The need for collocational aids

Existing linguistic tools are often of limited utility in assisting second language learners with collocations. Most spell checkers and grammar checkers can help correct errors made by native speakers, but offer no assistance for non-native errors. Futagi et al. (2008) note that common aids for second language learners namely, dictionaries and thesauri are often of limited value when the learner does not know the appropriate collocation and must sort through a list of synonyms to find one that is contextually appropriate. Yi et al. (2008) observe that language learners often use search engines to check if a phrase is commonly used by observing the number of results returned. However, search engines are not designed to offer alternative phrases that are more commonly used than the

Proceedings of The 2nd Workshop on Natural Language Processing Techniques for Educational Applications, pages 20–25,
Beijing, China, July 31, 2015.

learner's phrase (Park et al., 2008). Concordancers seem to be an alternative to search engines, but they retrieve too much information because they usually allow only single-word queries. Too much information might distract and confuse the user (Chen et al., 2014). Thus, a computer program that automatically identifies potential collocation errors and suggests corrections would be a more appropriate resource for second language learners.

A few researchers have proposed useful English corpus-based tools for correcting collocation errors (Futagi et al., 2008; Liu et al., 2009; Park et al., 2008; Chang et al., 2008; Wible et al., 2003; Dahlmeier and Ng, 2011). In a user study, Park et al. (2008) observed positive reactions from users when using their system. In another study, Liou et al. (2006) showed that the miscollocation aid proposed by Chang et al. (2008) can help learners improve their knowledge in collocations. One limitation is that these proposed tools rely on resources of limited coverage, such as dictionaries, thesauri, or manually constructed databases to generate the candidates. Another drawback is that most of these systems rely solely on well-formed English resources (except Wible et al., 2003) and do not actually take into account the learners' tendencies toward collocation errors.

3 Collocation Assistant

In the proposed system, we focused on providing Japanese collocation suggestions for potential collocation errors in Japanese noun-verb constructions. Given the noun-verb collocation input by a learner, the system first checks if it exists in the reference corpora. If not, the input is validated as a potential collocation error and a message is displayed to the user. Next, the system suggests more appropriate noun-verb collocations. For instance, if the learner types *夢を<u>する</u> (*yume wo <u>suru</u>* , lit. '<u>to do</u> a dream'), the system flags a collocation error. When the user clicks on "same noun", the system displays better collocations with the same noun input by the user, such as 夢を<u>見る</u> (*yume wo <u>miru</u>*, 'to dream') and 夢を持つ (*yume wo motsu*, 'to hold a dream'), as shown in Figure 1. Likewise, when the user clicks on "same verb", the system displays better collocations with the same verb input by the user. If the user clicks on "View all suggestions", all possible better collocations with the same noun or the same verb input by the user are displayed. Aside from the collocations, sentence examples for each phrase suggestion are displayed, showing the phrase in context with surrounding text. Showing phrases in context can be crucial in helping users determine which phrase is most appropriate (Park et al., 2008). Even if the learner's input is not flagged as an error, it will undergo the same correction process, since better collocations than the input might exist. In this case, the learner will check the ranked suggestions and sentence examples and choose the most appropriate expression. The current system does not detect which component (noun or verb) is wrong in a noun-verb construction. Therefore, the learner must specify which component would be corrected by the system. This has been the common evaluation setup in collocation error correction, which assumes that the error is already detected and more focus is given on correcting the identified errors. (Dahlmeier and Ng, 2011). In case the learner types only a noun or only a verb, the system will suggest collocations containing words that strongly collocate with this input.

3.1 Approach to collocation suggestion

Based on our previous study (Pereira et al., 2013), our Collocation Assistant generates collocation corrections by using noun and verb corrections extracted from a large annotated Japanese language learner corpus, Lang-8[1]. This approach to generating corrections achieved superior performance compared to methods that generate candidates based solely on the semantic relation of words. Using noun and verb corrections extracted from a learner corpus, our system can explore the learners' tendency to commit collocation errors. For ranking the collocation correction candidates, the tool uses the Weighted Dice coefficient (Kitamura and Matsumoto, 1997). This association measure achieved the best performance in our task among other association measures evaluated (i.e. pointwise mutual information, log-likelihood and dice coefficient).

3.2 Resources used for providing sentence examples

We used several monolingual and bilingual resources for providing useful sentence examples to users. These resources are:

Bilingual resources. 1) Tatoeba Corpus[2], a

[1] http://cl.naist.jp/nldata/lang-8/

[2] https://tatoeba.org/eng/

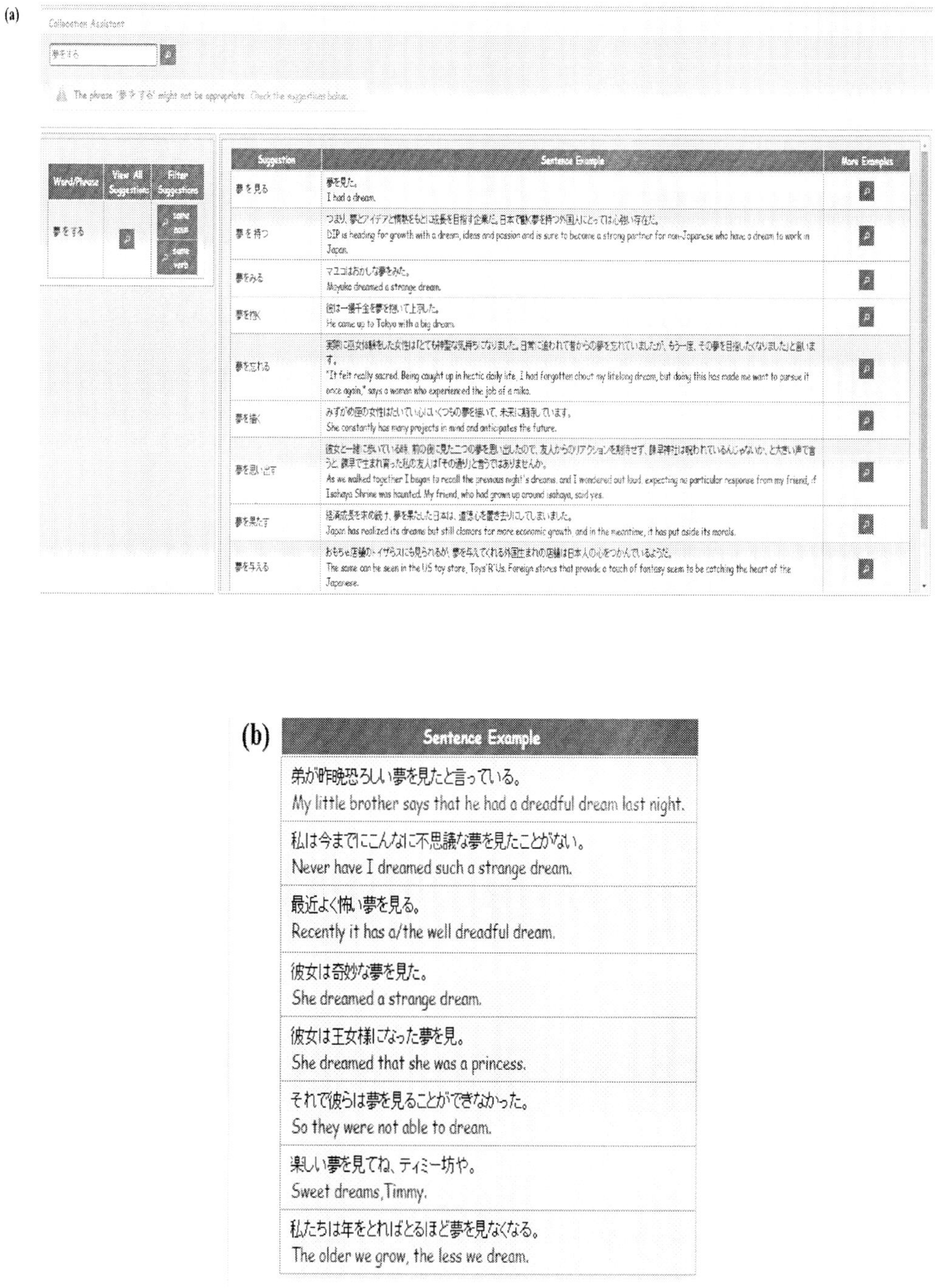

Figure 1: An example of collocation suggestions produced by the system given the erroneous collocation *夢をする (*yume wo suru*, lit. 'to do a dream') as input. (a) Collocation suggestions are shown on the left and an example sentence for each suggestion is shown on the right. In the example, 夢を見る(*yume wo miru*, 'to dream') is the correct collocation. (b) Further examples for each suggestion are shown when the user clicks on "More examples". In the example, further examples for the collocation 夢を見る(*yume wo miru*, 'to dream') are displayed.

free collaborative online database of example sentences geared towards foreign language learners. We used the Japanese-English sentences available in the website. 2) Hiragana Times (HT) Corpus[3], a Japanese-English bilingual corpus of magazine articles of Hiragana Times, a bilingual magazine written in Japanese and English to introduce Japan to non-Japanese, covering a wide range of topics (culture, society, history, politics, etc.). 3) Kyoto Wikipedia (KW) Corpus[4], a corpus created by manually translating Japanese Wikipedia articles (related to Kyoto) into English.

Monolingual resource: the Balanced Corpus of Contemporary Written Japanese (Maekawa, 2008) was used for the noun-verb expressions where no bilingual examples were available.

	# *jp* sentences	# *en* sentences
Tatoeba	203,191	203,191
HT	117,492	117,492
KW	329,169	329,169
BCCWJ	871,184	-

Table 1: Data used as sentence examples.

4 Preliminary User Study of the Collocation Assistant

We conducted a preliminary evaluation with JSL learners to gather their feedback on using the Collocation Assistant. The results gave us insights about the usefulness of the tool, and about the possible interesting evaluations that should be carried out in the future.

4.1 Participants

In this study, 10 JSL learners, all graduate students from the same institution as the authors were invited to participate. Participants' ages ranged from 24 to 33 years, and the average age was 27.5. Among the respondents, 2 were female and 8 were male, and they had different language backgrounds (Chinese, Indonesian, Tagalog, Swahili, Spanish, and Basque). Regarding their proficiency level, three were beginners, three were intermediate, and four were advanced learners, based on the Japanese-Language proficiency test certificate level they previously obtained. All participants were regular computer users.

[3]http://www.hiraganatimes.com/

[4]https://alaginrc.nict.go.jp/WikiCorpus/

4.2 Procedure

A collocation test was designed to examine whether or not the tool could help JSL learners find proper Japanese collocations. This included 12 Japanese sentences from the Lang-8 learner corpus and from another small annotated Japanese learner corpus, NAIST Goyo Corpus (Oyama, Komachi and Matsumoto, 2013). The sentences and their corrections were further validated by a professional Japanese teacher. Each sentence contained one noun-verb collocation error made by JSL learners. The participants were asked to use the Collocation Assistant to identify and correct the errors. Next, they were asked to write a small paragraph in Japanese and to use the tool if they needed. After performing the task, a survey questionnaire was also administered to better understand the learners' impressions of the tool. The questionnaire contained 43 questions answerable by a 7-point Likert-scale (with 7 labeled "strongly agree" and 1 labeled "strongly disagree"). The second part of the questionnaire contained 7 open-ended questions. Our survey questionnaire inquired on the difficulty of Japanese collocations, the usefulness of Collocation Assistant, the design of Collocation Assistant and the quality of the retrieved data.

4.3 Results on the Collocation Test and Survey Questionnaire

The participants successfully found corrections for an average of 8.9 (SD=1.6) out of 12 cases. The average time participants took to complete the task was 29 (SD=16) minutes. The average score of beginner and intermediate learners was 9.6 (SD=0.5). They scored higher than advanced learners, who obtained an average score of 8.2 (SD=2.0). Analyzing the log files of their interactions with the system, we observed that intermediate and beginner learners used the system 40% more times (on average) than the advanced learners. We noticed that two advanced learners tried to answer the questions without using the system when they felt confident about the answer, whereas the beginners and intermediate learners used the system for all sentences and obtained higher scores. The participants had difficulty in correcting two particular long sentences in the test. The noun-verb collocations in the sentences alone were not incorrect, but they were not appropriate in the context they appeared. The participants had difficulty in finding sentence examples close to the meaning of the sentences in the test. Although we need to evaluate this tool with a larger number of users, we observed that the system was effective in helping the learners choose the proper collocations. In the questionnaire administered, all participants acknowledged their difficulty in using Japanese collocations appropriately and stated that the software aids they used did not provide enough information about the meaning of Japanese phrases nor help in correcting errors in Japanese expressions. Their attitude toward the usefulness of Collocation Assistant was mostly positive and they thought the tool was useful to help choose the proper way to use Japanese expressions. Most participants considered the interface easy to use (M=6.3, SD=0.8). Regarding the quality of the retrieved data, the participants expressed satisfaction with the retrieved collocations, with an average score of 6.5 (SD=0.7). They also expressed satisfaction with the ranking of the collocations presented, with an average score of 5.8 (SD=0.6). Additionally, they reported that the sentence examples further helped them understand in which context an expression should be used. However, some participants expressed dissatisfaction with the complexity of some example sentences: some of the sentences were too long and difficult to understand. In the second part of the questionnaire, some participants stated that the Collocation Assistant could be helpful when learning new words and when one does not know which word combinations to use. They also suggested that the tool could be useful for teachers too when giving feedback to their students about the common errors they make and when providing alternative ways of expressing the same idea. Lastly, they suggested several improvements regarding the sentence examples and the interface: show shorter and simpler example sentences, highlithgt the user's input in the sentence examples and allow English search.

5 Conclusions

In this paper, we presented a collocational aid system for JSL learners. The tool flags possible collocation errors and suggests corrections by using corrections extracted from a large annotated Japanese language learner corpus. Our Collocation Assistant received positive feedback from JSL learners in a preliminary user study. The system can be used independently as a phrase dictionary, or it can be integrated into the writing component of some bigger CALL systems. For example, Collocation Assistant can be used by teachers as a way to obtain better understanding about learners' errors and help them provide better feedback to the students. One limitation of our experiments is the limited contextual information (only the noun, particle, and verb written by the learner). In the future, to verify our approach and to improve on our current results, we plan to consider a wider context size and other types of constructions (e.g., adjective-noun, adverb-verb, etc.). We also intend to investigate how to adjust the difficulty level of the sentences according to the user's proficienSolution cy level. Finally, we plan to conduct a more extensive evaluation with JSL learners to verify the usefulness of the tool in practical learning scenarios.

Acknowledgments

We would like to thank anonymous reviewers for their insightul comments and suggestions.

References

Chang, Y. C., Chang, J. S., Chen, H. J. and Liou, H. C. 2008. An automatic collocation writing assistant for Taiwanese EFL learners: A case of corpus-based NLP technology. *Computer Assisted Language Learning*, 21(3), 283–299. doi: 10.1080/09588220802090337.

Chen, M.-H., Huang, C.-C., Huang, S.-T., Chang, J.S. and Liou, H.-C. 2014. An Automatic Reference Aid for ImprovingEFL Learners' Formulaic Expressionsin Productive Language Use. *IEEE Transactions on Learning Technologies*, 01/2014; 7(1):57-68. doi:10.1109/TLT.2013.34.

Dahlmeier, D. and Ng, H. T. 2011. Correcting semantic collocation errors with L1-induced paraphrases. In *Proceedings of the Conference on Empirical Methods in Natural Language Processing*- (pp. 107-117). Edinburgh, Scotland, UK, July 27–31, 2011.

Futagi, Y., Deane, P., Chodorow, M. and Tetreault, J. 2008. A computational approach to detecting collocation errors in the writing of non-native speakers of English. *Computer Assisted Language Learning* 21(4), 353–367. doi: 10.1080/09588220802343561

Kitamura, M. and Matsumoto, Y. 1997. Automatic extraction of translation patterns in parallel corpora. Automatic extraction of translation patterns in parallel corpora. *Information Processing Society of Japan Journal*, 38 (4), 727–735.

Leacock, C., Chodorow, M., Gamon, M., and Tetreault, J. 2014. *Automated grammatical error detection for language learners*. Synthesis lectures on human language technologies, 7(1), 1-170.

Liou, H., Chang, J., Chen, H., Lin, C., Liaw, M., Gao, Z., Jang, J., Yeh, Y, Chuang, T. and You, G. (2006) 2006. Corpora processing and computational scaffolding for a Web-based English learning environment: The CANDLE Project. *CALICO Journal*, 24 (1), 77-95.

Liu, A. L. 2002. *A Corpus-based Lexical Semantic Investigation of VN Miscollocations in Taiwan Learners' English*. Master Thesis, Tamkang University, Taiwan.

Maekawa, K. 2008. Balanced Corpus of Contemporary Written Japanese. In *Proceedings of The 6th Workshop on Asian Language Resources*- (pp. 101–102). Association for Computational Linguistics, Stroudsburg, PA, USA.

Nesselhauf, N. 2003. The use of collocations by advanced learners of English and some implications for teaching. *Applied Linguistics*, 24, 223–242.

Oyama,H., Komachi, M. and Matsumoto, Y. 2013. Towards Automatic Error Type Classification of Japanese Language Learners' Writings. In *Proceedings of the 27th Pacific Asia Conference on Language, Information, and Computation*, pp.163-172, Taipei, Taiwan.

Park, T., Lank, E., Poupart, P. and Terry, M. 2008. "Is the Sky Pure Today?" AwkChecker: An Assistive Tool for Detecting and Correcting Collocation Errors. In *Proceedings of the 21th Annual Assotiation for Computing Machinery Symposium on User Interface Software and Technology*- pages 121-130. Monterey, CA, USA.

Pereira, L., Manguilimotan, E. and Matsumoto, Y. 2013. Automated Collocation Suggestion for Japanese Second Language Learners. In *Proceedings of the Student Research Workshop 51st Annual Meeting of the ACL*, pages 52-58, Sofia, Bulgaria.

Shei, C.-C. and Pain, H. 2000. An esl writer's collocational aid. *Computer Assisted Language Learning*, 13(2):167–182.

Wible, D., Kuo, C., Tsao, N., Liu, A. and Lin, H. 2003. Bootstrapping in a Language Learning Environment, *Journal of Computer-Assisted Learning*, 19(1), pp. 90-102. SSCI, LLBA.

Yi, X., Gao, J. and Dolan, W. A web-based English proofing system for English as a Second Language users. 2008. In *Proceedings of the 3rd International Joint Conference on Natural Language Processing*- pages 619–624. Association for Computational Linguistics, Stroudsburg, PA, USA.

Semi-automatic Generation of Multiple-Choice Tests from Mentions of Semantic Relations

Renlong Ai, Sebastian Krause, Walter Kasper, Feiyu Xu, Hans Uszkoreit
German Research Center for Artificial Intelligence
Alt-Moabit 91c, 10559 Berlin, Germany
{renlong.ai,skrause,kasper,feiyu,uszkoreit}@dfki.de

Abstract

We propose a strategy for the semi-automatic generation of learning material for reading-comprehension tests, guided by semantic relations embedded in expository texts. Our approach combines methods from the areas of information extraction and paraphrasing in order to present a language teacher with a set of candidate multiple-choice questions and answers that can be used for verifying a language learners reading capabilities. We implemented a web-based prototype showing the feasibility of our approach and carried out a pilot user evaluation that resulted in encouraging feedback but also pointed out aspects of the strategy and prototype implementation which need improvements.

1 Introduction

Computer assisted language learning (CALL) opens many new opportunities for language learners and teachers. In this paper, we focus on one often used tool of this area: reading-comprehension tests. Such tests are an important means for assessing a learner's current skill level by verifying his understanding of foreign-language texts. Some work in the area of CALL has focused on reducing the teacher's workload in context of reading-comprehension tests by inventing methods for the automatic scoring of such tests (see Section 5). In contrast, we propose a strategy for the semi-automatic *generation* of learning material for reading-comprehension tests, guided by semantic relations embedded in expository text. The multiple-choice exercises ask learners to choose from a list of statements about semantic relations the one which is actually expressed in a long free text. The exercises attempt to test whether the learners understand the text and have enough language knowledge for recognizing variants of expressions for the same semantic relations.

Our strategy combines technologies from different branches of NLP. A standard information extraction (IE) system is utilized to automatically recognize relevant entities and semantic relations among them in texts. The resulting mentions are used for the creation of (a) paraphrases of the actually mentioned facts and (b) natural-language statements expressing facts *not* mentioned in the original text, i. e., the sentence generation system takes linguistic patterns filled with entities as input and produces paraphrases as potential answer candidates. The multiple-choice exercises generated in this way are then presented to a language teacher, who has to go trough them and can reject a subset of these or can replace individual elements. This human-in-the-loop step is necessary because of the noise inherent to current NLP systems. We let the teacher choose the appropriate trade-off between correctness and content-coverage of the generated (candidate) questionnaires.

The proposed strategy is implemented in a web-based prototype system, with separate interfaces for teachers (for the preparation of exercises) and learners (for conducting the exercises). This prototype is capable of handling a number of selected semantic relations from the biographic and financial domains, illustrating the applicability of the approach for the frequent class of news articles from tabloid press and business news. Based on this prototype, we carried out a pilot user study to gather insights on the best directions for future development.

In summary, the contributions of this paper are as follows:

- A strategy for the semi-automatic generation of learning material for fact-centric reading-comprehension tests.
- A way of incorporating the idea of a human-

Proceedings of The 2nd Workshop on Natural Language Processing Techniques for Educational Applications, pages 26–33,
Beijing, China, July 31, 2015.

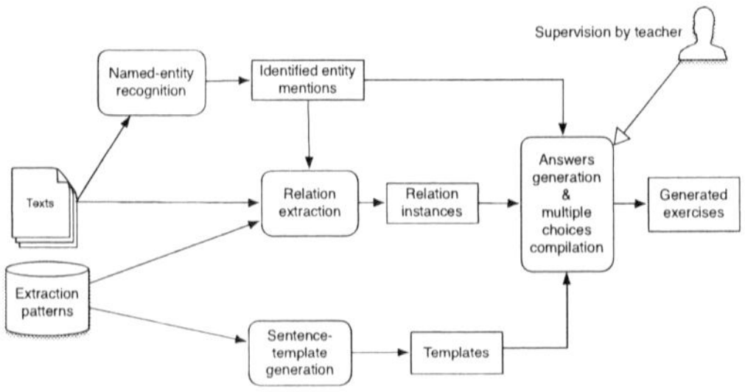

Figure 1: Workflow of exercise generation.

in-the-loop into the data flow of the strategy.

- A web-based prototype implementation of this approach, along with a pilot user study to explore directions for further development.

2 A workflow for automatic exercise generation

In this section, we present our generic approach towards the generation of candidate multiple-choice questions for given expository texts. Furthermore, we detail the steps necessary for a teacher to compile actual reading-comprehension exercises suitable for presentation to learners, given only our approach's resulting candidates.

2.1 Reading-comprehension exercises

The reading-comprehension exercises generated by our approach ask for relational facts mentioned in a text. In order to automatically identify these, we apply a series of processing steps, as depicted in Figure 1. In the first step, the input texts, e.g., news articles, are processed by a standard component for named-entity recognition (e.g., the well-known Stanford Named Entity Recognizer by Finkel et al. (2005)), in order to identify persons, organization, locations, etc. mentioned in the text, followed by application of a relation extraction system for the identification of facts.

The information about mentioned facts and entities is passed on to a further processing step in which a mentioned instance of a semantic relation is transformed into a natural-language statement, paraphrasing the original occurrence of the fact. Furthermore, the information about named-entity occurrences is used to create false statements about relations between the entities. For each fact identified in a text, four choices are provided as potential statements about the text, only one of them stating a fact actually mentioned.

2.2 Relation Extraction

A key part of our approach is the application of a *pattern-based* relation extraction (RE) system. Such systems, e.g., NELL (Carlson et al., 2010; Mitchell et al., 2015), PATTY (Nakashole et al., 2012), DARE (Xu et al., 2007), rely on lexico-syntactic patterns that pose restrictions on the surface level or grammatical level of sentences. Their underlying assumption is that whenever a given sentence matches a given pattern (i.e., a sentence template), the sentence expresses the pattern's corresponding semantic relation. This assumption does not always hold, hence the system output usually contains a certain amount of noise, which makes a human-in-the-loop necessary for high-precision applications.

Typically, RE systems associate patterns with a confidence score of some kind, allowing downstream components to trade precision for recall. At this step in our pipeline, we extract all the information the RE system can deliver, associate it with the extracting pattern's score, and pass it on to the next step.

One important aspect to consider is the amount of information such an approach can extract from texts. We believe that pattern-based RE systems provide enough facts for our approach as in principle any semantic relation between entities, such as kinship relations, can be detected. For example, given the following sentence, RE systems could extract the relation instance *marriage*(`Madonna, Guy Ritchie`) and pass it on to the next component:

Example 1: `As the skirls of a lone bagpiper gave way to the music of French pianist Katia Labèque and a local organist, the wedding ceremony of Madonna Louise Ciccone, 42, and film director Guy Ritchie, 32, began.`

2.3 Answer Generation

Given the relation instances and arguments identified in the previous step, candidates for questions and answers are automatically generated by filling arguments into sentence templates. These templates are created based on patterns that were used for relation extraction in the previous step, i.e., RE patterns are utilized for two purposes in our approach.

Depending on the specific kind of RE pattern, this step involves a few straight-forward processing steps, e.g., for the case of surface-level RE patterns it involves restoring correct inflections of potentially lemmatized lexical pattern elements; for the case of depenency-grammar based patterns it additionally includes a step of tree linearization, see, e.g., (Wang and Zhang, 2012).

In the following, we present some example sentence templates, used for the generation of multiple-choice tests[1]:

- *marriage* relation:
  - person `tied the knot with` person.
  - person `and` person `were married.`
- *parent-child* relation:
  - person `was raised by` parent.
  - parent `passed on the family gene to` person.
- *foundation* relation:
  - company `was founded by` person.
  - person `set up the first` company `(in` location`)`.

A multiple-choice question is generated for every identified relation mention involving two entities, where the questions are rather generic, e.g., *"Which one of the following four facts can be inferred from the text?"*. The respective correct answer is generated by filling the relation instance's arguments into a sentence template associated with the target relation. For the sentence in Example 1, a generated correct answer could be: "`Madonna Louise Ciccone and Guy Ritchie were in a wonderful marriage relation`".

Wrong answers are generated on the one hand by filling the arguments in templates for other target relations. For the case of the *parent-child* relation this yields "`Madonna Louise Ciccone passed on the family gene to Guy Ritchie.`". The second way wrong answers are created is by mixing in arguments from other relation instances, e.g., "`Madonna Louise Ciccone tied the knot with John Ritchie`".

To avoid the generation of answer options which are easy to identify as being made up, we use only entities for wrong answers which have at least one relationship with another entity mentioned in the same article. This means that, for the example scenario outlined by Example 1, celebrities who are only mentioned once, e.g., in a list of wedding guests, are not utilized.

As another measure to improve the quality of the wrong answer options, we ensure that the respective entities are mentioned relatively close to one another in the source text. The best case would be that they appear in the same sentence from which a relationship is extracted. Consider the following example sentence from which the instance *marriage*(`Madonna, Ritchie`) is extracted:

Example 2:

```
If Penn was Madonna's temperamental
match and boyfriend Carlos Leon, father
of Lourdes, her physical ideal, Ritchie
--- who reportedly calls his new wife
'Madge' in private --- is a man who
holds his own against his high-powered
bride.
```

Here, the approach would generate the following answer options:

- `Madonna and Ritchie had a wedding.` *(correct)*
- `Madonna tied the knot with Carlos Leon.`
- `Carlos Leon passed on the family gene to Ritchie.`
- `Lourdes was brought up by Penn.`

In order to identify the correct statement, learners need sufficient knowledge of both vocabulary and grammar, also they need to be able to resolve coreference relations between occurring entities.

Paraphrasing In order to create both challenging and motivating tests for language learners, the generated statements need to present the user with a large variety of ways to refer to semantic relations, i.e., repetitions should be avoided. We ensure this first of all by employing web-scale RE-pattern sets as a source for the sentence templates, were these sets often contain hundreds of different ways to express a given target relation (see Section 3).

To create even more variations, we also introduce paraphrasing technology to the system to reorder words in the patterns learned by relation extraction systems and produce a new sentence with the same meaning. For example, a sentence template "wife `had a kid from` husband" is formed from one of the patterns used in the *marriage* relation. The paraphrasing engine takes this template as input and provides templates with the same words in natural language, e.g., "`from` husband wife `had a kid`". Both templates are treated as valid and randomly chosen to create answers.

2.4 Human supervision

As already noted earlier, employing automatic information-extraction methods has the disadvantage of inevitable noise in the system output.

[1]Items with sans-serif font represent entity placeholders.

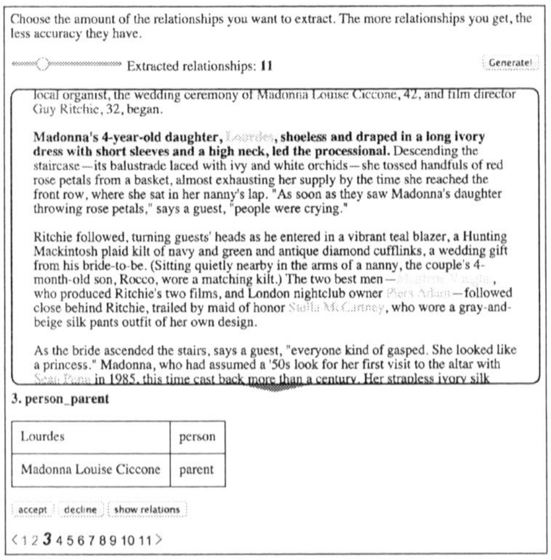

Figure 2: Interface for teacher step 1.

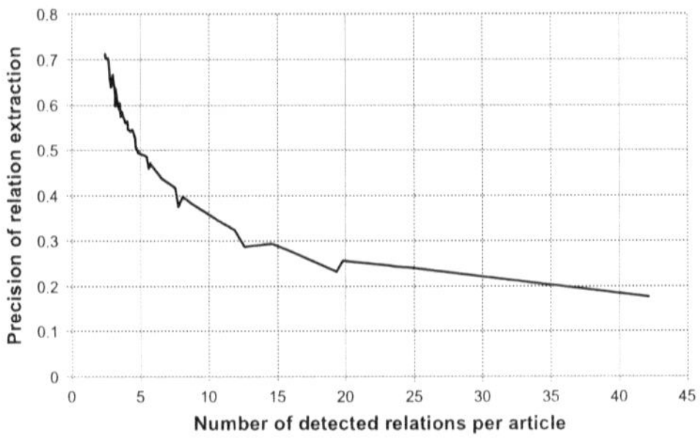

Figure 3: Precision/productivity trade-off

Given that the targeted users of the reading-comprehension exercises are language learners, it is necessary to include a step with human supervision into the data flow of our proposed system. All sentence templates, including those formulated from RE patterns and their variants created by the paraphrasing engine, are verified by teachers. Furthermore, teachers check the extracted relation instances to ensure they are actually mentioned in the text, then they verify the generated answers wrt. to grammaticality and adequacy for the context.

3 Prototype implementation

We have implemented a prototype of our system in order to test the feasibility of our proposed approach and to gather insights on future research directions, by carrying out user studies with it. The system is implemented as a browser-based application.

In principle, the approach can handle arbitrary texts. We tested it on a corpus of 140 English news articles (Krause et al., 2014), and measured the productivity of our approach for automatic question and answer generation. For these first experiments, we used the available gold-standard entity annotation. For the relation-extraction part, we applied the RE patterns of Moro et al. (2013) to automatically extract the relations between the annotated entities in the text. These patterns are based on the dependency-grammar analysis of sentences and were extracted from a large web corpus, hence they should provide enough variation for both the detection of relation mentions in texts as well as the generation of statements about such identified mentions. We used the patterns for three kinship relations in this experiment, namely the relations *marriage*, *parent-child*, *siblings*. As a means of automatic noise reduction, we work with a combination of training-support-based pattern filters and ones relying on the distribution of relation-relevant word senses in a lexico-semantic resource, as provided by Moro et al. (2013).

The paraphrasing engine in (Ai et al., 2014) is used in our system to generate sentence variants for the patterns, part of the process involves the utilization of the sentence generator by Wang and Zhang (2012), which produces linearizations for the dependency-tree-based patterns.

To reduce a teacher's work in examining the generated exercises, we provide a two-step user interface. In the first step, extracted relation instances for a given text are displayed and require validation by the user, as shown in Figure 2. The teacher can adjust the pattern-filter parameters in order to trade precision for recall, by moving the slider in the UI. Extracted relationships are shown below the text and teachers need to go through each of them, either accept them or decline them.

By choosing different parameter values for the filters, the number of relationships found by the extractor varies. The result of this trade-off for the employed corpus is illustrated in Figure 3. If the teacher tunes the relation-extraction component to its strictest setting, approximately three relation instances per article are found, out of which two are correct. If a user is willing to invest more time into question validation (i.e., the next step), it is possible to get more than twice as much facts of a lower average accuracy, hence a teacher would need more time to examine them.

In the second step of the teacher sub-workflow, generated questions and answers are presented for

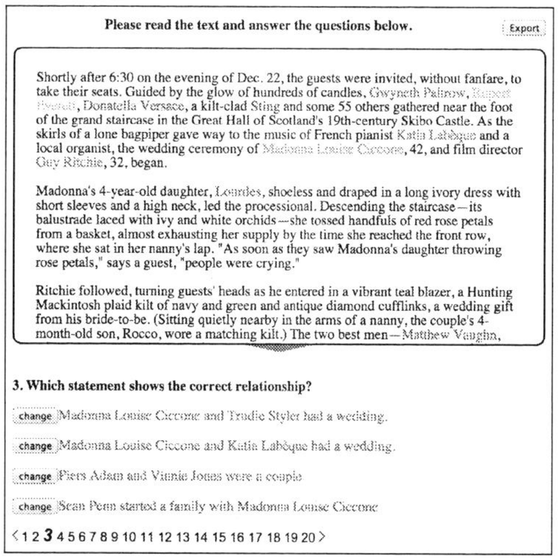

Figure 4: Interface for teacher step 2.

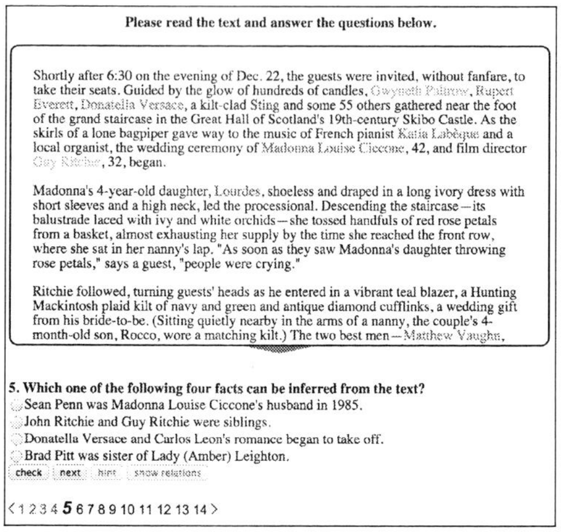

Figure 5: Example exercise, as generated by the prototype.

all previously accepted relation instances, see Figure 4. Teachers can check the answers for each question, and change them if they are, e.g., not consistent with the context induced by the article.

When teachers have verified all the questions and answers, they can press the *export* button to generate reading-comprehension exercises as shown in Figure 5. This is the interface that language learners use to interact with the system, i.e., access the teacher-approved exercises.

In order to find out the correct statements, learners need to firstly understand the semantic relations among the entities expressed in the texts and secondly have sufficient linguistic knowledge to understand the answer candidates which are paraphrases of the original sentences mentioned in the text. The paraphrases are namely linguistic variants at word (e.g., synonyms) or word-order level (e.g., topicalization). The interface provides feedback to the learners by marking the selected choice with green or red color depending on the correctness. In case a wrong answer is selected, the correct answer is shown to learners in green. If learners need more explanation, they can choose to click the *hint* button, which highlights the sentence with the relation instance mentioned in the correct answer. Furthermore, the system provides a visualization function which displays a graph with all recognized relations among the entities in the text.

4 Pilot user study

Two aspects of the implemented prototype were evaluated in separated tests with human subjects, i.e., the interface for language learners and the interface for teachers. For the tests with learners, our interests were to find out whether:

- ... the generated multiple-choice exercises fit the learners' expectations, e.g., with respect to user friendliness.
- ... the questions are of sufficient complexity, i.e., a learner's reading comprehension skills are actually tested.
- ... the system feedback after a wrong answer does help learners in figuring out the right answer.

For the tests with teachers, our evaluation tries to determine:

- ... if the prototype provides a user-friendly interface to generate exercises from texts.
- ... how teachers think about the step-by-step generation of exercises and if the teachers' requirements are met.
- ... if teachers agree such exercises would help users achieve their language-learning goals.

We set up a field test for users in which we asked them to work with the respective interface in an online version of the prototype and to fill out a provided online questionnaire after the test. Questions in the interview for usability and acceptability are composed based on ISO NORM 9241/10, which checks compliance to ergonomic requirements for screen work places, for example self-descriptiveness, controllability, conformity with user expectations and suitability for individualization. For this pilot study, we had five students act as teachers and language learners and asked them to take the questionnaire.

The following table lists the questions used in the interview:

The interface gives a clear concept of what there is to do.	5-Step Likert Scale (Agreement)
I can adjust the layout to suit my preferences.	5-Step Likert Scale (Agreement)
Generally, I feel no challenge in answering the questions.	5-Step Likert Scale (Agreement)
It is possible to answer the questions without fully understanding the article text, e.g. by concluding the correct answer from certain properties of the text.	5-Step Likert Scale (Agreement)
I can easily tell apart the correct answer from the wrong ones, without looking at the article text at all.	5-Step Likert Scale (Agreement)
The "hint" function makes it easier to figure out the correct answer.	5-Step Likert Scale (Agreement)
What has to be changed?/What did you like?	Open

Table 1: Questionnaire for learners.

The interface provides self-explained instructions.	5-Step Likert Scale (Agreement)
I can easily check the validity of the extracted relationships from the corresponding sentences in the article.	5-Step Likert Scale (Agreement)
I can easily change answers in the generated questions if I find any of them not proper.	5-Step Likert Scale (Agreement)
I myself would create similar questions from these articles without this tool.	5-Step Likert Scale (Agreement)
What are your expectations from such a tool? What would you suggest?	Open

Table 2: Questionnaire for teachers.

The summarized evaluation results are as follows:

- The language learners find the exercise interface intuitive and suitable for a quick start on the exercises.
- Questions in the exercises are somewhat too easy to answer. Advanced learners are able to infer the correct answer without looking at the article text.
- The "hint" functionality is perceived ambiguously. While all users agree that such a functionality is helpful in principle, only some of the learners think the way it is implemented is helpful.
- Teachers find the multi-step exercise generation confusing, however, after one or two attempts they get familiar with it and can conveniently filter relation instances and modify answers.
- Generally, teachers think this is the kind of exercise they would create based on the given articles.

The results from the learner interviews indicate several problematic aspects of the prototype. Besides a usability issue with insufficient feedback during exercise conduction, an aspect mentioned frequently by the users relates to the complexity of the generated exercises. Since our testers are mainly advanced English learners, the exercises were relatively easy to solve for them. Apart from their English skill level, they also mentioned that answers with incorrect or less plausible gender statements are easy to exclude. For example an answer *"Guy Richtie gave birth to Loudres."* is obviously false. We believe that such problems can be fixed by few, relation-specific heuristics, i.e., stricter rules on patterns. Another reason why questions tend to be easy is that the topic of the articles in our test set is celebrity gossip, i.e., an area which many people are familiar with, hence learners could answer questions based only on their prior knowledge, not their understanding of the text.

As for the tool for teachers, in the future we will provide clearer instructions so that teachers will not get lost in the process of creating exercises. According to the teachers, although some articles contain rich amounts of relations, they are not a good fit for a reading-comprehension exercise because of other aspects of the text. They also reported that at times none of the suggested answer options was acceptable; to solve this issue, we will add the option to freely edit the provided answer candidates, including the chance to compose totally new ones. In sum, the interview feedback from the teachers shows that despite the need for manual supervision, the overall prototype is perceived in a positive way.

5 Related work

The work presented in this paper is part of a growing body of approaches in computer-assisted language learning (CALL). The methods in this area aim to support (second) language learners through various means, among them methods for error correction (e.g., pronunciation training) or providing them with exercises for practicing existing language skills, while some approaches focus on reducing the workload of language teachers related to preparation and verification of exercises.

An example from the area of text-based CALL is the work of Uitdenbogerd (2014), who present systems for finding or generating exercise texts of a complexity level appropriate to the learner's current skill level, e.g., by reordering existing text elements wrt. difficulty or finding texts which make use of only appropriate vocabulary. Similar work is reported by Sheehan et al. (2014), who classify texts wrt. different metrics (academic vocabulary, syntactic complexity, concreteness, cohesion, among others) in order to identify texts for specific complexity levels.

An area receiving particular focus in the literature is the task of reading comprehension. Typically, language learners are asked to provide a short free-text summary for, e.g., a news article. A teacher then has to manually verify whether the learner was capable of understanding the text and correctly summarized the main content. Some CALL systems support the teacher in this task by automatically scoring the learner's summary wrt. the original article text or compared to a teacher-provided gold-standard summary, see for example (Hahn and Meurers, 2012; Madnani et al., 2013; Horbach et al., 2013; Koleva et al., 2014).

Equally relevant to our work is the approach of Gates (2008), who automatically generated WH-questions for reading-comprehension tests through a transformation of the parse tree of selected sentences from the article text, as well as Riloff and Thelen (2000), who developed a rule-based system for the automatic answering of questions in a reading-comprehension setting.

Our focus is the automatic generation of multiple-choice reading-comprehension exercises. This exercise type is a standard tool for educational tests and has, compared to short-answer summaries, the benefit that once created such tests require relatively few work on the teacher's side in order to assess a learner's skill level. At the core of our approach is the application of existing information-extraction approaches, mainly from the sub-area of relation extraction, for the identification of facts in texts which are suitable for checking a learner's understanding of a foreign language. In addition to the work of Moro et al. (2013), which we employed in our prototype implementation, many more relation extraction systems exist that could be utilized in our setting, either from traditional relation extraction (Carlson et al., 2010; Mitchell et al., 2015) or the open-IE paradigm (Fader et al., 2011; Pighin et al., 2014).

6 Conclusion and outlook

In this paper, we present a semi-automatic approach to the generation of reading-comprehension exercises, which builds on existing strategies from the areas of information extraction and paraphrasing. A user evaluation of a prototype implementation provided some evidence for the feasibility of the approach, albeit it also showed that the quality and particularly the difficulty of the generated questions needs to improve.

For the future, we plan to implement further prototypes which will employ additional relation-extraction and paraphrasing systems, and which will support a broader range of fact types. Furthermore, we want to enlarge the lexical and syntactic variability of the generated answers and would like to reduce the amount of required teacher supervision, in order to make the approach better suited for real-world applications.

Another line of future work could focus on injecting more indirectness into the question-answer generation, i.e., the system should not only ask for facts explicitly referenced in the text but should also check a language learners conclusion capabilities, which require a deeper understanding of language than fact finding. A possible way to implement this may be the integration of textual-entailment methods. For example, the system might ask about a particular *parent-child* relation not directly mentioned in the text, which the system could infer from a mentioned relation between *siblings* and another (different) instance of relation *parent-child*. This can help to generate exercises testing for more sophisticated reading-comprehension capabilities of language learners.

Acknowledgments

This research was partially supported by the German Federal Ministry of Education and Research (BMBF) through the projects ALL SIDES (01IW14002) and Deependance (01IW11003).

References

Renlong Ai, Marcela Charfuelan, Walter Kasper, Tina Klüwer, Hans Uszkoreit, Feiyu Xu, Sandra Gasber, and Philip Gienandt. 2014. Sprinter: Language technologies for interactive and multimedia language learning. In *LREC*.

Andrew Carlson, Justin Betteridge, Bryan Kisiel, Burr Settles, Estevam R. Hruschka, and Tom M. Mitchell.

2010. Toward an Architecture for Never-Ending Language Learning. In *Twenty-Fourth AAAI Conference on Artificial Intelligence*, pages 1306–1313.

Anthony Fader, Stephen Soderland, and Oren Etzioni. 2011. Identifying Relations for Open Information Extraction. In *Proceedings of the Conference on Empirical Methods in Natural Language Processing*, EMNLP '11, pages 1535–1545, Stroudsburg, PA, USA. Association for Computational Linguistics.

Jenny Rose Finkel, Trond Grenager, and Christopher Manning. 2005. Incorporating non-local information into information extraction systems by gibbs sampling. In *Proceedings of the 43rd Annual Meeting of the Association for Computational Linguistics (ACL'05)*, pages 363–370, Ann Arbor, Michigan, June. Association for Computational Linguistics.

Donna M. Gates. 2008. Automatically generating reading comprehension look-back strategy: Questions from expository texts. Master's thesis, Carnegie Mellon University.

Michael Hahn and Detmar Meurers. 2012. Evaluating the meaning of answers to reading comprehension questions: A semantics-based approach. In *Proceedings of the Seventh Workshop on Building Educational Applications Using NLP (BEA)*, pages 326–336, Montréal, Canada, June. Association for Computational Linguistics.

Andrea Horbach, Alexis Palmer, and Manfred Pinkal. 2013. Using the text to evaluate short answers for reading comprehension exercises. In *Second Joint Conference on Lexical and Computational Semantics (*SEM), Volume 1: Proceedings of the Main Conference and the Shared Task: Semantic Textual Similarity*, pages 286–295, Atlanta, Georgia, USA, June. Association for Computational Linguistics.

Nikolina Koleva, Andrea Horbach, Alexis Palmer, Simon Ostermann, and Manfred Pinkal. 2014. Paraphrase detection for short answer scoring. In *Proceedings of the third workshop on NLP for computer-assisted language learning (NLP4CALL)*.

Sebastian Krause, Hong Li, Feiyu Xu, Hans Uszkoreit, Robert Hummel, and Luise Spielhagen. 2014. Language resources and annotation tools for cross-sentence relation extraction. In *LREC*.

Nitin Madnani, Jill Burstein, John Sabatini, and Tenaha O'Reilly. 2013. Automated scoring of a summary-writing task designed to measure reading comprehension. In *Proceedings of the Eighth Workshop on Innovative Use of NLP for Building Educational Applications (BEA)*, pages 163–168, Atlanta, Georgia, June. Association for Computational Linguistics.

T. Mitchell, W. Cohen, E. Hruschka, P. Talukdar, J. Betteridge, A. Carlson, B. Dalvi, M. Gardner, B. Kisiel, J. Krishnamurthy, N. Lao, K. Mazaitis, T. Mohamed, N. Nakashole, E. Platanios, A. Ritter, M. Samadi, B. Settles, R. Wang, D. Wijaya, A. Gupta, X. Chen, A. Saparov, M. Greaves, and J. Welling. 2015. Never-ending learning. In *Proceedings of the Conference on Artificial Intelligence (AAAI)*.

Andrea Moro, Hong Li, Sebastian Krause, Feiyu Xu, Roberto Navigli, and Hans Uszkoreit. 2013. Semantic rule filtering for web-scale relation extraction. In *ISWC*.

Ndapandula Nakashole, Gerhard Weikum, and Fabian M. Suchanek. 2012. PATTY: A taxonomy of relational patterns with semantic types. In Jun'ichi Tsujii, James Henderson, and Marius Pasca, editors, *Proceedings of the 2012 Joint Conference on Empirical Methods in Natural Language Processing and Computational Natural Language Learning, EMNLP-CoNLL 2012, July 12-14, 2012, Jeju Island, Korea*.

Daniele Pighin, Marco Cornolti, Enrique Alfonseca, and Katja Filippova. 2014. Modelling events through memory-based, open-ie patterns for abstractive summarization. In *Proceedings of the 52nd Annual Meeting of the Association for Computational Linguistics, ACL 2014, Volume 1: Long Papers*, pages 892–901, Baltimore, MD, USA, June.

Ellen Riloff and Michael Thelen. 2000. A rule-based question answering system for reading comprehension tests. In *Proceedings of the 2000 ANLP/NAACL Workshop on Reading Comprehension Tests As Evaluation for Computer-based Language Understanding Sytems - Volume 6*, ANLP/NAACL-ReadingComp '00, pages 13–19, Stroudsburg, PA, USA. Association for Computational Linguistics.

Kathleen M. Sheehan, Irene Kostin, Diane Napolitano, and Michael Flor. 2014. The TextEvaluator tool: Helping teachers and test developers select texts for use in instruction and assessment. *The Elementary School Journal*, 115(2):184–209, December.

Alexandra Uitdenbogerd. 2014. Tools for supporting language acquisition via extensive reading. In *Proceedings of the 1st Workshop on Natural Language Processing Techniques for Educational Applications (NLP-TEA-1) at the 22nd International Conference in Computer Education (ICCE 2014)*.

Rui Wang and Yi Zhang. 2012. Sentence realization with unlexicalized tree linearization grammars. In *Proceedings of COLING 2012: Posters*, Mumbai, India, December.

Feiyu Xu, Hans Uszkoreit, and Hong Li. 2007. A seed-driven bottom-up machine learning framework for extracting relations of various complexity. In *Proceedings of the 45th Annual Meeting of the Association of Computational Linguistics*, page 584–591, Prague, Czech Republic, June. Association for Computational Linguistics.

Interactive Second Language Learning from News Websites

Tao Chen[1] **Naijia Zheng**[1] **Yue Zhao**[1]
Muthu Kumar Chandrasekaran[1] **Min-Yen Kan**[1,2*]
[1]School of Computing, National University of Singapore
[2]NUS Interactive and Digital Media Institute, Singapore
{taochen,muthu.chandra,kanmy}@comp.nus.edu.sg
{znj472982642,immortalzhaoyue}@gmail.com

Abstract

We propose WordNews, a web browser extension that allows readers to learn a second language vocabulary while reading news online. Injected tooltips allow readers to look up selected vocabulary and take simple interactive tests.

We discover that two key system components needed improvement, both which stem from the need to model context. These two issues are real-world word sense disambiguation (WSD) to aid translation quality and constructing interactive tests. For the first, we start with Microsoft's Bing translation API but employ additional dictionary-based heuristics that significantly improve translation in both coverage and accuracy. For the second, we propose techniques for generating appropriate distractors for multiple-choice word mastery tests. Our preliminary user survey confirms the need and viability of such a language learning platform.

1 Introduction

Learning a new language from language learning websites is time consuming. Research shows that regular practice, guessing, memorization (Rubin, 1975) as well as immersion into real scenarios (Naiman, 1978) hastens the language learning process. To make second language learning attractive and efficient, we interleave language learning with the daily activity of online news reading.

Most existing language learning software are either instruction-driven or user-driven. Duolingo[1] is a popular instruction-driven system that teaches through structured lessons. Instruction driven systems demand dedicated learner time on a daily basis and are limited by learning materials as lesson curation is often labor-intensive.

In contrast, many people informally use Google Translate[2] or Amazon Kindle's Vocabulary Builder[3] to learn vocabulary, making these prominent examples of user-driven systems. These systems, however, lack the rigor of a learning platform as they omit tests to allow learners to demonstrate mastery. In our work, we merge learning and assessment within the single activity of news reading. Our system also adapts to the learner's skill during assessment.

We propose a system to enable online news readers to efficiently learn a new language's vocabulary. Our prototype targets Chinese language learning while reading English language news. Learners are provided translations of open-domain words for learning from an English news page. In the same environment – for words that the system deems mastered by the learner – learners are assessed by replacing the original English text in the article with their Chinese translations and asked to translate them back given a choice of possible translations. The system, **WordNews**, deployed as a Chrome web browser extension, is triggered when readers visit a preconfigured list of news websites (*e.g.*, CNN, BBC).

A key design property of our WordNews web browser extension is that it is only active on certain news websites. This is important as news articles typically are classified with respect to a news

* This research is supported by the Singapore National Research Foundation under its International Research Centre @ Singapore Funding Initiative and administered by the IDM Programme Office.

[1]https://www.duolingo.com
[2]https://translate.google.com
[3]http://www.amazon.com/gp/help/customer/display.html?nodeId=201733850

Proceedings of The 2nd Workshop on Natural Language Processing Techniques for Educational Applications, pages 34–42,
Beijing, China, July 31, 2015.

category, such as *finance*, *world news*, and *sports*. If we know which category of news the learner is viewing, we can leverage this contextual knowledge to improve the learning experience.

In the development of the system, we discovered two key components that can be affected by this context modeling. We report on these developments here. In specific, we propose improved algorithms for two components: **(i)** for translating English words to Chinese from news articles, **(ii)** for generating distractors for learner assessment.

2 The WordNews Chrome Extension

Our method to directly enhance the web browser is inspired by earlier work in the computer-aided language learning community that also uses the web browser as the delivery vehicle for language learning. WERTi (Metcalf and Meurers, 2006; Meurers et al., 2010) was a monolingual, user-driven system that modified web pages in the target language to highlight or remove certain words from specific syntactic patterns to teach difficult-to-learn English grammar.

Our focus is to help build Chinese vocabulary for second language learners fluent in English. We give a running scenario to illustrate the use of WordNews. When a learner browses to an English webpage on a news website, our extension either selectively replaces certain original English words with their Chinese translation or underlines the English words, based on user configuration (Figure 1, middle). While the meaning of the Chinese word is often apparent in context, the learner can choose to learn more about the replaced/underlined word, by mousing over the word to reveal a definition tooltip (Figure 1, left) to aid mastery of the Chinese word. Once the learner has encountered the target word a few times, WordNews assesses learner's mastery by generating a multiple choice translation test on the target word (Figure 1, right). Our learning platform thus can be viewed as three logical use cases: *translating*, *learning* and *testing*.

Translating. We pass the main content of the webpage from the extension client to our server for candidate selection and translation. As certain words are polysemous, the server must select the most appropriate translation among all possible meanings. Our initial selection method replaces any instance of words stored in our dictionary. For translation, we check the word's stored meanings against the machine translation of each sentence obtained from the Microsoft Bing Translation API[4] (hereafter, "Bing"). Matches are deemed as correct translations and are pushed back to the Chrome client for rendering.

Learning. Hovering the mouse over the replacement Chinese word causes a tooltip to appear, which gives the translation, pronunciation, and simplified written form, and a `More` link that loads additional contextual example sentences (that were previously translated by the backend) for the learner to study. The `More` link must be clicked for activation, as we find this two-click architecture helps to minimize latency and the loading of unnecessary data. The server keeps record of the learning tooltip activations, logging the enclosing webpage URL, the target word and the user identity.

Testing. After the learner encounters the same word a pre-defined number $t = 3$ times, WordNews generates a multiple choice question (MCQ) test to assess mastery. When the learner hovers over the replaced word, the test is shown for the learner to select the correct answer. When an option is clicked, the server logs the selection and updates the user's test history, and the client reveals the correct answer.

2.1 News Categories

As our learning platform is active only on certain news websites, we can model the news category (for individual words and whole webpages) as additional evidence to help with tasks. Of particular importance to WordNews is the association of words to a news category, which is used downstream in both word sense disambiguation (Section 3) and the generation of distractors in the interactive tests (Section 4). Here, our goal is to automatically find highly relevant words to a particular news category – *e.g.*, "what are typical *finance* words?"

We first obtain a large sample of categorized English news webpages, by creating custom crawlers for specific news websites (*e.g.* CNN). We use a seed list of words that are matched

[4]`https://www.bing.com/translator`

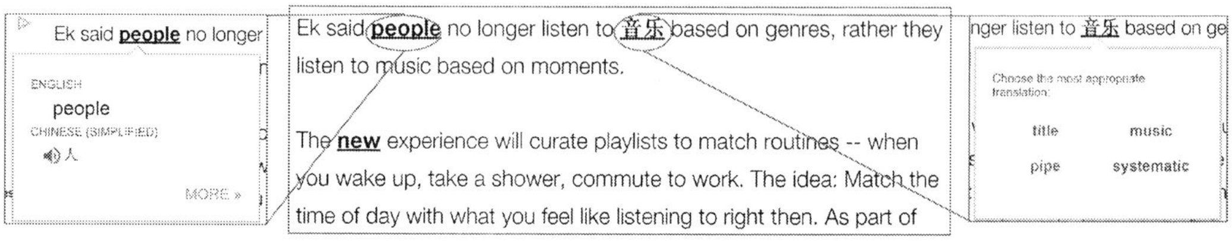

Figure 1: Merged screenshots of our Chrome extension on the CNN English article *Spotify wants to be the soundtrack of your life*. Underlined components are clickable to yield tooltips of two different forms: (left) a definition for learning, (right) a multiple-choice interactive test.

Table 1: News category alignment between English and Chinese.

English Category	Chinese Category	Example Words
1. Entertainment	Entertainment	"superstar", "明星"
2. World	Military, International, Social	"attacks", "军事"
3. Finance	Finance	"investment", "财富"
4. Sports	Sports	"score", "比赛"
5. Fashion	Beauty & Health	"jewelry", "时髦"
6. Technology	Technology	"cyber", "互联网"
7. Travel		"natural"

against a target webpage's URL. If any match, the webpage is deemed to be of that category. For example, a webpage that has the seed word "football" in its URL is deemed of category "Sports". Since the news category is also required for Chinese words for word sense disambiguation, we must perform a similar procedure to crawl Chinese news (*e.g.*, BaiduNews[5]) However, Chinese news sites follow a different categorization scheme, so we first manually align the categories based on observation (see Table 1), creating seven bilingual categories: namely, "World", "Technology", "Sports", "Entertainment", "Finance", "Fashion" and "Travel".

We tokenize and part-of-speech tag the main body text of the categorized articles, discarding punctuation and stopwords. For Chinese, we segment words using the Stanford Chinese word segmenter (Chang et al., 2008). The remaining words are classified to a news category based on document frequency. A word w is classified to a category c if it appears more often (a tunable threshold δ^6) than its average category document frequency. Note that a word can be categorized to multiple categories under this scheme.

3 Word Sense Disambiguation (WSD) Component

Our extension needs to show the most appropriate translation sense based on the context. Such a translation selection task – cross-lingual word sense disambiguation – is a common problem in machine translation. In this section, we describe how we improved WordNews' WSD capabilities through a series of six approaches.

The context evidence that we leverage for WSD comes in two forms: the news category of the target word and its enclosing sentence.

3.1 Bilingual Dictionary and Baseline

WordNews's server component includes a bilingual lexicon of English words with possible Chinese senses. The English words in our dictionary is based on the publicly-available College English Test (CET 4) list, which has a breadth of about 4,000 words. We augment the list to include the relative frequency among Chinese senses, with their part-of-speech, per English word.

Our baseline translation uses the most frequent sense: for an English word to be translated, it chooses the most frequent relative Chinese translation sense c from the possible set of senses C.

[5] `http://news.baidu.com`

[6] We empricially set δ to 10.

Table 2: Example translations from our approaches to WSD. Target words are italicized and correct translations are bolded.

English Sentence	Dictionary	Baseline	POS	Machine Translation		
				Substring	Relax	Align
(1) ... a very *close* friend of ...	verb: 关闭, 合, 关 ... adj: 密切, ... 亲密 ...	关闭	密切	**亲密**	**亲密**	**亲密**
(2) ... kids can't *stop* singing ...	verb: 停止, 站, 阻止, 停 ...	**停止**	阻止	**停止**	**停止**	**停止**
(3) ... about Elsa being happy and *free* ...	adj: 免费, 自由, 游离, 畅, 空闲的...	免费	免费	**自由**	**自由**	**自由**
(4) ... why Obama's *trip* to my homeland is meaningful ...	noun: 旅, 旅程 ... 旅游 ...	旅	旅	旅	**旅行**	**旅行**
(5) ... winning more points in the *match* ...	noun: 匹配, 比赛, 赛, 敌手, 对手, 火柴 ...	匹配	匹配	**比赛**	**比赛**	**比赛**
(6) ... *state* department spokeswoman Jen Psaki said that the allies ...	noun: 态, 国, 州, ... verb: 声明, 陈述, 述, 申明 ... 发言 ... adj: 国家的 ...	态	态	发言	发言人	**国家**

This method has complete coverage over the CET 4 list (as the word frequency rule always yields a prospective translation), but as it lacks any context model, it is the least accurate.

3.2 Approach 1: News Category

Topic information has been shown to be useful in WSD (Boyd-Graber et al., 2007). For example, consider the English word *interest*. In finance related articles, "interest" is more likely to carry the sense of "a share, right, or title in the ownership of property" ("利息" in Chinese), over other senses. Therefore, analysing the topic of the original article and selecting the translation with the same topic label might help disambiguate the word sense. For a target English word e, for each prospective Chinese sense $c \in C$, choose the first (in terms of relative frequency) sense that has the same news category as the containing webpage.

3.3 Approach 2: Part-of-Speech

Part-of-Speech (POS) tags are also useful for word sense disambiguation (Wilks and Stevenson, 1998) and machine translation (Toutanova et al., 2002; Ueffing and Ney, 2003). For example, the English word "book" can function as a verb or a noun, which gives rise to two different dominant senses: "reserve" ("预定" in Chinese) and "printed work" ("书"), respectively. As senses often correspond cross-lingually, knowledge of the English word's POS can assist disambiguation. We employ the Standford log-linear Part-of-Speech tagger (Toutanova et al., 2003) to obtain the POS tag for the English word, whereas the POS tag for target Chinese senses are provided in our dictionary. In cases where multiple candidate Chinese translations fit the same sense, we again break ties using relative frequency of the prospective candidates.

3.4 Approaches 3–5: Machine Translation

Neighbouring words provide the necessary context to perform WSD in many contexts. In our work, we consider the sentence in which the target word appears as our context. We then acquire its translation from Microsoft Bing Translator using its API. As we access the translation as a third party, the Chinese translation comes as-is, without the needed explicit word to locate the target English word to translate in the original input sentence. We need to perform alignment of the Chinese and English sentences in order to recover the target word's translation from the sentence translation.

Approach 3 – Substring Match. As potential Chinese translations are available in our dictionary, a straightforward use of substring matching recovers a Chinese translation; *i.e.*, check whether the candidate Bing translation is a substring of the Chinese translation. If more than one candidate matches, we use the longest string match heuristic and pick the one with the longest match as the final output. If none matches, the system does not output a translation for the word.

Approach 4 – Relaxed Match. The final rule in the substring match method unfortunately fires often, as the coverage of WordNews's lexicon is limited. As we wish to offer correct translations that are not limited by our lexicon, we relax our substring condition, allowing the Bing translation to be a superset of a candidate translation in our dictionary (see Example 4 in Table 2, where the Bing translation "旅行" is allowed to be relaxed to match the dictionary "旅"). To this end, we must know the extent of the words in the translation. We first segment the obtained Bing translation with the Stanford Chinese Word Segmenter, and then use string matching to find a Chinese translation c. If more than one candidate matches, we heuristically use the last matched candidate. This technique significantly augments the translation range of our extension beyond the reach of our lexicon.

Approach 5 – Word Alignment. The relaxed method runs into difficulties when the target English e's Chinese prospective translations which come from our lexicon generate several possible matches. Consider Example 6 in Table 2. The target English word "state" has corresponding Chinese entries "发言" and "国家的" in our dictionary. For this reason, both "国家" ("country", correct) and "发言人" ("spokeswoman", incorrect) are relaxed matches. As relaxed approach always picks up the last candidate, "发 言人" is the final output, which is incorrect.

To address this, we use the Bing Word Alignment API[7] to provide a possibly different prospective Chinese sense c. In this example, "state" matches "国家" ("country", correct) from word alignment, and the final algorithm chooses "国家" as the output.

[7] https://msdn.microsoft.com/en-us/library/dn198370.aspx

Table 3: WSD performance over our test set.

	Coverage	Accuracy
Baseline	**100%**	57.3%
News Category	2.0%	7.1%
POS	94.5%	55.2%
Bing – Substring	78.5%	79.8%
Bing – Relaxed	75.7%	80.9%
Bing – Align	76.9%	**97.4%**

3.5 Evaluation

To evaluate the effectiveness of our proposed methods, we randomly sampled 707 words and their sentences from recent CNN[8] news articles, manually annotating the ground truth translation for each target English word. We report both the **coverage** (*i.e.*, the ability of the system to return a translation) and **accuracy** (*i.e.*, whether the translation is contextually accurate).

Table 3 shows the experimental results for the six approaches. As expected, frequency-based baseline achieves 100% coverage, but a low accuracy (57.3%); POS also performs similarly . The category-based approach performs the worst, due to low coverage. This is because news category only provides a high-level context and many of the Chinese word senses do not have a strong topic tendency.

Of most promise is our use of web based translation related APIs. The three Bing methods iteratively improve the accuracy and have reasonable coverage. Among all the methods, the additional step of word alignment is the best in terms of accuracy (97.4%), significantly bettering the others. This validates previous work that sentence-level context is helpful in WSD.

4 Distractor Generation Component

Assesing mastery over vocabulary is the other key functionality of our prototype learning platform. The generation of the multiple choice selection test requires the selection of alternative choices aside from the correct answer of the target word. In this section, we investigate a way to automatically generate such choices (called *distractors* in the literature) in English, given a target word.

[8] http://edition.cnn.com

4.1 Related Work

Multiple choice question (MCQ) is widely used in vocabulary learning. Semantic and syntactic properties of the target word need to be considered while generating their distractors. In particular, (Pho et al., 2014) did an analysis on real-life MCQ corpus, and validated there are syntactic and semantic homogeneity among distractors. Based on this, automatic distractor generation algorithms have been proposed.

For instance, (Lee and Seneff, 2007) generate distractors for English prepositions based on collocations, and idiosyncratic incorrect usage learned from non-native English corpora. Lärka (Volodina et al., 2014) – a Swedish language learning system – generates vocabulary assessment exercises using a corpus. They also have different modes of exercise generation to allow learning and testing via the same interface. (Susanti et al., 2015) generate distractors for TOEFL vocabulary test using WordNet and word sense disambiguation given a target word. While these approaches serve in testing mastery, they do not provide the capability for learning new vocabulary in context. The most related prior work is WordGap system (Knoop and Wilske, 2013), a mobile application that generates MCQ tests based on the text selected by users. WordGap customizes the reading context, however, the generation of distractors – based on syntactic and semantic homogeneity – is not contextualized.

4.2 Approach

WordNews postulates "a set of suitable distractors" as: 1) having the same form as the target word, 2) fitting the sentence's context, and 3) having proper difficulty level according to user's level of mastery. As input to the distractor generation algorithm, we provide the target word, its part-of-speech (obtained by tagging the input sentence first) and the enclosing webpage's news category. We restrict the algorithm to produce distractors matching the input POS, and which match the news category of the page.

We can design the test to be more difficult by choosing distractors that are more similar to the target word. By varying the semantic distance, we can generate tests at varying difficulty levels. We quantify similarity by using the Lin distance (Lin, 1998) between two input candidate concepts in WordNet (Miller, 1995):

$$sim(c1, c2) = \frac{2 * logP(lso(c1, c2))}{logP(c1) + logP(c2)} \quad (1)$$

where $P(c)$ denotes the probability of encountering concept c, and $lso(c1, c2)$ denotes the lowest common subsumer synset, which is the lowest node in the WordNet hierarchy that is a hypernym of both $c1$ and $c2$. This returns a score from 0 (completely dissimilar) to 1 (semantically equivalent).

If we use a target word e as the starting point, we can use WordNet to retrieve related words using WordNet relations (hypernyms/hyponyms, synonyms/antonyms) and determine their similarity using Lin distance.

We empirically set 0.1 as the similarity threshold – words that are deemed more similar than 0.1 are returned as possible distractors for our algorithm. We note that Lin distance often returns a score of 0 for many pairs and the threshold of 0.1 allows us to have a large set of distractors to choose from, while remaining fairly efficient in run-time distractor generation.

We discretize a learner's knowledge of the word based on their prior exposure to it. We then adopt a strategy to generate distractors for the input word based learners' knowledge level:

Easy: The learner has been exposed to the word at least $t = 3$ times. Two distractors are randomly selected from words that share the same news category as the target word e. The third distractor is generated using our algorithm.

Hard: The learner has passed the Easy level test $x = 6$ times. All three distractors are generated from the same news category, using our algorithm.

4.3 Evaluation

The WordGap system (Knoop and Wilske, 2013) represents the most related prior work on automated distractor generation, and forms our baseline. WordGap adopts a knowledge-based approach: selecting the synonyms of synonyms (also computed by WordNet) as distractors. They first select the most frequently used word, $w1$, from the target word's synonym set, and then select the synonyms of $w1$, called $s1$. Finally, WordGap selects the three most frequently-used words from $s1$ as distractors.

We conducted a human subject evaluation of distractor generation to assess its fitness for use. The subjects were asked to rank the feasibility of a distractor (inclusive of the actual answer) from a given sentential context. The contexts were sentences retrieved from actual news webpages, identical to WordNews's use case.

We randomly selected 50 sentences from recent news articles, choosing a noun or adjective from the sentence as the target word. We show the original sentence (leaving the target word as blank) as the context, and display distractors as choices (see Figure 2). Subjects were required to read the sentence and rank the distractors by plausibility: 1 (the original answer), 2 (most plausible alternative) to 7 (least plausible alternative). We recruited 15 subjects from within our institution for the survey. All of them are fluent English speakers, and half are native speakers.

We evaluated two scenarios, for two different purposes. In both evaluations, we generate three distractors using each of the two systems, and add the original target word for validation (7 options in total, conforming to our ranking options of 1–7).

Since we have news category information, we wanted to check whether that information alone could improve distractor generation. Evaluation 1 tests the WordGap baseline system versus a **Random News** system that uses random word selection. It just uses the constraint that chosen distractors must conform to the news category (be classified to the news category of the target word).

In our Evaluation 2, we tested our **Hard** setup where our algorithm is used to generate all distractors against WordGap. This evaluation aims to assess the efficacy of our algorithm over the baseline.

4.3.1 Results and Analysis

Each question was answered by five different users. We compute the average ranking for each choice. A lower rating means a more plausible (harder) distractor. The rating for all the target words is low (1.1 on average) validating their truth and implying that the subjects answered the survey seriously, assuring the validity of the evaluation.

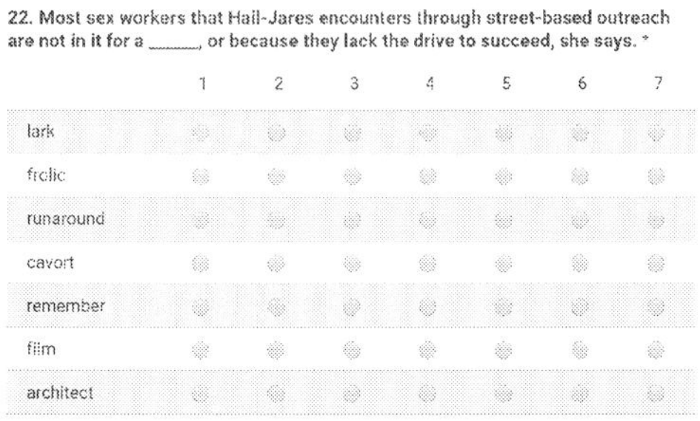

Figure 2: Sample distractor ranking question.

For each question, we deem an algorithm to be the winner if its three distractors as a whole (the sum of three average ratings) are assessed to be more plausible than the distractors by its competitor. We calculate the number of wins for each algorithm over the 50 questions in each evaluation.

Table 4: WordGap vs. Random News. Lower scores are better.

	# of wins	Avg. score
WordGap	27	3.84
Random News	23	4.10

Table 5: WordGap vs. WordNews Hard. Lower scores are better.

	# of wins	Avg. score
WordGap	21	4.16
WordNews Hard	29	3.49

We display the results of both evaluations in Table 4 and Table 5. We see that the WordGap baseline outperforms the random selection, constrained solely by news category, by 4 wins and a 0.26 lower average score. This shows that word news category alone is insufficient for generating good distractors. When a target word does not have a strong category tendency, *e.g.*, "venue" and "week", the random news method cannot select highly plausible distractors.

In the second table, our distractor algorithm significantly betters the baseline in both number of

Table 6: Distractors generated by WordGap and WordNews Hard for example question in Figure 2. The identified news category for the enclosing webpage was Entertainment.

System	**Distractor**	**Lin Dist.**	**Avg. Rate**
Target Word	lark		1.33
WordGap	frolic		3.33
	runaround		5.67
	cavort		4.17
WordNews Hard	art	0.154	1.67
	film	0.147	3.33
	actress	0.217	4.83

wins (8 more) and average score (0.67 lower). This further confirms that context and semantic information are complementary for distractor generation. As we mentioned before, a good distractor should fit the reading context and have a certain level of difficulty. Finally, in Table 6 we show the distractors generated for the target word "lark" in the example survey question (Figure 2).

5 Platform Viability and Usability Survey

We have thus far described and evaluated two critical components that can benefit from capturing the learner's news article context. In the larger context, we also need to check the viability of second language learning intertwined with news reading. In a requirements survey prior to the prototype development, two-thirds of the respondents indicated that although they have interest in learning a second language, they only have only used language learning software infrequently (less than once per week) yet frequently read news, giving us motivation for our development.

Post-prototype, we conducted a summative survey to assess whether our prototype product satisfied the target niche, in terms of interest, usability and possible interference with normal reading activities. We gathered 16 respondents, 15 of which were between the ages of 18–24. 11 (the majority) also claimed native Chinese language proficiency.

The respondents felt that the extension platform was a viable language learning platform (3.4 of 5; on a scale of 1 "disagreement" to 5 "agreement") and that they would like to try it when available for their language pair (3 of 5).

In our original prototype, we replaced the original English word with the Chinese translation. While most felt that replacing the original English with the Chinese translation would not hamper their reading, they still felt a bit uncomfortable (3.7 of 5). This finding prompted us to change the default learning tooltip behavior to underlining to hint at the tooltip presence.

6 Conclusion

We described WordNews, a client extension and server backend that transforms the web browser into a second language learning platform. Leveraging web-based machine translation APIs and a static dictionary, it offers a viable user-driven language learning experience by pairing an improved, context-sensitive tooltip definition service with the generation of context-sensitive multiple choice questions.

WordNews is potentially not confined to use in news websites; one respondent noted that they would like to use it on arbitrary websites, but currently we feel usable word sense disambiguation is difficult enough even in the restricted news domain. We also note that respondents are more willing to use a mobile client for news reading, such that our future development work may be geared towards an independent mobile application, rather than a browser extension. We also plan to conduct a longitudinal study with a cohort of second language learners to better evaluate WordNews' real-world effectiveness.

References

Jordan Boyd-Graber, David Blei, and Xiaojin Zhu. 2007. A Topic Model for Word Sense Disambiguation. In *Proceedings of the 2007 Joint Conference on Empirical Methods in Natural Language Processing and Computational Natural Language Learning*, EMNLP-CoNLL'07, pages 1024–1033.

Pi-Chuan Chang, Michel Galley, and Christopher D. Manning. 2008. Optimizing Chinese Word Segmentation for Machine Translation Performance. In *Proceedings of the Third Workshop on Statistical Machine Translation*, StatMT'08, pages 224–232.

Susanne Knoop and Sabrina Wilske. 2013. WordGap-Automatic Generation of Gap-filling Vocabulary Exercises for Mobile Learning. In *Proceedings of Second Workshop NLP Computer-Assisted Language Learning*, pages 39–47.

John Lee and Stephanie Seneff. 2007. Automatic generation of cloze items for prepositions. In *INTERSPEECH*, pages 2173–2176.

Dekang Lin. 1998. An information-theoretic definition of similarity.

Vanessa Metcalf and Detmar Meurers. 2006. Generating web-based english preposition exercises from real-world texts. Presentation at EUROCALL, September. http://purl.org/dm/handouts/eurocall06-metcalf-meurers.pdf.

Detmar Meurers, Ramon Ziai, Luiz Amaral, Adriane Boyd, Aleksandar Dimitrov, Vanessa Metcalf, and Niels Ott. 2010. Enhancing authentic web pages for language learners. In *Proceedings of the NAACL HLT 2010 Fifth Workshop on Innovative Use of NLP for Building Educational Applications*, pages 10–18. Association for Computational Linguistics.

George A. Miller. 1995. WordNet: A Lexical Database for English. *Communications of the ACM*, 38(11):39–41.

Neil Naiman. 1978. *The Good Language Learner*, volume 4. Multilingual Matters.

Van-Minh Pho, Thibault André, Anne-Laure Ligozat, B Grau, G Illouz, Thomas François, et al. 2014. Multiple choice question corpus analysis for distractor characterization. In *9th International Conference on Language Resources and Evaluation (LREC 2014)*.

Joan Rubin. 1975. What the "good language learner" can teach us. *TESOL quarterly*, pages 41–51.

Yuni Susanti, Ryu Iida, and Takenobu Tokunaga. 2015. Automatic generation of english vocabulary tests. In *Proceedings of the 7th International Conference on Computer Supported Education (CSEDU 2015)*, pages 77–78.

Kristina Toutanova, H Tolga Ilhan, and Christopher D Manning. 2002. Extensions to HMM-based Statistical Word Alignment Models. In *Proceedings of the 2002 Conference on Empirical Methods in Natural Language Processing*, EMNLP EMNLP'02, pages 87–94.

Kristina Toutanova, Dan Klein, Christopher D. Manning, and Yoram Singer. 2003. Feature-rich Part-of-speech Tagging with a Cyclic Dependency Network. In *Proceedings of the 2003 Conference of the North American Chapter of the Association for Computational Linguistics on Human Language Technology*, NAACL '03, pages 173–180.

Nicola Ueffing and Hermann Ney. 2003. Using POS Information for Statistical Machine Translation into Morphologically Rich Languages. In *Proceedings of the 10th Conference on European Chapter of the Association for Computational Linguistics*, EACL'03, pages 347–354.

Elena Volodina, Ildikó Pilán, Lars Borin, and Therese Lindström Tiedemann. 2014. A flexible language learning platform based on language resources and web services. *Proceedings of LREC 2014*.

Yorick Wilks and Mark Stevenson. 1998. The Grammar of Sense: Using Part-of-speech Tags As a First Step in Semantic Disambiguation. *Natural Language Engineering*, 4(2):135–143.

Bilingual Keyword Extraction and its Educational Application

Chung-Chi Huang
LTI, CMU
5000 Forbes Ave.
Pittsburgh, PA, USA
u901571@gmail.com

Mei-Hua Chen
FLL
Tunghai University
Taichung, Taiwan
chen.meihua@gmail.com

Ping-Che Yang
Institute for
Information Industry
Taipei, Taiwan
maciaclark@iii.org.tw

Abstract

We introduce a method that extracts keywords in a language with the help of the other. The method involves estimating preferences for topical keywords and fusing language-specific word statistics. At run-time, we transform parallel articles into word graphs, build cross-lingual edges for word statistics integration, and exploit PageRank with word keyness information for keyword extraction. We apply our method to keyword analysis and language learning. Evaluation shows that keyword extraction benefits from cross-language information and language learners benefit from our keywords in reading comprehension test.

1 Introduction

Keyword extraction algorithms (KEA) have been developed to extract keywords for content understanding, event tracking, or opinion mining. However, most of them calculate article-level word keyness in *a* single language. The articles' counterparts in *another* language may have different keyword candidates in mind since languages differ in grammar, phrase structure, and word usage, all of which play a role in word keyness statistics, thus keyword analysis.

Consider the English article in Figure 1. Monolingual KEA, based solely on the English content, may not identify the best keyword set. A better set might be obtained by consulting the article in more than a language (e.g., the Chinese counterparts) in that language divergence such as phrasal structure (i.e., word order), and word usage and word repetition (resulting from word translation or word sense) lead to different views on keywords across languages. Example English-Chinese divergence in Figure 1 includes the word order in the phrase *social reintegration* and *重返社會* (*social* translated to *社會* and *reintegration* inversely to *重返*), many-to-one mapping/translation e.g. both *prosthesis* and *artificial limbs* translated to *義肢*, and one-to-many mapping e.g. *physical* respectively translated to *物理* and *身體* in context *physical therapist* and *physical rehabilitation*. We hypothesize that, with the differences in languages, language-specific word statistics might be fused to contribute to keyword analysis.

We present a system, *BiKEA*, that learns to identify keywords in a language with the help of the other. The cross-language information is expected to reinforce language similarities and respect language dissimilarities, and better understand articles in terms of keywords. An example keyword analysis of an English article is shown in Figure 1. *BiKEA* has aligned the parallel articles at word level and determined the topical keyword preference scores for words. *BiKEA* learns these topic-related scores during training by analyzing a collection of articles.

At run-time, *BiKEA* transforms an article in a language into PageRank word graph. To hear another side of the story, *BiKEA* also constructs word graph from its counterpart in another language. These two graphs are then bridged over bilingually equivalent nodes. The bridging is to take language divergence into account and

Proceedings of The 2nd Workshop on Natural Language Processing Techniques for Educational Applications, pages 43–48,
Beijing, China, July 31, 2015.

The English Article: I've been in Afghanistan for 21 years. I work for the Red Cross and I'm a physical therapist. My job is to make arms and legs -- well it's not completely true. We do more than that. We provide the patients, the Afghan disabled, first with the physical rehabilitation then with the social reintegration. It's a very logical plan, but it was not always like this. For many years, we were just providing them with artificial limbs. It took quite many years for ...

Its Chinese Counterpart: 我在阿富汗已經 21 年。我為紅十字會工作，我是一名物理治療師。我的工作是製作胳膊和腿--恩，這不完全是事實。 我們做的還不止這些。我們提供給患者，阿富汗的殘疾人，首先是身體康復, 然後重返社會。這是一個非常合理的計劃， 但它並不是總是這樣。多年來，我們只是給他們 提供義肢。花了很多年的程序才讓這計劃成為現在的模樣。...

Word Alignment Information: physical (物理), therapist (治療師), social (社會), reintegration (重返), physical (身體), rehabilitation (康復), prosthesis (義肢), ...

Scores of Topical Keyword Preferences for Words:
(English) prosthesis: 0.32; artificial leg: 0.21; physical therapist: 0.15; rehabilitation: 0.08; ...
(Chinese) 義肢: 0.41; 物理治療師: 0.15; 康復: 0.10; 阿富汗: 0.08, ...

English Keywords from Bilingual Perspectives:
prosthesis, artificial, leg, rehabilitation, orthopedic, ...

Figure 1. An example *BiKEA* keyword analysis for an English article.

to allow for language-wise interaction over word statistics. At last, *BiKEA* iterates in bilingual context with word keyness scores to find keywords.

2 Related Work

Keyword extraction has been actively applied to many NLP tasks: document categorization (Manning and Schutze, 2000), indexing (Li et al., 2004), and text mining on social networking services ((Li et al., 2010); (Zhao et al., 2011); (Wu et al., 2010)).

The body of KEA focuses on learning word statistics in document collection. Approaches such as tfidf and entropy, using local document and/or across-document information, pose strong baselines (Liu et al. (2009) and Gebre et al. (2013)). On the other hand, Mihalcea and Tarau (2004) apply PageRank, connecting words locally, to extract essential words. In our work, we integrate globally learned keyword preferences into PageRank to identify keywords.

Recent work has been incorporating semantics into PageRank. For example, Liu et al. (2010) construct PageRank synonym graph to accommodate words with similar meaning. And Huang and Ku (2013) weigh PageRank edges based on nodes' degrees of reference. In contrast, we bridge PageRank word graphs from parallel articles to facilitate re-distribution or interaction of the word statistics of the involved languages.

In studies more closely related to our work, Liu et al. (2010) and Zhao et al. (2011) present PageRank algorithms leveraging article topic information for keyword identification. The main differences from our current work are that the article topics we exploit are specified by humans, not automated systems, and that our PageRank graphs are built and connected bilingually.

In contrast to the previous research on topic modeling (e.g., Zhao and Xing (2007)) and keyword extraction, we present a keyword extraction algorithm that learns topical keyword preferences and bilingually inter-connects PageRank graphs. The bilinguality is to help predict better keywords taking into account the perspectives of the languages involved including the language similarities and dissimilarities. We also use our keywords for educational purpose like reading comprehension.

3 BiKEA

3.1 Problem Statement

We focus on identifying keywords of a given article in a language with the help of the other. Keyword candidates are returned as the output of the system. The returned keyword list can be examined by humans (e.g., for keyword evaluation or language learning), or passed on to article recommendation systems for article retrieval. Therefore, our goal is to return a reasonable-sized set of keyword candidates that contain the given article's essential terms. We now formally describe the problem that we are addressing.

Problem Statement: We are given a bilingual parallel article collection of various topics from social media (e.g., TED), an article ART^e in language *e*, and its counterpart ART^c in language *c*. Our goal is to determine a set of words that are likely to contain important words of ART^e. For this, we take into account word keyness w.r.t. ART^e's topic and bridge language-specific statistics of ART^e and ART^c via bilingual information (e.g., word alignments) such that cross-lingual diversities are valued in extracting keywords in *e*.

3.2 Topical Keyword Preferences

We attempt to estimate language-wise keyword preferences with respect to a wide range of article topics. Basically, the estimation is to calculate word significance in a domain topic. Our learning process has following four stages.

In the first two stages of the learning process, we generate two sets of article and word information. The input to these stages is a set of articles and their domain topics. The output is a set of pairs of article ID and word in the article, e.g., (ID_ART^e=1,w^e=*prosthesis*) in language *e* or (ID_ART^c=1,w^c=*義肢*) in language *c*, and a set of pairs of article topic and word in the article, e.g., (tp^e=*disability*,w^e=*prosthesis*) in *e* and (tp^e=*disability*,w^c=*義肢*) in *c*. Note that the topic information is shared across languages, and that, to respect language diversities, words' topical significance is calculated within their specific language and the original language-independent word statistics will later be fused and interact at run-time.

The third stage estimates keyword preferences for words across articles and domain topics using aforementioned (*ART*,*w*) and (*tp*,*w*) sets. In our paper, simple yet effective tfidf estimation is used: *tfidf*(*w*)=*freq*(*ART*,*w*)/*appr*(*ART'*,*w*) where term frequency in an article is divided by its appearance in the article collection to distinguish important words from common words.

tfidf takes global information (i.e., article collection) into account, and will be used as keyword preference model in PageRank at run-time which locally connects words (i.e., within articles).

3.3 Run-Time Keyword Extraction

Once language-specific keyword preference scores for words are learned, they are stored for run-time reference. *BiKEA* then uses the procedure in Figure 2 to fuse word statistics across languages to determine keyword list for a given article. In this procedure machine translation technique i.e., IBM word aligner is exploited to glue statistics in the involved languages and make bilingually motivated random-walk algorithm (i.e., PageRank) possible.

```
procedure PredictKW(ART^e,ART^c,KeyPrefs,WA,α,N)
//Construct language-specific word graph for PageRank
(1) EW^e=constructPRwordGraph(ART^e)
(2) EW^c=constructPRwordGraph(ART^c)
//Construct inter-language bridges
(3) EW=α × EW^e+(1-α) × EW^c
      for each word alignment (w_i^c, w_j^e) in WA
        if IsContWord(w_i^c) and IsContWord(w_j^e)
(4a)       EW[i,j]+=1 × BiWeight^cont
        else
(4b)       EW[i,j]+=1 × BiWeight^noncont
(5) normalize each row of EW to sum to 1
//Iterate for PageRank
(6) set KP_{1×v} to
          [KeyPrefs(w_1), KeyPrefs(w_2), ...,KeyPrefs(w_v)]
(7) initialize KN_{1×v} to [1/v,1/ v, ...,1/v]
      repeat
(8a) KN'=λ × KN × EW+(1-λ) × KP
(8b) normalize KN' to sum to 1
(8c) update KN with KN' after the check of KN and KN'
      until maxIter or avgDifference(KN,KN') ≤ smallDiff
(9) rankedKeywords=Sort words in decreasing order of KN
      return the N rankedKeywords in e with highest scores
```

Figure 2. Extracting keywords at run-time.

```
procedure constructPRwordGraph(ART)
(1) EW_{v×v}=0_{v×v}
      for each sentence st in ART
        for each word w_i in st
          for each word w_j in st where i<j and j-i ≤ WS
            if not IsContWord(w_i) and IsContWord(w_j)
(2a)          EW[i,j]+=1 × m
            elif not IsContWord(w_i) and not IsContWord(w_j)
(2b)          EW[i,j]+=1 × (1/m)
            elif IsContWord(w_i) and not IsContWord(w_j)
(2c)          EW[i,j]+=1 × (1/m)
            elif IsContWord(w_i) and IsContWord(w_j)
(2d)          EW[i,j]+=1 × m
      return EW
```

Figure 3. Constructing PageRank word graph.

In Steps (1) and (2) of Figure 2 we construct PageRank word graphs for the article ART^e in language *e* and its counterpart ART^c in language *c*. They are built independently using the procedure in Figure 3 to respect language properties (such as subject-verb-object or subject-object-verb structure). In the algorithm of Figure 3, **EW** stores normalized edge weights for word w_i and w_j (Step (2)). And **EW** is a *v* by *v* matrix where *v* is the vocabulary size of ART^e and ART^c. Note that the graph is directed (from words to words that follow) and edge weights are words' co-occurrences within window size *WS*. Additionally we incorporate edge weight multiplier m>1 to propagate more PageRank scores to content words.

Then, Step (3) in Figure 2 linearly combines word graphs $\mathbf{EW}^e$ and $\mathbf{EW}^c$ using α. We use α to balance language properties/statistics, and *BiKEA* backs off to monolingual KEA if α is one.

In Step (4) for each word alignment (w_i^c, w_j^e), we construct a link between the word nodes with the weight *BiWeight*. The inter-language link is expected to reinforce language similarities and respect language divergence while the weight is to facilitate cross-language statistics interaction. Word alignments *WA* are derived using IBM models 1-5 (Och and Ney, 2003). Based on the directional word-aligned entry (w_i^c, w_j^e), the inter-language link is directed from w_i^c to w_j^e, i.e. from language *c* to *e*. The fusion or bridging of PageRank graphs across languages is expected to help keyword extraction in language *e* with the statistics in language *c*. Although alternative approach can be used for bridging, our approach is intuitive, and most importantly in compliance with the directional spirit of PageRank.

Step (6) sets keyword preference model **KP** using topical preference scores from Section 3.2, while Step (7) initializes **KN** of PageRank scores or, in our case, word keyness scores. Then we distribute keyness scores until **KN** converges. In each iteration, a word's keyness score is the linear combination of its keyword preference score and the sum of the propagation of its inbound words' previous PageRank scores. For the word w_j^e in ART^e, any edge (w_i^e,w_j^e) in ART^e, and any edge (w_k^c,w_j^e) in *WA*, its new PageRank score is computed as

$$\mathbf{KN}'[1,j] = \lambda \times \left(\begin{array}{c} \alpha \times \sum_{i \in v} \mathbf{KN}[1,i] \times \mathbf{EW}^e[i,j] + \\ (1-\alpha) \times \sum_{k \in v} \mathbf{KN}[1,k] \times \mathbf{EW}[k,j] \end{array} \right) + (1-\lambda) \times \mathbf{KP}[1,j]$$

Once the iterative process stops, we rank words according to their final keyness scores and return *N* top-ranked words in language *e* as keyword candidates of the given article ART^e.

4 Experiments

4.1 Data Sets

We collected 3.8M-word English transcripts along with their Chinese counterparts from TED for our experiments. GENIA tagger (Tsuruoka and Tsujii, 2005) was used to lemmatize and part-of-speech tag the English transcripts while CKIP (Ma and Chen, 2003) was used to segment the Chinese.

Fifty parallel articles (approximately 2,500 words per article) were randomly chosen and manually annotated with English keywords for keyword analysis.

4.2 Evaluation on Keywords

Table 1 summarizes the keyword extraction results of the baseline *tfidf* and our best systems on the test set. The evaluation metrics are precision, mean reciprocal rank, and nDCG (Jarvelin and Kekalainen, 2002).

As we can see, monolingual PageRank (*PR*) and bilingual PageRank (*BiKEA*), using global information tfidf, outperform *tfidf*. They relatively boost nDCG by 21% and P by 55%. MRR's also indicate their superiority: their top-two candidates are often keywords vs. the 2nd-ranked from *tfidf*. Encouragingly, *BiKEA+tfidf* achieves better performance than the strong monolingual *PR+tfidf*, further improving nDCG relatively by 7.4% and MRR relatively by 9.4%.

Overall, topical keyword preferences and inter-language bridging in PageRank which values language properties/statistics, help keyword extraction.

@*N*=5	P	MRR	nDCG
tfidf	.256	.547	.587
PR+tfidf	.396	.663	.712
BiKEA+tfidf	.412	.725	.765

@*N*=7	P	MRR	nDCG
tfidf	.211	.550	.587
PR+tfidf	.337	.669	.720
BiKEA+tfidf	.348	.728	.770

@*N*=10	P	MRR	nDCG
tfidf	.162	.555	.594
PR+tfidf	.282	.669	.719
BiKEA+tfidf	.302	.730	.760

Table 1. System performance across *N*'s.

4.3 Application to Language Learning

The role of highlighting keywords in reading comprehension has been attracting interest in the field of language learning and educational psychology (Nist and Hogrebe, 1987; Peterson 1991; Silvers and Kreiner, 1997). In this paper, we further examine keywords in the context of computer assisted language learning. Specifically, we applied our automatic *BiKEA* to keyword highlighting in reading comprehension and intended to see how much language learners can benefit from *BiKEA* keywords in reading comprehension test.

This is really a two-hour presentation I give to high school students, cut down to three minutes. And it all started one day on a plane, on my way to TED, seven years ago. And in the seat next to me was a high school student, a teenager, and she came from a really poor family. And she wanted to make something of her life, and she asked me a simple little question. She said, "What leads to success?" And I felt really badly, because I couldn't give her a good answer. So I get off the plane, and I come to TED. And I think, jeez, I'm in the middle of a room of successful people! So why don't I ask them what helped them succeed, and pass it on to kids?

So here we are, seven years, 500 interviews later, and I'm gonna tell you what really leads to success and makes TEDsters tick. And the first thing is passion. Freeman Thomas says, "I'm driven by my passion." TEDsters do it for love; they don't do it for money.

Carol Coletta says, "I would pay someone to do what I do." And the interesting thing is: if you do it for love, the money comes anyway.

Work! Rupert Murdoch said to me, "It's all hard work. Nothing comes easily. But I have a lot of fun." Did he say fun? Rupert? Yes!

TEDsters do have fun working. And they work hard. I figured, they're not workaholics. They're workafrolics.

Good! Alex Garden says, "To be successful put your nose down in something and get damn good at it." There's no magic; it's practice, practice, practice.

And it's focus. Norman Jewison said to me, "I think it all has to do with focusing yourself on one thing."

And push! David Gallo says, "Push yourself. Physically, mentally, you've gotta push, push, push." You gotta push through shyness and self-doubt.

Goldie Hawn says, "I always had self-doubts. I wasn't good enough; I wasn't smart enough. I didn't think I'd make it."

Now it's not always easy to push yourself, and that's why they invented mothers. (Laughter) Frank Gehry -- Frank Gehry said to me, "My mother pushed me."

Serve! Sherwin Nuland says, "It was a privilege to serve as a doctor."

Now a lot of kids tell me they want to be millionaires. And the first thing I say to them is: "OK, well you can't serve yourself; you gotta serve others something of value. Because that's the way people really get rich."

Ideas! TEDster Bill Gates says, "I had an idea: founding the first micro-computer software company." I'd say it was a pretty good idea. And there's no magic to creativity in coming up with ideas -- it's just doing some very simple things. And I give lots of evidence.

Persist! Joe Kraus says, "Persistence is the number one reason for our success." You gotta persist through failure. You gotta persist through crap! Which of course means "Criticism, Rejection, Assholes and Pressure." (Laughter)

So, the big -- the answer to this question is simple: Pay 4,000 bucks and come to TED. Or failing that, do the eight things -- and trust me, these are the big eight things that lead to success. Thank you TEDsters for all your interviews!

Figure 4. The English TED transcript used in our reading comprehension test.

In our case study, we asked an English professor to set a multiple-choice reading comprehension test based on one English TED transcript (See Figure 4) and recruited 26 second-year college students learning English as a second language. Their proficiency in English was estimated to be of pre-intermediate level.

These students were randomly and evenly divided into experimental (reading the English transcript with *BiKEA* keywords) and control group (reading without). Promisingly, our keywords helped the students: students in the experimental group achieved better averaged test score (.82) than those in the control group (.74). Relatively, the improvement was 10%. Moreover, post-study survey indicated that 90% of the participants found our keywords helpful for their article reading and key concept grasping. We are analyzing the influence of the highlighted *BiKEA* keywords on the high-performing students as well as the low-performing students in the test.

5 Summary

We have introduced a method for extracting keywords in bilingual context. The method involves automatically estimating topical keyword preferences and bridging language-specific PageRank word statistics. Evaluation shows that the method can yield better keywords than strong monolingual KEA. And a case study indicates that language learners benefit from our keywords in reading comprehension test. Admittedly, using our keywords for educational purposes needs further experiments.

Acknowledgement

This study is conducted under the "Online and Offline integrated Smart Commerce Platform (2/4)" of the Institute for Information Industry which is subsidized by the Ministry of Economic Affairs of the Republic of China.

References

B. G. Gebre, M. Zampieri, P. Wittenburg, and T. Heskens. 2013. Improving native language identification with tf-idf weighting. In *Proceedings of the NAACL Workshop on Innovative Use of NLP for Building Educational Applications*, pages 216-223.

Scott A. Golder and Bernardo A. Huberman. 2006. Usage patterns of collaborative tagging systems. *Information Science*, 32(2): 198-208.

Harry Halpin, Valentin Robu, and Hana Shepherd. 2007. The complex dynamics of collaborative tagging. In *Proceedings of the WWW*, pages 211-220.

Chung-chi Huang and Lun-wei Ku. 2013. Interest analysis using semantic PageRank and social interaction content. In *Proceedings of the ICDM Workshop on Sentiment Elicitation from Natural Text for Information Retrieval and Extraction*, pages 929-936.

Kalervo Jarvelin and Jaana Kekalainen. 2002. Cumulated gain-based evaluation of IR technologies. *ACM Transactions on Information Systems*, 20(4): 422-446.

Philipp Koehn, Franz Josef Och, and Daniel Marcu. 2003. Statistical phrase-based translation. In *Proceedings of the North American Chapter of the Association for Computational Linguistics*, pages 48-54.

Quanzhi Li, Yi-Fang Wu, Razvan Bot, and Xin Chen. 2004. Incorporating document keyphrases in search results. In *Proceedings of the Americas Conference on Information Systems*.

Zhenhui Li, Ging Zhou, Yun-Fang Juan, and Jiawei Han. 2010. Keyword extraction for social snippets. In *Proceedings of the WWW*, pages 1143-1144.

Marina Litvak and Mark Last. 2008. Graph-based keyword extraction for single-document summarization. In *Proceedings of the ACL Workshop on Multi-Source Multilingual Information Extraction and Summarization*, pages 17-24.

F. Liu, D. Pennell, F. Liu, and Y. Liu. 2009. Unsupervised approaches for automatic keyword extraction using meeting transcripts. In *Proceedings of the NAACL*, pages 620-628.

Zhengyang Liu, Jianyi Liu, Wenbin Yao, and Cong Wang. 2010. Keyword extraction using PageRank on synonym networks. In *Proceedings of the ICEEE*, pages 1-4.

Zhiyuan Liu, Wenyi Huang, Yabin Zheng, and Maosong Sun. 2010. Automatic keyphrase extraction via topic decomposition. In *Proceedings of the EMNLP*, pages 366-376.

Wei-Yun Ma and Keh-Jiann Chen. 2003. Introduction to CKIP Chinese word segmentation system for the first international Chinese word segmentation bakeoff. In *Proceedings of the ACL Workshop on Chinese Language Processing*.

Chris D. Manning and Hinrich Schutze. 2000. *Foundations of statistical natural language processing*. MIT Press.

Rada Mihalcea and Paul Tarau. 2004. TextRank: Bringing orders into texts. In *Proceedings of the EMNLP*, pages 404-411.

S. L. Nist and M. C. Hogrebe. 1987. The role of underlining and annotating in remembering textual information. *Reading Research and Instruction*, 27(1): 12-25.

Franz Josef Och and Hermann Ney. 2003. A systematic comparison of various statistical alignment models. *Computational Linguistics*, 29(1): 19-51.

Divya Padmanabhan, Prasanna Desikan, Jaideep Srivastava, and Kashif Riaz. 2005. WICER: a weighted inter-cluster edge ranking for clustered graphs. In *Proceedings of the IEEE/WIC/ACM WI*, pages 522-528.

S. E. Peterson. 1991. The cognitive functions of underlining as a study technique. *Reading Research and Instruction*, 31(2): 49-56.

V. L. Silvers and D. S. Kreiner. 1997. The effects of pre-existing inappropriate highlighting on reading comprehension. *Reading Research and Instruction*, 36(3): 217-223.

Yoshimasa Tsuruoka and Jun'ichi Tsujii. 2005. Bidirectional inference with the easiest-first strategy for tagging sequence data. In *Proceedings of the EMNLP*, pages 467-474.

Peter D. Turney. 2000. Learning algorithms for keyphrase extraction. *Information Retrieval*, 2(4): 303-336.

Wei Wu, Bin Zhang, and Mari Ostendorf. 2010. Automatic generation of personalized annotation tags for Twitter users. In *Proceedings of the NAACL*, pages 689-692.

B. Zhao and E. P. Xing. 2007. HM-BiTAM: Bilingual topic exploration, word alignment, and translation. In *Proceedings of the NIPS*.

Wayne Xin Zhao, Jing Jiang, Jing He, Yang Song, Palakorn Achananuparp, Ee-Peng Lim, and Xiaoming Li. 2011. Topical keyword extraction from Twitter. In *Proceedings of the ACL*, pages 379-388.

Annotating Entailment Relations for Shortanswer Questions

Simon Ostermann, Andrea Horbach, Manfred Pinkal
Department of Computational Linguistics, Saarland University, Saarbrücken, Germany
(simono|andrea|pinkal)@coli.uni-saarland.de

Abstract

This paper presents an annotation project that explores the relationship between textual entailment and short answer scoring (SAS). We annotate entailment relations between learner and target answers in the Corpus of Reading Comprehension Exercises for German (CREG) with a fine-grained label inventory and compare them in various ways to correctness scores assigned by teachers. Our main finding is that although both tasks are clearly related, not all of our entailment tags can be directly mapped to SAS scores and that especially the area of partial entailment covers instances that are problematic for automatic scoring and need further investigation.

1 Introduction

Reading comprehension exercises are a standard task in foreign language education: Students read a text in the language they are learning and answer questions about it. With the advent of computer-based language learning courses, the automatic scoring of such shortanswer questions has become an important research topic (for an overview see Burrows et al. (2015); Ziai et al. (2012)), not only for reading and listening comprehension in the context of foreign language learning, but also e.g. in science questions for native speaker students.

It has been often noted that the SAS task is related to the task of recognizing textual entailment (RTE, e.g. Mohler et al. (2011), Sukkarieh and Blackmore (2009), Dzikovska et al. (2013b)). RTE is the task to decide whether there is an inference relation between two texts; in the case of SAS, these texts are the learner answer (LA), given by a student, and a teacher-specified target answer (TA, i.e. a sample solution). An entailment relation between two texts A and B is given if people reading A and B would infer that whenever A is true, B is most likely true as well (Dagan et al., 2013).

Consider the following example:[1]

(1) **Q:** Why did Julchen come to the kitchen?
TA: She came to the kitchen because of the noise her parents made.
LA: She came to the kitchen because Mr. and Mrs. Muschler became out of breath from laughing.

In this example, the LA textually (but not logically) entails the TA. In a strictly logical sense of entailment, laughing until you are out of breath does not entail making noise. However, it seems plausible to many people that laughing in that way makes a lot of noise. Such a learner answer that is more specific than the target answer – and thus entails the target answer – is likely to be scored as correct by a teacher.

In some aspects, SAS for reading comprehension in a language learning scenario differs from a standard textual entailment scenario: Whereas in standard RTE, two texts are compared, in the SAS scenario the additional context of the question has to be accounted for in terms of information structure and resolution of anaphora and ellipses. Additionally, when processing learner language one often has to deal with ungrammatical sentences and orthographical variance that are challenging for many NLP tools, up to the extent that it is sometimes difficult to understand what the learner wanted to express with an answer (the so-called *target hypothesis*).

In this study, we want to explicitly assess the relation between RTE labels and correctness scores assigned by teachers. We assume that they are related, but we expect that the relation is not a direct

[1] All examples are taken from the CREG corpus and translated by the authors preserving linguistic errors whenever possible.

Proceedings of The 2nd Workshop on Natural Language Processing Techniques for Educational Applications, pages 49–58,
Beijing, China, July 31, 2015.

mapping. We expect, for example, that, if a LA entails a TA and vice versa at the same time, i.e. if they are paraphrases, then the LA will probably be scored as correct by a teacher. On the other hand, the fact that there is only some partial conceptual overlap between a LA and a TA does not constitute entailment, but is in some instances enough for an answer to be scored as correct by a teacher.

We present in this paper the first part of an annotation project that aims at investigating the relationship between SAS and RTE and that compares existing binary correctness scores annotated by teachers to RTE annotations that have been conducted without the correctness or quality of the learner answer in mind. (In future work, we will also look at the relation between reading texts and learner answers.)

Understanding these relations better will potentially help us to leverage techniques from RTE for the task of SAS in a more efficient way and to shed light on the the way teachers score shortanswer questions.

This paper makes the following contributions:

- We provide a fine-grained annotation of the Corpus of Reading Comprehension Exercises in German (CREG) (Ott et al., 2012) with 7 textual entailment labels that specify the entailment relations between learner answers and target answers.

- We provide an evaluation of our annotations that compares how our label distribution corresponds to the distribution of binary teacher scores in CREG.

- State of the art binary scoring approaches label only about 86% of the corpus correctly (Hahn and Meurers, 2012). In order to understand the challenges of automatic scoring better, we evaluate which instances in terms of our entailment annotation labels are most problematic for automatic scoring with a binary label.

- We will further explore the relation between textual entailment and SAS by comparing, how well features from shortanswer scoring tasks can be used to learn our classification.

2 Related Work

Recognizing textual entailment and automatic shortanswer scoring are two related tasks in which text pairs are labeled with the relation between them:

The RTE task in its original formulation (Dagan and Glickman, 2004) is a binary classification task deciding whether a *text t* entails a *hypothesis h*. The two-way task has been extended to a 3-way task involving the labels *Entailed*, *Contradicted* and *Unknown* (Giampiccolo et al., 2007). Annual RTE shared tasks led to a growing community with a large number of approaches, cf. (Dagan et al., 2013). MacCartney and Manning (2009a) proposed an extension of the classification schema to a much more fine-grained inventory of 7 semantic relations that expresses additional concepts such as *equivalence* and *reverse entailment* and also inspired our label set.

In SAS, the task is to assign a student answer a score that specifies the correctness of the answer. Many approaches to SAS compare learner answers given by a student to target answers specified by a teacher and rely on some measure of surface or semantic overlap between them (e.g. Bailey and Meurers (2008); Meurers et al. (2011); Mohler et al. (2011)) or measure whether teacher-specified aspects of a correct answer (so-called facets) are addressed in the learner answer (Nielsen et al., 2008).

In SAS corpora, the label for an answer is a binary score, stating whether the LA is correct or incorrect. Some data sets also provide annotations with points from an integer scale (e.g. Mohler and Mihalcea (2009) or the kaggle SAS competition [2]). Other data use more meaningful diagnostic labels such as Ott et al. (2012) and Bailey and Meurers (2008) that provide feedback to the learner.

In our study, we primarily rely on binary correctness scores for our comparisons. For the RTE task, we see LA and TA as text and hypothesis and expect that entailment will correlate with correctness: While a LA paraphrasing the TA should definitely count as correct, making the LA more specific should not make it incorrect either. However, omitting crucial information from the TA will potentially make the LA incorrect.

SemEval-2013 task 7 (Dzikovska et al., 2013b) took a first step in bringing together the RTE and the SAS community in a task to label student answers to explanation and definition questions with 5 RTE-labels. The data set used there (Dzikovska et al., 2012) focuses on science questions (Nielsen

[2]https://www.kaggle.com/c/asap-sas/data

et al., 2008) and physics questions from tutorial dialogues (Dzikovska et al., 2010), i.e. in contrast to our scenario they deal with native speakers – thus avoiding problems in processing learner language – and the questions do not refer to a specific reading text. Most importantly, our perspective on the relation between SAS and RTE also differs from the SemEval definition: The SemEval task uses RTE labels that are constructed from labels assigned by teachers as meaningful feedback to students. They assume that there is a direct mapping from RTE labels to binary teacher scores and construct their binary data set from collapsing those labels. Their approach is backed up by a small feasibility study that shows the correspondence of the RTE and SAS label sets in their setting. In our study, we consider RTE and SAS as different tasks and want to explore their relation. We therefore compare labeling from a RTE perspective and scoring from a teacher's point of view.

Both within the context of the SemEval task and already before, RTE approaches have been used for SAS. Levy et al. (2013) try to recognize *partial entailment* based on the facet approach by Nielsen et al. (2008) and aim at exploring its possible impact on recognizing full entailment relations on learner data as part of the SemEval-2013 task 7. Consequently, they also see the tasks of RTE and SAS as equivalent. In contrast to this, Mohler et al. (2011) present a SAS approach that uses techniques from RTE (e.g. a dependency graph matching approach, cf. Haghighi et al. (2005)), but clearly point out that although their system uses those methods, it cannot be seen as RTE system.

3 Annotations

3.1 Data Set

We use the Corpus of Reading Comprehension Exercises in German (CREG) (Ott et al., 2012), a prominent resource for shortanswer scoring data for German as a Foreign Language, as basis for our annotations. It contains 1032 learner answers (half of which have been scored as correct, the other half as incorrect by teachers), answering 177 different questions about a total of 32 texts together with teacher-specified target answers. Sometimes the corpus contains more than one target answer for a question. In such cases the corpus provides annotations that link every learner answer to exactly one best-fitting target answer. We use these annotations in creating LA-TA pairs for our annotations.

3.2 LA-TA Annotation Scheme

The aim of this first part of our annotation project is to investigate the textual entailment relations between TAs and LAs.

We use an extended and slightly modified version of the entailment classes proposed by MacCartney and Manning (2009b) that we adapted to our scenario of answer pairs, instead of self-contained text pairs (or even sentence pairs as in the early RTE tasks). Our labels are as follows:

paraphrase: TA and LA are paraphrases, i.e. express the same semantic content.

entailment: The LA textually entails the TA, i.e. it is more specific than the TA.

reverse entailment: The TA textually entails the LA.

partial entailment: There is a semantic overlap between TA and LA but there is no clear entailment relation in any direction[3].

contradiction: LA and TA are mutually exclusive, i.e. they cannot both be true at the same point in time.

topical non-entailment: The LA is in principle a valid answer to the question (it is *on-topic*) but there is no semantic overlap to the TA that would qualify it for one of the other entailment categories.

off-topic: While answers with any of the previous labels addressed the right question, i.e. were *on-topic*, for this label, the LA is *off-topic*[4] , i.e. it either answers a different question or is a non-answer and therefore cannot be compared to the TA.

Table 1 gives examples for all entailment types.

Note that our label set is a refinement of the classical 3-way entailment definition: While our *entailment* and *paraphrase* labels (if considering the LA to be the *text* and the TA to be the *hypothesis* in the classical RTE problem) correspond to *entailment* in the 3-way task, and our *contradiction* label directly corresponds to *contradictions* in classical RTE, all our other labels refine the *unknown* class.

[3]The *partial entailment* relation is discussed in more detail in Nielsen et al. (2009) and Levy et al. (2013)

[4]Note that this label is similar to the notion of incongruence introduced by von Stechow (1990).

Label	Question	Target Answer	Learner Answer
paraphrase	How much does BA earn monthly?	BA earns less than 300 Euro in a month.	less than 300 Euro monthly
entailment	What can you do in Dresden apart from sightseeing?	You can take a walk by the waterfront.	You can enjoy a relaxing walk by the waterfront.
reverse entailment	Where did the halo originate from?	The halo originated from the light out of the oven.	It originated from the oven.
partial entailment	List two places where one can sit outside!	there are two large terraces and a sunny garden.	In the garden or forest area.
contradiction	Is the apartment located in a new or an old building?	The apartment is in a new building.	The apartment is in an old building.
topical-non-entailment	What was the topic of the survey?	The survey was about things you can't do without.	The topic was usage of the Internet.
off-topic	Who made lawn gnomes famous?	Philipp Griebel made lawn gnomes famous.	It was famous in the Thuringian.

Table 1: Examples for the 7 entailment annotation labels

Due to the difference between classical RTE settings and the task and data we use, our annotation manual contains some guidelines that differ from those for a standard textual entailment task:

Learner Language Issues: One feature of the data that makes the annotation in general difficult is the fact that the LAs in CREG often come in an ungrammatical form or use lexically inappropriate material since they are formulated by language learners. Similarly to teachers in a short answer grading task, our annotators were instructed to ignore such errors. That means they had to implicitly build a so-called *target hypothesis* for each learner answer, i.e. an error-free version of what the learner presumably wanted to express (cf. Ellis (1994)), a task which is known to be problematic even for experienced teachers (Lüdeling, 2008).

Therefore, depending on the interpretation of the annotator, the chosen label can differ, as is illustrated by the following example:

(2) **Q:** Where and when could most garden gnomes be found?
TA: Most garden gnomes could be found in the postwar period in West Germany.
LA: Die Gartenzwerge setzte aus den Wald.
a) The garden gnomes released in the woods.
b) The garden gnomes sets out of the woods.

The LA in this example is ungrammatical and could either be interpreted as "The garden gnomes [were] released into the woods" or "The garden gnomes put [something] out of the woods", leading to *topical non-entailment* as the most plausible label for the first (a) and *off-topic* for the second (b) interpretation.

Note, that the label *contradiction* is not an option for this answer: Although the question presupposes that there is only one correct answer and the topical reading of the learner answer gives a different location than the TA, the two locations "western Germany" and "in the forest" are not mutually exclusive, but the learner answer rather addresses a different type of location than the TA. A clear case of a contradictory answer is instead the following LA: "Most garden gnomes could be found between 1948 and 1952 in the GDR", because GDR refers to a different location than western Germany.

Annotating Answers in Relation to the Question: In contrast to other RTE data sets that compare two texts, our data has the form of answer pairs with both answers referring to the same question. The question is made available to the annotators to resolve anaphoric expressions such as pronouns occurring in the answers and to expand answers in the form of ellipses to *full answers*: Semantic material introduced by the question is explicitly addressed in a *full answer* and omitted in a *term answer* (cf. the example for *paraphrase* in table 1) in the terminology of e.g. Krifka (2001), following von Stechow and Zimmermann (1984). Otherwise, the annotators were instructed to treat short and full answers in the same way. Specifically, only semantic content which has not been introduced by the question should be taken into consideration when deciding between partial entailment and topical-non-entailment. In doing so, we want to avoid that a learner answer is already partially entailed by the TA as soon as it is on-topic and repeats material from the question.

3.3 Annotation Process

All material has been double-annotated by two German native speakers with a background in linguistics using the *WebAnno* annotation tool (Yimam et al., 2013). The annotators were shown the question together with each LA-TA pair, but could not see the corresponding text and did not know whether a LA has been graded as correct or incorrect. We did so to avoid that they would explicitly or implicitly base their labelling decision on the knowledge of whether an answer is correct or supported by the text. Cases of disagreement have been additionally annotated by a third annotator and then be resolved through majority voting. Instances where all three annotators gave a different label have been resolved by one of the authors.

4 Evaluation

This section presents an analysis of our RTE annotations and comparisons to SAS scores.

4.1 Agreement

Our annotators reached a Cohen's Kappa of *0.69* which – according to Landis and Koch (1977) – indicates *substantial agreement*. The confusion matrix is given in table 2. Our results show that the labels *paraphrase*, *entailment* and *reverse entailment* can be reliably identified by the annotators. However, the confusion matrix highlights 2 problems: First, the identification of *partial entailment* is not trivial, as can be seen from a relatively high rate of misclassifications between *partial entailment* and almost any other label. Second, it is challenging to tell apart the three entailment classes *contradiction*, *off-topic* and *topical non-entailment*. As these labels – as we will later see – primarily belong to answers scored as incorrect, we will refer to them as *negative entailment* labels. When collapsing the three labels , our Kappa score improves to *0.78*.

4.2 Comparison of Teacher Scores and Entailment Labels

Figure 1 shows the distribution of our entailment labels compared to the binary CREG labels that indicate whether an answer is correct or incorrect. We can see that some of our labels clearly correspond to correct (paraphrase, entailment) or incorrect answers (contradiction, off-topic, topical-non-entailment). From the definition of these labels, this is an expected result: Whenever a LA is a paraphrase of a TA or more specific than a TA it should be correct and whenever a LA contradicts the TA, does not answer the question or answers the question without overlap with the target answer, it is most likely incorrect. However, the labels *partial entailment* and *reverse entailment* cannot be as easily mapped to binary scores, providing evidence for the existence of some substantial differences between the two tasks of RTE and SAS. These two labels have in common, that only some information from the TA is entailed by the LA (while in *partial entailment* the LA additionally entails information not present in the TA). One possible explanation why such answers sometimes are still scored as correct is that often TAs are formulated in an exhaustive way and more elaborate than the teacher would expect the learner to answer. It is not clear however from the TA which facts are necessary to make the LA correct and which facts are not. Example 3 shows one such answer pair, where the binary label is *correct*, although the entailment type clearly is *reverse entailment*. [5]

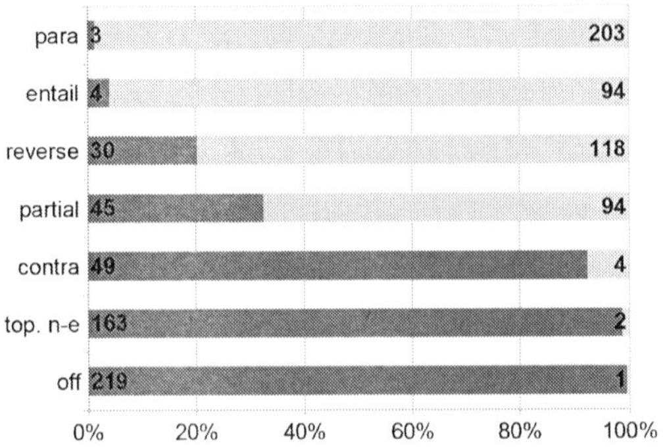

Figure 1: Distribution of entailment labels over binary labels, relative and absolute values (correct: light grey, incorrect: dark grey).

(3) **Q:** What is needed for paper production?
TA: You need wood, water and energy to produce paper.

[5] An answer just stating *water is needed* does not occur in our corpus, but we would consider it plausible that teachers label such an answer as incorrect, due to the the more prominent role of wood in the paper production process.

	para	entail	reverse	partial	contra	top. n-e	off
para	180	4	12	9	0	2	0
entail	6	78	0	15	0	2	0
reverse	7	5	112	28	2	1	3
partial	5	8	15	75	8	3	10
contra	0	0	0	2	47	1	1
top. n-e	1	0	2	10	35	100	30
off	0	1	3	3	5	31	169

Table 2: Confusion matrix between the two annotators for our labels. Abbreviations: **para**phrase, **entail**ment, **reverse** entailment, **partial** entailment, **contra**diction, **top**ical **n**on-**e**ntailment, **off**-topic.

LA: Wood is needed for paper production.

There are a few curious cases of label score combinations that seem implausible, such as answers with a negative entailment label that are scored as correct answer. The following example (4) illustrates this. While our schema clearly labels the LA as *off-topic*, since question material is paraphrased in a wrong way, the teacher decided to accept the answer by implicitly substituting the location of *Erfurt* with *Frankfurt*.

(4) **Q:** For how long does the company hold a branch at Frankfurt?
TA: The company holds a branch at Frankfurt for 15 years.
LA: It holds a branch at Erfurt for 15 years.

Similarly, there are rare examples of *entailment* or *paraphrase* items that are labeled as *incorrect*. Example 5 shows one such pair, where, both for the entailment label and the correctness score, different options are plausible depending on the interpretation of *warm light* (temperature vs. colour):

(5) **Q:** Why did the man put the wood into the plate oven?
TA: He put the wood into the oven to make the room warmer.
LA: For a warm light through the room.

The findings from this evaluation show that, in our labeling scenario, SAS and RTE are two separate tasks – in contrast to findings by Dzikovska et al. (2013a), who assume that the two tasks do not differ essentially from each other. Thus, their label set contains labels for scoring the LA and exploring its entailment relation simultaneously: They distinguish the label *correct* for complete paraphrases of the TA – which they expect to be the only correct type of answers – and *Partially_correct_incomplete* for LAs that lack information; furthermore *Contradictory* and *Irrelevant* for answers that are on-topic, but either contradictory to the TA or containing the wrong information; and finally *Non_domain* for answers that do not address the question. Our labels are slightly more fine grained: *Partial entailment* has no correspondence in their 5-way label set, but forms for our data the most interesting case for further investigation because of its coverage of both correct and incorrect answers. There is also no correspondence for our *entailment* label. From a SAS perspective, the difference between *paraphrase* and *entailment* seems not to be crucial, as both labels almost exclusively cover answers that are scored binary as correct in our data.

	correct	missing concept	extra concept	blend	non-answer
para	194	7	3	2	0
entail	73	3	16	6	0
reverse	74	53	1	20	0
partial	50	37	8	46	0
contra	1	10	0	42	0
top. n-e	1	15	1	148	0
off	1	40	0	175	4

Table 3: Confusion matrix for teacher assessments and entailment labels.

In addition to binary scores, the CREG corpus also contains a 5-way set of teacher scores (Ott et al. (2012), following Bailey and Meurers (2008)): In these annotations, *missing concept* and *extra concept* were used if the answer missed important information or contained additional, not necessary information, respectively. Therefore we would expect them to match our *reverse entailment* and *entailment* labels, while their *correct* label should correspond to our *paraphrase*. The label *blend* is a combination of *missing* and *extra concept*, seemingly similar to our *partial entailment*. The label

non-answer was used for LAs that did not address the question as with our *off-topic*.
From the label descriptions, we would have expected to see a good fit between the two label sets. Instead, we find that a clear mapping between our labels and the 5-way scores is not possible, as can be seen in the confusion matrix in table 3. Similar to the comparison to the SemEval7 labels, this is mainly the case because the 5-way scores mix aspects of SAS and RTE in an unsuitable way.

5 Machine Learning Experiments

We explore the relation between RTE and SAS through a series of machine learning evaluations. In the first part, we evaluate a SAS classifier asking which LAs in terms of entailment type are most difficult for automatic labeling. We then present a modeling experiment that explores the impact of using our entailment labels as features for a SAS system and finally a series of experiments that aim at testing how well entailment information is modeled by alignment-based machine learning features.

For all experiments, we used the *Logistic* classifier in the *Weka* package, that is based on a logistic regression algorithm (Hall et al., 2009). We use alignment-based features in a re-implementation of Meurers et al. (2011) that reaches an accuracy of 86% on CREG. All experiments were evaluated via leave-one-out cross validation.

Task Setting	Accuracy	Kappa
teacher-alignment	*0.861*	*0.723*
teacher-entailment	*0.922*	*0.843*
entailment-7	*0.473*	*0.36*
entailment-5	*0.641*	*0.489*
entailment-3	*0.749*	*0.562*
entailment-2	*0.837*	*0.668*

Table 5: Overview of the classifier performances Abbreviations: **teacher** scores as class with **alignment** features and alignment+**entailment** features. 7-way **entailment** type as class and collapsed entailment class sets by combining entailment types into **5**, **3** or **2** classes, all with alignment features

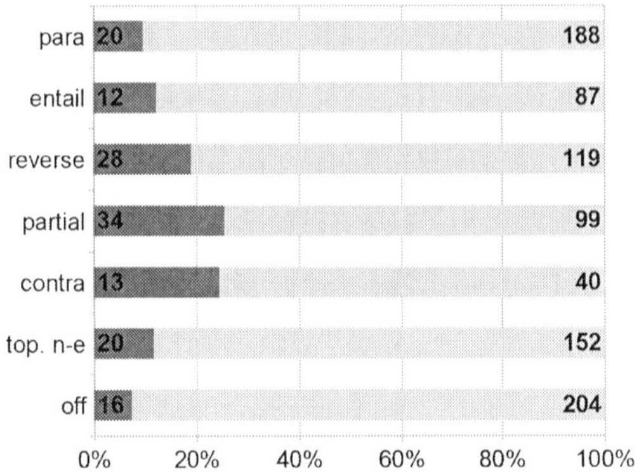

Figure 2: Correctly (light grey) and incorrectly (dark grey) classified instances per entailment class, relative and absolute values.

5.1 Distribution of correctly and incorrectly automatically scored instances over the entailment types

We investigate if some of the entailment types are challenging for a SAS system. Figure 2 shows the distribution of incorrectly classified instances over our entailment types.

In general, LAs that are labeled with *partial entailment* or *reverse entailment* are more problematic for the SAS model than the other labels. This observation reminds of the finding that these labels do not clearly correspond to one correctness score: An alignment based SAS model that covers among its features the percentage of TA tokens and chunks covered in the LA can not differentiate whether a unit not covered was crucial or not. The machine learner also struggles in general with the *contradiction* class. This is because many contradicting answer pairs still provide a high overlap but differ in just a small but critical detail.

Our finding again underlines the difficulty which the evaluation of the semantic overlap between two texts, as can be found in the *partial entailment* group, poses to SAS approaches and reinforces the need for more sophisticated semantic features for modeling these entailment phenomena and consequently for a better shortanswer scoring.

5.2 Can entailment classes improve an SAS feature set?

We enhanced the feature set used by the classifier with our annotated entailment label as an ad-

real \ classified	para	entail	reverse	partial	contra	top. n-e	off	recall
para	136	11	26	18	1	3	11	*0.66*
entail	20	44	2	24	0	1	7	*0.449*
reverse	24	1	82	17	0	1	23	*0.554*
partial	20	15	20	46	0	9	32	*0.324*
contra	5	2	7	7	1	3	28	*0.019*
top. n-e	2	3	10	13	2	16	119	*0.097*
off	6	3	14	7	1	26	163	*0.741*
precision	*0.638*	*0.557*	*0.51*	*0.348*	*0.2*	*0.271*	*0.426*	

Table 4: Confusion matrix for the machine learner on our labels with precision and recall for all classes.

ditional feature in order to explore whether our annotations, could they be determined automatically, would be helpful in a SAS task. This raises the classifier's performance from *86.1%* (*κ=0.723*) to *92.2%* (*κ=0.843*), as can be seen in table 5. Although we showed that the RTE and SAS scenario differ substantially, this outcome emphasizes that they also have a lot in common.

However, the obvious problem here is that the usage of a manually annotated feature is comparable to the use of a human oracle and is therefore not feasible for a fully automatic approach. Thus, further research has to concentrate on how we can automatically model entailment types computationally. To do so, we will for example try to enhance the current TA-LA alignment based SAS approach. This leads to the question in how far the model is already able to predict our entailment types. One first evaluation trial of this question is presented in the next section.

5.3 Are entailment relations learnable with an SAS system?

In this last set of experiments we address the question in how far the automatic prediction of entailment labels is possible with the feature sets of an alignment based SAS approach. Although the focus in an educational application would be the automatic scoring of the correctness of a LA rather than its entailment relation to its TA, this experiment might shed additional light on the relatedness of the two tasks.

We therefore train our classifier on the LA data and use the entailment labels as class, which leads to an accuracy of *47%* (table 5) and a kappa indicating *poor agreement*. The confusion matrix for this classification (table 4) shows that the machine learner especially struggles with labeling the negative classes, because the features it uses are computed based on the alignment between TA and LA, while the question is not taken into account. Therefore the machine learner is unable to decide if an answer addresses the question or not. *Partial entailment* poses a large difficulty again as well, resulting in an F1-Score of *0.336* (*P=0.348/R=0.324*) for that class. In contrast, the F1-Score for paraphrase reaches a modest level of *0.649* (*P=0.638/R=0.66*).

To narrow down the difficulties for our machine learner, we stepwise collapsed our entailment labels, by first subsuming the negative entailment classes *topical non-entailment*, *off-topic* and *contradiction* as one class, which leads to only 5 entailment classes and an accuracy of *64.1%*. In the next step, we subsumed *entailment*, *reverse entailment* and *paraphrase* under one "positive" label, but left partial entailment out, which lead to 3 classes (positive, negative, partial) and an accuracy of *74.9%*. Finally, we added *partial entailment* to the positive class and achieved a performance of *83.7%*. Although it is in general not surprising that the performance increases as the number of labels decreases, it is interesting that the inclusion or exclusion of *partial entailment* has a rather high impact on the performance.

6 Conclusions and Future Work

This paper presented a study that labels LA TA pairs from the CREG corpus with a set of fine-grained textual entailment annotations. Our main finding is that there is a clear correspondence between some textual entailment classes and a binary correctness score. But there is also an area that needs further investigation. This concerns the *partial* and *reverse entailment* cases and illustrates that the tasks of RTE and SAS are related, but not equivalent for our scenario.

One next step will be to investigate the structure of answers that are labeled as *partial* or *reverse entailment* as those instances seem to be particularly problematic for automatic SAS. For advances in automatic scoring it is important to determine which parts of a target answer are crucial for a correct LA and which are not.

In the next step of this annotation project, we will focus on the relation between reading texts and answers. We expect that the combination of this variant of the RTE setting with our current annotations helps us to gather further insights into the nature of shortanswer questions.

Acknowledgements

We thank the three anonymous reviewers for their helpful comments. We also thank our annotators Fernando Ardente, Sophie Henning and Maximilian Wolf for their help with this study and alexis Palmer for valuable feedback for our annotation guidelines.

This work was funded by the Cluster of Excellence "Multimodal Computing and Interaction" of the German Excellence Initiative.

References

Stacey Bailey and Detmar Meurers. 2008. Diagnosing meaning errors in short answers to reading comprehension questions. In *Proceedings of the Third ACL Workshop on Innovative Use of NLP for Building Educational Applications*, page 107115, Columbus, Ohio, USA, June.

Steven Burrows, Iryna Gurevych, and Benno Stein. 2015. The eras and trends of automatic short answer grading. *International Journal of Artificial Intelligence in Education*, 25(1):60–117.

Ido Dagan and Oren Glickman. 2004. Probabilistic textual entailment: Generic applied modeling of language variability.

Ido Dagan, Dan Roth, Mark Sammons, and Fabio Massimo Zanzotto. 2013. *Recognizing Textual Entailment: Models and Applications*. Synthesis Lectures on Human Language Technologies. Morgan & Claypool Publishers.

Myroslava O. Dzikovska, Johanna D. Moore, Natalie Steinhauser, Gwendolyn Campbell, Elaine Farrow, and Charles B. Callaway. 2010. Beetle ii: A system for tutoring and computational linguistics experimentation. In *Proceedings of the ACL 2010 System Demonstrations*, ACLDemos '10, pages 13–18, Stroudsburg, PA, USA. Association for Computational Linguistics.

Myroslava O Dzikovska, Rodney D Nielsen, and Chris Brew. 2012. Towards effective tutorial feedback for explanation questions: A dataset and baselines. In *Proceedings of the 2012 Conference of the North American Chapter of the Association for Computational Linguistics: Human Language Technologies*, pages 200–210. Association for Computational Linguistics.

Myroslava O. Dzikovska, Rodney Nielsen, Chris Brew, Claudia Leacock, Danilo Giampiccolo, Luisa Bentivogli, Peter Clark, Ido Dagan, and Hoa Trang Dang. 2013a. Semeval-2013 task 7: The joint student response analysis and 8th recognizing textual entailment challenge. **SEM 2013: The First Joint Conference on Lexical and Computational Semantics*.

Myroslava O Dzikovska, Rodney D Nielsen, Chris Brew, Claudia Leacock, Danilo Giampiccolo, Luisa Bentivogli, Peter Clark, Ido Dagan, and Hoa T Dang. 2013b. Semeval-2013 task 7: The joint student response analysis and 8th recognizing textual entailment challenge. Technical report, DTIC Document.

Rod Ellis. 1994. *The Study of Second Language Acquisition*. Oxford University Press.

Danilo Giampiccolo, Bernardo Magnini, Ido Dagan, and Bill Dolan. 2007. The third pascal recognizing textual entailment challenge. In *Proceedings of the ACL-PASCAL Workshop on Textual Entailment and Paraphrasing*, RTE '07, pages 1–9, Stroudsburg, PA, USA. Association for Computational Linguistics.

Aria Haghighi, Andrew Y. Ng, and Christopher D. Manning. 2005. Robust textual inference via graph matching. In *Proceedings of Human Language Technology Conference and Conference on Empirical Methods in Natural Language Processing*, pages 387–394, Vancouver, British Columbia, Canada, October. Association for Computational Linguistics.

Michael Hahn and Detmar Meurers. 2012. Evaluating the meaning of answers to reading comprehension questions - a semantics-based approach. *The 7th Workshop on the Innovative Use of NLP for Building Educational Applications.*

Mark Hall, Eibe Frank, Geoffrey Holmes, Bernhard Pfahringer, Peter Reutemann, and Ian H. Witten. 2009. The weka data mining software: An update. *SIGKDD Explor. Newsl.*, 11(1):10–18, November.

Manfred Krifka. 2001. For a structured meaning account of questions and answers. *Audiatur Vox Sapientia. A Festschrift for Arnim von Stechow*, pages 287–319.

J. Richard Landis and Gary G. Koch. 1977. The measurement of observer agreement for categorical data. *Biometrics*, 33(1):pp. 159–174.

Omer Levy, Torsten Zesch, Ido Dagan, and Iryna Gurevych. 2013. Recognizing partial textual entailment. In *Proceedings of the 51st Annual Meeting of the Association for Computational Linguistics*, page 451455, Sofia, Bulgaria, August 4-9.

Anke Lüdeling. 2008. Mehrdeutigkeiten und kategorisierung: Probleme bei der annotation von lernerkorpora. *Fortgeschrittene Lernervarietäten*, pages 119–140.

Bill MacCartney and Christopher D Manning. 2009a. An extended model of natural logic. In *Proceedings of the eighth international conference on computational semantics*, pages 140–156. Association for Computational Linguistics.

Bill MacCartney and Christopher D. Manning. 2009b. An extended model of natural logic. In *Proceedings of the Eighth International Conference on Computational Semantics*, IWCS-8 '09, pages 140–156, Stroudsburg, PA, USA. Association for Computational Linguistics.

Detmar Meurers, Ramon Ziai, Niels Ott, and Stacey Bailey. 2011. Integrating parallel analysis modules to evaluate the meaning of answers to reading comprehension questions. *Special Issue on Free-text Automatic Evaluation. International Journal of Continuing Engineering Education and Life-Long Learning (IJCEELL)*, 21(4):355–369.

Michael Mohler and Rada Mihalcea. 2009. Text-to-text semantic similarity for automatic short answer grading. In *Proceedings of the 12th Conference of the European Chapter of the Association for Computational Linguistics*, EACL '09, pages 567–575, Stroudsburg, PA, USA. Association for Computational Linguistics.

Michael Mohler, Razvan Bunescu, and Rada Mihalcea. 2011. Learning to grade short answer questions using semantic similarity measures and dependency graph alignments. In *Proceedings of the 49th Annual Meeting of the Association for Computational Linguistics: Human Language Technologies-Volume 1*, pages 752–762. Association for Computational Linguistics.

Rodney D Nielsen, Wayne Ward, James H Martin, and Martha Palmer. 2008. Annotating students' understanding of science concepts. In *LREC*.

Rodney D. Nielsen, Wayne Ward, and James H. Martin. 2009. Recognizing entailment in intelligent tutoring systems. *Natural Language Engineering*, 15:479–501.

Niels Ott, Ramon Ziai, and Detmar Meurers. 2012. Creation and analysis of a reading comprehension exercise corpus: Towards evaluating meaning in context. In Thomas Schmidt and Kai Wörner, editors, *Multilingual Corpora and Multilingual Corpus Analysis*, Hamburg Studies in Multilingualism (HSM). Benjamins, Amsterdam. to appear.

Jana Zuheir Sukkarieh and John Blackmore. 2009. c-rater: Automatic content scoring for short constructed responses. In *FLAIRS Conference*.

Arnim von Stechow and Thomas Ede Zimmermann. 1984. Term answers and contextual change. *Linguistics*, 22:3–40.

Arnim von Stechow, 1990. *Discourse Particles*, chapter Focusing and Background Operators.

Seid Muhie Yimam, Iryna Gurevych, Richard Eckart de Castilho, and Chris Biemann. 2013. Webanno: A flexible,web-based and visually supported system for distributed annotations. In *Proceedings of the 51st Annual Meeting of the Association for Computational Linguistics (System Demonstrations) (ACL 2013)*, pages 1–6, Stroudsburg, PA, USA, August. Association for Computational Linguistics.

Ramon Ziai, Niels Ott, and Detmar Meurers. 2012. Short answer assessment: Establishing links between research strands. In *Proceedings of the 7th Workshop on Innovative Use of NLP for Building Educational Applications (BEA7)*, pages 190–200, Montreal, Canada. Association for Computational Linguistics.

An Automated Scoring Tool for Korean Short-Answer Questions Based on Semi-Supervised Learning

Min-Ah Cheon
Korea Maritime and Ocean University
minah014@outlook.com

Hyeong-Won Seo
Korea Maritime and Ocean University
wonn24@gmail.com

Jae-Hoon Kim
Korea Maritime and Ocean University
jhoon@kmou.ac.kr

Eun-Hee Noh
Korea Institute for Curriculum and Evaluation
noro@kice.re.kr

Kyung-Hee Sung
Korea Institute for Curriculum and Evaluation
Kelly9147@kice.re.kr

EunYong Lim
Korea Institute for Curriculum and Evaluation
elim@kice.re.kr

Abstract

Scoring short-answer questions has disadvantages that may take long time to grade and may be an issue on consistency in scoring. To alleviate the disadvantages, automated scoring systems are widely used in America or Europe, but, in Korea, there has been researches regarding the automated scoring. In this paper, we propose an automated scoring tool for Korean short-answer questions using a semi-supervised learning method. The answers of students are analyzed and processed through natural language processing and unmarked-answers are automatically scored by machine learning methods. Then scored answers with high reliability are added in the training corpus iteratively and incrementally. Through the pilot experiment, the proposed system is evaluated for Korean and social subjects in Programme for National Student Assessment. We have showed that the processing time and the consistency of grades are promisingly improved. Using the proposed tool, various assessment methods have got to be development before applying to school test fields.

1. Introduction

Multiple choice items can be more efficient and reliably scored than short-answer questions (Case and Swason, 2002). For this reason, questions of large-scale testing generally are multiple choice questions such as College Scholastic Ability Test (CSAT). Multiple choice questions, however, have a serious disadvantage that the limited types of knowledge, so that Korea Institute of Curriculum and Evaluation (KICE) should provide short-answer questions. The short-answer questions are difficult to score in an economical, efficient, and reliable scoring (Latifi et al., 2013). One of possible solution for such problems is using the machine learning technology of automated essay scoring (AES), e.g. Project Essay Grader (PEG) , Intelligent Essay Assessor (IEA), e-Rater and Bayesian Essay Test Scoring sYstem (BESTY) (Attali and Burstein, 2006, Shermis and Burstein, 2003).

The goal of the paper is to propose an automated scoring tool for Korean short-answer questions using semi-supervised learning. The tool consists of three components: User interface, Language analysis, Scoring. The user interface component allows users human raters interact with other components and controls them. The language analysis component analyzes and processes the answers of students through natural language processing modules like spacing normalizers, morphological analyzers, and parsers. Finally, the scoring component first grades unmarked-answers by machine learning methods and then iteratively and incrementally adds the scored answers with high reliability in the training corpus. Through the pilot experiment, the proposed system is evaluated for Korean and social subjects in Programme for National Student Assessment. We have showed that the processing time and the consistency of grades are

Proceedings of The 2nd Workshop on Natural Language Processing Techniques for Educational Applications, pages 59–63,
Beijing, China, July 31, 2015.

promisingly improved. The rest of the paper is structured as follows: Section 2 describes the proposed tool. The experiments carried out with the proposed system are discussed in Section 3. Finally, Section 4 draws conclusions and discusses future works.

2. Korean Automated Scoring Tool

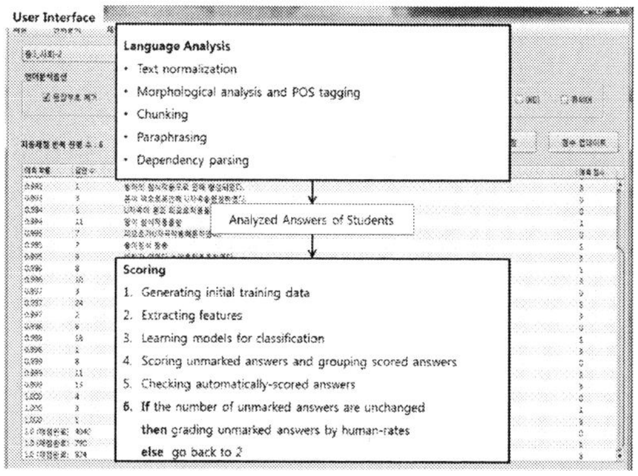

Figure 1. The overall architecture of the proposed tool

The overall architecture of Korean automated scoring tool is given in Figure 1. The tool consists of three components: User interface, Language analysis, Scoring. The user interface component allows users as human raters interact with other components and controls them and we do not describe more details of this component because it is not important for readers to understand it. The language component and the scoring component will be described in sequent subsection in more detail.

2.1. Language analysis

As mentioned before, the language analysis component analyzes and processes the answers of students through natural language processing modules: Text normalization, Morphological analysis and POS tagging, Chunking, Paraphrasing, Dependency parsing as you can see in Figure 2. All modules in the language analysis component is implemented in Python 3.

Text normalization is composed of spacing normalization and spelling correction. Like English, Korean language uses white spaces as separators of words called Eojeol, which is a sequence of characters and represent an inflected word. Students as well as educated persons can often make spacing errors because the regulation is so flexible. The spacing normalization is performed using maximum entropy model (Berger et al., 1996). The spelling correction is implemented using Levenshtein distance algorithm. The morphological analyzer is implemented using the modified CYK algorithm (Kim, 1983) and the pre-analyzed data. The POS tagging is to find the longest path on the weighted network (Kim, 1998). The weighted network is made of a lattice structure constructed by using the morphological analysis results, contextual probability, and lexical probability. The chunker is based on the maximum entropy model and a chunking dictionary. The paraphrasing replaces consecutive words or phrases with representative words or phrases. We perform a small scale of paraphrasing, for example, synonyms, endings, and particles. The purpose of the paraphrasing is twofold. First, it helps to alleviate data sparseness of dependency parsing. Second, it increases the accuracy of automated scoring. The dependency parsing finds direct syntactic relationships between words by connecting head-modifier pair into a tree structure and is implemented by the MaltParser (Niver, 2008). Actually we use just dependency relations as one of features, described in the next subsection, but not the tree structure.

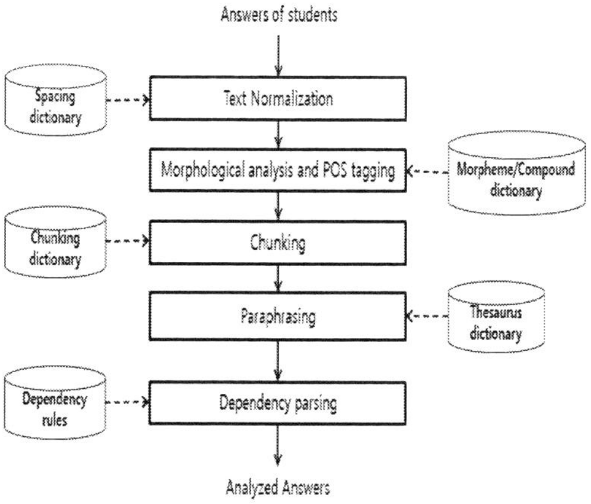

Figure 2. The processing order in the language analysis component

2.2. Scoring

The scoring component first grades unmarked-answers by machine learning methods and then iteratively and incrementally adds the scored answers with high reliability in the training corpus. The process order in the scoring component is shown in Figure 3.

The scoring component is based on a semi-supervised learning (Chapelle et al., 2006), which is halfway between supervised learning and unsupervised learning. It uses a small amount of labeled data and a large amount of unlabeled data. Actually, a grade in scoring can be considered a label in automated scoring. In other words, automated scoring classifies grades as labels from students' answers. The scoring component comprises six steps described in the follows.

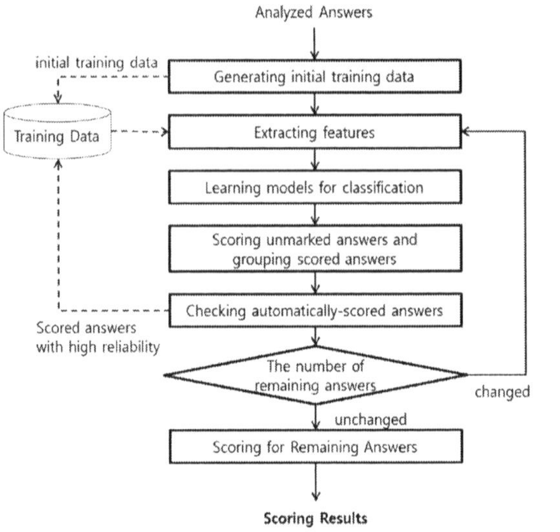

Figure 3. The processing order in the scoring component

The first step is to generate initial training data by the human raters who grade high frequency answers as many as they want. The graded answers will be the initial training data.

The second is to extract features for machine learning. We use word features, syntactic features, and dependency relation features. A word feature is a content word, a syntactic feature comprises a content word and a syntactic relation like Subj and Obj. A dependency relation feature is composed of a triplet of a dependent, a governor of features consists of TF-IDF which is widely used in information retrieval.

The third step is to generate learning model for classification. We use two classification models: Logistic regression model and k-NN (k-Nearest Neighbors) model. The logistic regression model is used to classify answers as well as to get the probability of classification. The k-NN model is used to increase the reliability of classification by comparing the result with that of logistic regression classifier.

The fourth step is to grade unmarked answers and to group the scored answers. We classify grades of unmarked answers using the two learning models. If the two results are same and if the predictive probability as the regression probability is greater than a threshold, the scored answers are considered as correct scoring results which are candidates added in the training corpus. The threshold is arbitrarily set by human-raters (default is 0.99) through the user interface and is automatically decreased by 0.03 during iteration. The interval value can also be determined through the user interface. Each group of scored answers has the same probability and is showed as one row on the user interface in order that it is easy to check whether the scored answer is correct.

The fifth step is check whether the automatically-scored answers are correct. The Human-raters have to confirm the results. If there is some wrong results, the human raters should correct them or put back them into unmarked answers. After that, the confirmed results are added to the training data. The system repeats the second step to the fifth step until the number of unmarked answers is unchanged. Repeating this process can increase the amount of training data, thus both reliability and accuracy of automated scoring are increased.

Finally the sixth step is to manually grade still-unmarked answers by human-raters.

3. Pilot Experiments

3.1. Experimental setting

We have evaluated the proposed tool on the short-answer questions which are selected from "Programme for National Student Assessment (KICE, 2013)". The eleven items are from subjects such as Korean and social. The number of students' answers in each item is 1000. All the answers are composed only one sentence.

The correct answers as gold standards are graded by experts throughout three rounds. The round defines as grading the same problem by two experts in subjects. If scored results of the two experts are different, other experts perform the round again. The round is repeated by three times.

We use Pearson's correlation coefficient (Corey, 1998), Cohen's Kappa coefficient (Carletta, 1996; Fleiss, 2003) and an accuracy which generally used from information retrieval. For example, interpreting any kappa value can be considered as follows: $\kappa < 0.4$ (poor), $0.4 \leq \kappa < 0.75$ (fair to good), and $0.75 \leq \kappa$ (excellent).

Table 1. Results of Evaluation

-		Pearson's correlation coefficient (r)		Kappa correlation coefficient (κ)		Accuracy (%)	
subject	**Item no.**	**H-G**	**S-G**	**H-G**	**S-G**	**H-G**	**S-G**
Korean: Middle school	2-(1)	0.96	0.82	0.90	0.80	98.6	97.3
	2-(2)	0.97	0.93	0.91	0.87	97.5	96.1
	4-(2)	0.97	0.93	0.93	0.81	96.9	92.0
Korean: High school	2-(1)	0.99	1.00	0.99	1.00	99.5	100.0
	2-(2)	0.98	0.87	0.98	0.87	99.5	96.3
	4-(1)	0.99	0.88	0.97	0.83	98.6	91.5
	5-(2)	0.99	0.93	0.99	0.88	99.1	92.3
	6-(1)	0.98	0.94	0.98	0.94	98.9	97.2
	6-(2)	1.00	0.90	0.98	0.84	98.9	92.4
Social: Middle school	4-(3)	0.86	0.95	0.85	0.95	96.8	99.0
	8	1.00	0.92	0.99	0.93	99.8	97.8
Average (standard derivation)		**0.97 (0.04)**	**0.92 (0.05)**	**0.95 (0.05)**	**0.88 (0.06)**	**98.6 (1.04)**	**95.6 (3.05)**

As another example, interpreting r can be considered as follows: r ≤ 0.2 (very small), 0.2 < r ≤ 0.4 (small), 0.4 < r ≤ 0.6 (medium), and 0.6 < r ≤ 0.8 (large), r ≤ 0.8 (very large).

3.2. Experiment Results

Table 1 shows performance evaluation results of the proposed tool. In the Table 1, H-G stands for human-rater and gold standard and S-G for our system and gold standard.

The average of Pearson's correlation coefficient between results of our system and gold standards (S-G) is 0.92. It means a strong positive linear relationship between the automated scores as results of our system and the gold standard scores, therefore it can be mostly similar to our automatic grading and gold standards. The average of Kappa correlation coefficient is 0.88, so results of our system are broadly same like standard scores. The accuracy of the answer that contains negative expressions and the inversion of word order is relatively low as compared to other answers. According to report of KICE (Noh et al., 2014), this system can save significant time and cost in comparison with scoring methods of human raters.

4. Conclusion

We have presented an automated scoring tool for Korean short-answer questions based on semi-supervised learning. The tools use several NLP technologies for analyzing answers of students, and some machine learning methods of logistic regression and k-NN algorithm for automated scoring. The scoring process is iterative and incremental under the semi-supervised learning. The experimental results show that the proposed automated scoring tool is very promising in automated scoring for the short-answer questions.

In future work, we will be going to study a method for increasing the accuracy of our automated tool and to find a way to minimize the intervention of the human-raters.

Acknowledgements

This work was partly supported by KICE (Korea Institute of Curriculum & Evaluation) and the IT R&D program of MSIP/KEIT. [10041807, Development of Original Software Technology for Automatic Speech Translation with Performance 90% for Tour/International Event focused on Multilingual Expansibility and based on Knowledge Learning]

Reference

Y. Attali and J. Burstein. 2006. Automated Essay Scoring with E-rater. *The Journal of Technology, Learning, and Assessment*, 4(3):12-15.

A. Berger, S. A. Della Pietra, and V. J. Della Pietra. 1996. A Maximum Entropy Approach to Natural Language Processing. *Computational Linguistics*, 22(1):39-71.

J. Carletta. 1996. Assessing Agreement on Classification Tasks: The Kappa Statistic. *Computational Linguistics*, 22(2):249-254.

S. M. Case and D. B. Swason. 2002. Constructing Written Test Questions for the Basic and Clinical Sciences. *National board of Medical Examiners.*

O. Chapelle, B. Schölkopf,and A. Zien. 2006. *Semi-Supervised Learning*. The MIT Press Cambridge, Massachusetts London, England, pages 1-3.

D. M. Corey, W. P. Dunlap and M. J. Burke. 1998. Averaging Correlations: Expected Values and Bias in Combined Pearson rs and Fisher's z Transformations. *J. Gen. Psychol.*, 125:245-261.

J. L. Fleiss, B. Levin, M.C. Paik (Eds.). 2003. Statistical methods for rates and propositions 3rd. *John Wiley & Sons, Inc.*, pages 598-626.

KICE. 2013. *Programme for National Student Assessment*. Korean Institute of Curriculum & Evaluation.

J. Kim. 1998. Korean Part-of-Speech Tagging using a Weighted Network. *Journal of the Korea Information Science Society (B): Software and Applications*, 25(6):951-959.

S. Kim. 1987. *A Morphological Analyzer for Korean Language with Tabular Parsing Method and Connectivity Information*. MS Thesis, Department of Computer Science, Korea Advanced Institute of Science and Technology, pages 21-37.

S. M. F. Latifi, Q. Guo, M. J. Gierl, A. Mousavi, K. Fung. 2013. Towards Automated Scoring using Open-source Technologies. In *Proceedings of the 2013 Annual Meeting of the Canadian Social for the Study of Education Victoria, British Columbia*, pages 1-27.

J. Nivre, 2008. Algorithms for Deterministic Incremental Dependency Parsing. *Computational Linguistics*, 34(4):513-553.

E. Noh, S. Lee, E. Lim, K. Sung and S. Park, 2014. Development of Automatic Scoring System for Korean Short-answer question and Verification of Practicality. Korean Institute of Curriculum & Evaluation, page 87-120.

M. D. Shermis and J. Burstein. 2003. *Automated Essay Scoring: A Cross-Disciplinary Perspective*. Lawrence Erlbaum Associates, Cambridge, England, MIT Press.

A System for Generating Multiple Choice Questions: With a Novel Approach for Sentence Selection

Mukta Majumder
Computer Centre, Vidyasagar University
Midnapore, West Bengal, India-721102
mukta_jgec_it_4@yahoo.co.in

Sujan Kumar Saha
Computer Science and Engg. Department
BIT, Mesra, Jharkhand, India-835215
sujan.kr.saha@gmail.com

Abstract

Multiple Choice Question (MCQ) plays a major role in educational assessment as well as in active learning. In this paper we present a system that generates MCQs automatically using a sports domain text as input. All the sentences in a text are not capable of generating MCQs; the first step of the system is to select the informative sentences. We propose a novel technique to select informative sentences by using topic modeling and parse structure similarity. The parse structure similarity is computed between the parse structure of an input sentence and a set of reference parse structures. In order to compile the reference set we use a number of existing MCQs collected from the web. Keyword selection is done with the help of occurrence of domain specific word and named entity word in the sentence. Distractors are generated using a set of rules and name dictionary. Experimental results demonstrate that the proposed technique is quite accurate.

1 Introduction

MCQ generation is the task of generating questions from various text inputs, having prospective learning content. MCQ is a popular assessment tool used widely in various levels of educational assessment. Apart from assessment MCQ also acts as an effective instrument in active learning. It is studied that, in active learning classroom framework conceptual understanding of the students can be boosted by posing MCQs on the concepts just taught (Mazur, 1997; Nicol 2007). Thus the MCQ is becoming an important aspect for next generation learning, training and assessment environments.

Generation of Multiple Choice Question manually is a time-consuming and tedious task which also requires domain expertise. Therefore an automatic MCQ generation system can leverage the active learning and assessment process. Consequently automatic MCQ generation became a popular research topic and a number of systems have been developed (Coniam 1997; Mitkov, Ha, & Karamanis, 2006; Karamanis, Ha, & Mitkov, 2006; Pino, Heilman, & Eskenazi, 2008; Agarwal & Mannem, 2011). Generation of MCQ automatically consists of three major steps; (i) selection of sentences from which question can be generated, (ii) identification of the keyword which is the correct answer and (iii) generation of distractors that are the wrong answers (Delphine Bernhard, 2010).

All the sentences of a textual document cannot be the candidates for being question sentences or stems. The sentence that contains sufficient and quality information can act as MCQ stem; moreover keyword and corresponding distractors should be available. Hence the target is to select only the informative sentences from which factual MCQs can be generated for testing the content knowledge of the learner. Therefore, selection of sentence has been playing a pioneer role in automatic MCQ generation task. But unfortunately in the literature we have found that the sentence selection task has become unable to achieve adequate attention from the researchers. As a result, the sentence selection task is confined in a limited number of approaches by using only a set of rules or checking the occurrence of a set of pre-defined features and pattern. Success of such approaches suffers from

Proceedings of The 2nd Workshop on Natural Language Processing Techniques for Educational Applications, pages 64–72,
Beijing, China, July 31, 2015.

the quality of the rules or features and thus become extremely domain reliant.

In this paper we propose an efficient technique for informative sentence selection and generation of MCQs from the selected sentences. Here we select the informative sentences based on certain words that are important to define the domain or topic and parse structure similarity. The proposed system is robust and expected to work in a wide range of domains. As input to the system we consider the Wikipedia and news article which are trusted sources of information. To generate a MCQ from a sentence, first we perform a set of pre-processing tasks like, converting complex and compound sentences into simple sentences and co-reference resolution. Then we use topic modeling as another pre-processing step that finds the subject words or topics of the domain and check whether the sentence contains any of these topics. This will reduce our overhead in subsequent steps. We have found that two sentences contain similar parse structures, are generally of similar type and carry same type of facts. Therefore, parse structure of a sentence may play an important role in sentence selection. We collect a set of MCQs available in the Internet in the domain of interest and form sentences from them. Here we like to mention that we have chosen sports domain specially cricket as a case study because of wide availability of existing MCQs in this domain. We obtain parse structures of these sentences and the common structures are saved as a reference set. Next we compare the parse tree of an input sentence with the reference set structures. If the sentence has structural similarity with any of the reference set structures then it is considered as an informative sentence for MCQ stem generation.

Next we perform other subtasks namely, keyword selection and distractor generation. Keyword selection is done by a rule based approach based on cricket domain specific words and named entities (NE) in the sentence. Generation of distractors is done using a gazetteer list based approach. The following sections present the details of the system.

2 Previous Work

Generating Multiple Choice Question automatically is a relatively new and important research area and potentially useful in Education Technology. Here we first discuss a few systems for MCQ generation.

Coniam (1997) presented one of the earlier attempts of MCQ generation. They used word frequencies for an analyzed corpus in the various phases of the development. They matched parts-of-speech and word frequency of each test item with similar word class and word frequency options to construct the test items. Mitkov and Ha (2003) and Mitkov et al. (2006) used NLP techniques like shallow parsing, term extraction, sentence transformation and computation of semantic distance in their works for generating MCQ semi automatically from an electronic text. They did term extraction from the text using frequency count, generated stems using a set of linguistic rules, and selected distractors by finding semantically close concepts using WordNet. Brown (2005) developed a system for automatic generation of vocabulary assessment questions. They used WordNet for finding definition, synonym, antonym, hypernym and hyponym in order to generate the questions as well as the distractors. Aldabe et al. (2006) and Aldabe and Maritxalar (2010) developed systems to generate MCQ in Basque language. They have divided the task into six phases: selection of text (based on learners and length of texts), marking blanks (manually), generation of distractors, selection of distractors, evaluation with learners and item analysis. Papasalouros et al. (2008) proposed an ontology based approach for development of an automatic MCQ system. Agarwal et al. (2011) presented a system that automatically generates questions from natural language text using discourse connectives.

As in this paper we focus on sentence selection, next we like to discuss the sentence selection strategies used in various works. In order to MCQ stem generation different types of rules have been defined manually or semi-automatically for selecting informative sentences from a corpus; these are discussed as follows. Mitkov et al. (2006) selected sentences if they contain at least one term, is finite and is of SVO or SV structure. Karamanis et al. (2006) implemented a module to select clause, having some specific terms and filtering out sentences which having inappropriate terms for multiple choice test item generation (MCTIG). For sentence selection Pino et al. (2008) used a set of criteria like, number of clause, well-defined context, probabilistic context-free grammar score and number of tokens. They also manually computed a sentence score based on occurrence of these criteria in a given sentence and select the sentence as informative if the score is higher than a threshold. For sentence selection Agarwal and Mannem (2011) used a number of features like:

is it first sentence, contains token that occurs in the title, position of the sentence in the document, whether it contains abbreviation or superlatives, length, number of nouns and pronouns etc. But they have not clearly reported what should be optimum value of these features or how the features are combined or whether there is any relative weight among the features. Kurtasov (2013) applied some predefined rules that allow selecting sentences of a particular type. For example, the system recognizes sentences containing definitions, which can be used to generate a certain category of test exercise. For 'Automatic Cloze-Questions Generation' Narendra et al. (2013) in their paper directly used a summarizer, MEAD for selection of important sentences. Bhatia et al. (2013) used pattern based technique for identifying MCQ sentences from Wikipedia. Apart from these rule and pattern based approaches we also found an attempt on using supervised machine learning technique for stem selection by Correia et al. (2012). They used a set of features like parts-of-speech, chunk, named entity, sentence length, word position, acronym, verb domain, known-unknown word etc. to run Support Vector Machine (SVM) classifier. Another approach was presented by Majumder and Saha (2015), which used named entity recognition, based rule mining along with syntactic structure similarity for sentence selection.

3 Pre-processing on Input Text

MCQ is generally made from a simple sentence but we have found that many of the Wikipedia and news article sentences are long, complex and compound in nature. Moreover, a number of these sentences are having coreference issues. Our system first aims to identify informative sentences from Wikipedia and news articles for stem generation. The proposed technique is based on parse structure similarity; hence the structure of the sentences plays a major role in the task. In order to obtain better structural similarity we first apply a few pre-processing steps that are discussed below.

3.1 Co-reference Resolution and Simple Sentence Generation

First preprocessing step we employ is transforming complex and compound sentences into simple form. Moreover, to resolve the coreference issues we perform corefernce resolution. Coreference has been defined as, referring of the same object (e.g., person) by two or more expressions in a corpus. For generating question the referent must be identified from such sentences. We consider the following sentence as an example.

The 2012 ICC World Twenty20 was the fourth ICC World Twenty20 competition that took place in Sri Lanka from 18 September to 7 October 2012 which was won by the West Indies.

This sentence is complex in nature and it has coreference problem. In this sentence 'that' and 'which' are referring to '2012 ICC World Twenty20'. A simple sentence is built up from one independent clause where a compound or complex sentence is consisted of at least two clauses. So the task is to split complex or compound sentence into clauses that can form simple sentences.

To convert the sentence into simple form we use the openly available 'Stanford CoreNLP Suite[1]'. The tool is not directly converting the complex and compound sentences into simple ones. It provides the parse result of the example sentence in Stanford typed dependency (SD) notations (Marneffe et al., 2008). We analyze the dependency structure provided by the tool in order to convert it. We use 'Stanford Deterministic Coreference Resolution System', which is basically a module of the 'Stanford CoreNLP Suite', for coreference resolution. Finally we get the following simple sentences from the aforementioned example sentence.

Simple1: The 2012 ICC World Twenty20 was the fourth ICC World Twenty20 competition.

Simple2: The 2012 ICC World Twenty20 took place in Sri Lanka from 18 September to 7 October 2012.

Simple3: The 2012 ICC World Twenty20 was won by the West Indies.

3.2 Subject or Topic Word Identification and Potential Candidate Sentence Selection

The sentence selection strategy for MCQ stem generation is based on parse tree similarity. We need to compare an input sentence with reference set of structures for selecting it as the basis of a MCQ. But the size of such input text is huge. Therefore comparing these vast numbers of sentences with reference structures will be a gigantic task. To reduce this overhead we have taken the help of topic modeling which can identify the topic words of the domain and if the test sentence is not containing a topic then reject it. We also found that the sentence with the topic word

[1] http://nlp.stanford.edu/software/corenlp.shtml

is more informative than the sentences which are not containing any domain or topic specific words. This approach will identify a set of potential candidate sentences and simplifies the task of parse tree comparison.

We use the openly available Topic Modeling Tool (TMT)[2] to identify the topic words as well as the distribution of these words in the sentences. We run the topic modeling tool on the Wikipedia pages and news articles that we considered as input for sentence selection, and get the topic words. Some of the identified topic words are, 'World Cup', 'World Twenty20', 'Champions Trophy', 'Knock Out Tournament', 'Indian Premier League or IPL' etc. Now we check whether an input sentence is containing any of these topic words or not.

4 Sentence Selection for MCQ Stem Generation

The syntactic structure can play a key role in sentence selection for MCQ. The parse tree of a particular question sentence is able to retrieve many informative sentences have similar structure. For example, the aforementioned Wikipedia sentence 'Simple3' (in Section 3.1) is defining the fact that a team has won a series/tournament. The parse structure of the sentence is similar with many sentences carrying 'team wins series' fact. The sentences like '1983 ICC World Cup was won by India.', '2006 ICC Champions Trophy was won by Australia.' have similar parse trees and these can be retrieved if the parse structure shown in Figure 1 is considered as a reference structure. From this observation we aim to collect a set of such syntactic structures that can act as the reference for retrieving new sentences from the web.

4.1 Reference Sentence Formation

For the parse tree matching we require a reference set of parse structures with which the input sentences will be compared. We compile the reference set from existing MCQs. We found that in the sports domain a large number of MCQs are available in the Internet. We collect about 400 MCQs for the reference set creation.

As we have discussed earlier, a MCQ is mainly composed of a stem and a few options. Generally the stems are interrogative in nature. Our system is supposed to identify informative sentences from Wikipedia and news articles. Most of the sentences in Wikipedia pages and news articles are assertive. In order to get the structural similarity the reference sentences and the input sentences should be in same form. Therefore we convert the collected stems into assertive form. For this conversion we replace the 'wh' phrase or the blank space of the stem by the first alternative of the option set. For example:

MCQ: Which country won the first World Cup Cricket tournament held in England in 1975?

a) England b) India c) Australia d) Pakistan e) West Indies

Reference Sentence: England won the first World Cup Cricket tournament held in England in 1975.

Here we like to mention that in this phase our target is to compile a reference set containing a number of grammatically correct sentences, not to extract the fact from the existing MCQ. Even if the first option is not the correct answer of the given question, out target of reference set creation is satisfied. The set of sentences generated using the approach is referred as 'reference sentence'.

4.2 Parse Tree Comparison

We generate the parse tree of the reference set sentences using the openly available Stanford Parser 3 . In the sports domain the questions (MCQs) deal with the facts embedded in the sentences. Therefore, the tense information of the sentences is not so important for question formation but tense information leads to alter the parse structure. For example, *'In the 2012 season Sourav Ganguly has been appointed as the Captain for Pune Warriors India.'* and *'In the 2013 season Graeme Smith was announced as the captain for Surrey County Cricket Club.'* the two sentences are describing similar type of fact but parse structure is different due to the difference in verb form. This type of phenomena occurs in 'noun' subclasses also: singular noun vs plural noun, common noun vs proper noun etc. For the sake of parse tree matching we have used a coarse-grain tagset where a set of subcategories of a particular word class is mapped into one broader category. From the original Penn Treebank Tagset (Santorini, 1990) used in Stanford Parser we derive the new tagset and modify the sentences accordingly. For this purpose first we create parse trees and replace the tags or words according to the new tagset in the pare structures.

[2] http://code.google.com/p/topic-modeling-tool/

[3] http://nlp.stanford.edu/software/lex-parser.shtml

For example, we map VBZ-VBN (has been), VBD (was) and VBG (chasing) into 'VB'; similarly 'NN', 'NNS', 'NNP' and 'NNPS' are mapped into 'NN' etc.

Once we get the parse trees of the reference sentences and test sentences, we need to find the similarity among them. In order to find the similarity in these parse trees we have proposed the Parse Tree Matching (PTM) Algorithm.

The algorithm is basically trying to find whether the sentences have similar structure. The parse tree matching algorithm considers only the non-leaf nodes during the matching process. All other words that occur as leaf of the tree are not playing any role in the parse tree matching.

Algorithm 1: Parse Tree Matching (PTM) Algorithm
input : Parse Tree T1, Parse Tree T2
output : 1 if T1 is similar with T2, 0 otherwise

```
1. T1 and T2 are using the coarse-grain tagset.
2. Set Cnode1 as root of T1 and Cnode2 as root of T2;
3. if (label (Cnode1) = label (Cnode2) and number of
   children (Cnode1) = number of children (Cnode2))
   then
4.   n=number of children of Cnode1;
5.   for (i= 1 to n) do
6.       if both Cnode1_child_i and Cnode2_child_i
     are non-leaf then
7.           if label(Cnode1_child_i
             )!=label(Cnode2_child_i)
8.           then return 0 and exit;
9.       end
10.      if Only one of Cnode1_child_i and
         Cnode2_child_i is leaf then
11.          return 0 and exit;
12.      end
13.  end
14.  Increase level by 1, update Cnode1 and Cnode2,
     and Go to Step 4;
15.  return 1;
16. else
17.  return 0 and exit;
18. end
```

We have found that some of the reference sentences are having similar parse structures. Therefore first we run the PTM Algorithm among these parse trees generated from the reference set of sentences to find the unique set of structures. During this phase argument 'T1' of the algorithm is a parse tree of the reference set sentence and the argument 'T2' is the parse tree of another reference set sentence. We run this algorithm for several iterations: by keeping 'T1' fixed and varying 'T2' for all the parse trees.

The sentences for which the matches are found are basically of similar type and we keep only one of these in the reference set and discard the others. By applying the procedure finally we generate the reduced set of parse structures.

Once the reference structures are finalized, we used them for finding new Wikipedia and news article sentences which have similar structure. For this purpose we run the proposed PTM Algorithm repeatedly in the same way as mentioned above. Here we set the argument 'T1' as the parse structure of a test sentence and argument 'T2' as a reference structure. We fix 'T1' and vary the 'T2' among the reference set structures until a match is found or we come to the end of the reference set. If a match is found then the sentence (whose structure is 'T1') is selected.

1998 ICC Knock Out Trophy was won by South Africa.

```
(ROOT
 (S
  (NP (CD 1998) (NN ICC) (NN Knock) (NN Out)
(NN Trophy))
  (VP (VB was)
   (VP (VB won)
    (PP (IN by)
     (NP (NN South) (NNP Africa)))))
  (. .)))
```

Figure 1. Reference Structure One

Figure 1 is a reference structure and Figure 2 and Figure 3 are showing two input structures. When the PTM Algorithm is executed a match is found in between Figure 1 and Figure 2. The other input structure (Figure 3) does not have similarity with any of the reference trees.

The 2002 ICC Champions Trophy was held in Sri Lanka.

```
(ROOT
 (S
  (NP (DT The) (CD 2002) (NN ICC) (NN Cham-
pions) (NN Trophy))
  (VP (VB was)
   (VP (VB held)
    (PP (IN in)
     (NP (NN Sri) (NN Lanka)))))
  (. .)))
```

Figure 2. Input Structure which matches with reference set

After this phase we have successfully selected a set of sentences which is used to form MCQ stems. Keyword extraction and distractors generation are also done from these selected sentences. Question generation, keyword extraction and distraction are discussed as follows.

5 Keyword Identification, Question Formation and Distractors Generation

A MCQ consists of a stem along with the option set which contains a keyword and distractors.

Therefore we need to identify the keyword and form the distractors to generate a multiple choice question.

```
The Kolkata Knight Rider is the champions, having won the IPL 2014.
(ROOT
 (S
  (NP (DT The) (NN Kolkata) (NN Knight) (NN
Rider))
  (VP (VB is)
   (NP (DT the) (NN champions))
   (, ,)
   (S
    (VP (VB having)
     (VP (VB won)
      (NP (DT the) (NNP IPL) (CD 2014))))))
  (. .)))
```

Figure 3. Input Structure which does not matches with reference structure

5.1 Keyword Identification

Keyword identification is the next phase where we select the word (or n-gram) that has the potential to become the right answer of the MCQ. We have found that some particular patterns are followed by these potential sentences which are having some specific named entities (NEs). For the identification of these keys we have taken the help of the named entity recognition (NER) system developed by Majumder and Saha (2014). And the domain specific words like, tournament, series, trophy, captain, wicket, bowler, batsman, wicket-keeper, umpire, pitch, opening ceremony, etc are very important to identify these patterns in the sentences. Therefore we have also compiled a list of such domain specific words. For example, "opening ceremony was held in" pattern retrieves sentences containing the name of the location (city name or ground name) where the opening ceremony of a tournament was held. Therefore the key for this pattern is the location name in the retrieved sentence. Similarly, "the man of the tournament" pattern extracts sentences having the name of the player who got the man of the tournament in a particular tournament. Here the key for the pattern is the person name. The pattern "team won the tournament/series" is retrieving the team or country name that won the series or tournament; therefore the corresponding key is the country or team or franchise name. The sentences are tagged using the NER system and the corresponding entity is selected as the key.

5.2 Question Formation

After the keyword is identified we can form the question by replacing it with proper 'wh-word'. We have also consulted the parse tree structure of the sentence to bring the 'wh-word' at the appropriate position in the stem of the MCQ. For different type of keyword appropriate 'wh-word' is selected. For example if the category is location then the 'wh-word' is where; similarly, for person: who, for date: when, for number: how many etc.

5.3 Distractors Generation

Distractors are closely related to keyword. These are the distraction for the right answer in a MCQ. In this cricket domain majority of the distractors are named entity. Here first we identify the class of the key and search for a few close members using a gazetteer list based approach.

We compile a few gazetteer lists using the web. In this cricket domain the major categories of key (or, distractors) are: person name (cricketer, bowler, batsman, wicketkeeper, captain, board president, team owner etc.), organization name (country name, franchise name, cricket boards like ICC etc.), event name (cup, tournament, trophy, championship etc.), location name (cricket ground, city etc.). For each of the name categories we extract lists of names from relevant websites. For example, for cricketers we search the Wikipedia, Yahoo! Cricket and Espncricinfo player's lists. Then we search the key in these lists to determine the class of the key.

For each name category we select a set of attributes. The Wikipedia pages normally contain an information template on the title (at the top-right portion of the page) that contains a set of properties defining the class. Additionally, majority of the cricket related pages contain a table for summarizing the topic. Those fields of the tables are extracted to become member of the attribute set. For example, if we consider the category batsman, the attribute set may include date-of-birth, span, team name, batting style, last match, total run, batting average, strike rate, number of century, number of half-century, highest score etc. The detailed strategy is discussed as follows.

Next we search for a list of related tokens of the same category in the Wikipedia. For a cricketer key we run a search query "list of <national side> cricketers"; if the 'is-captain' attribute value is true, then the query is "List of <national side> national cricket captains". From the search result in Wikipedia pages we extract a set of similar entities. *Similar entity* is defined as the entities that have certain attribute value same as the *key*. We have predefined a set of attributes as 'important' for each class. For the *cricketer* class we consider the attributes *country*, *span* (overlapping), *batting average* (difference less than ten) or *bowling average* (difference less than five). Similarly, for the *ground* class we use only the *country* attribute; for the *team* class we consider the *country* and common *trophy/tournament* attributes as important. The entities which have match in important attributes are considered as candidate distractor. And from these candidate distractors we randomly pick three to four entities as the list of distractors.

6 Result and Discussion

We have already mentioned that the system is tested on cricket related Wikipedia pages and news article. In order to evaluate the performance of the sentence selection module we consider the quality of the retrieved sentence - whether this is really able to act as a MCQ stem.

There is no benchmark or gold- standard data in the task. In order to evaluate the performance of the system we have taken a few Wikipedia pages and news articles as input on which we run the system. The question formation capability of the retrieved sentences is examined by a set of human evaluators. The evaluators count the number of sentences that are potential to become the basis of a MCQ ('correct retrieval'). The average of the percentage of correct retrieval is considered as the accuracy of the system.

For computing the accuracy of the system we consider six Wikipedia pages. These are the pages on 2003, 2007, 2011 ICC Cricket World Cup, ICC Champions Trophy, IPL 2014 and T20 World Cup 2014 and four sports news articles from The Times of India, a popular English daily of India related to the T20 World Cup 2014, namely, 'Sri Lankans Lord Over India', 'Yuvi cuts a sorry figure in final', 'Virat, the lone man standing for India' and 'Mahela, Sangakkara bow out on a high'. Only the text portions of these pages are taken as input that contains a total of ~795 sentences. From these input text ~508 sentences were selected after the topic word based filtering. Then we apply the parse tree matching algorithm which finally considers 112 sentences. These sentences are examined by five human evaluators. They consider 105, 104, 103, 106 and 104 sentences respectively as correct retrieval. Therefore the accuracy of the system is 93.21%. Table 1 summarizes the accuracy of the system.

Input Sentence	Sentence After TMT	Sentence After PTMA	Evaluators Judgment	% Accuracy
~795	508	112	Evaluator1: 105	93.21%
			Evaluator2: 104	
			Evaluator3: 103	
			Evaluator4: 106	
			Evaluator5: 104	

Table 1: Performance of the developed System

From the evaluation score given by the human evaluators it is clear that the proposed system is capable of retrieving quality sentences from an input document. In addition to the correct retrievals, the system also selects a few sentences that are not considered as 'good' by the evaluators. We have analyzed these sentences. As for example we have listed the following sentences:

Netherlands and Canada were both appearing in the Cricket World Cup for the second time.

Ireland had been the best-performing associate member since the previous World Cup.

These sentences are containing the topic words and matching with the reference set structures. But these are missing out of some important information for which the fact is incomplete. The time or year related information is missing in both the sentences. A modified topic modeling system may be used to consider a tournament name with year is a topic but only the tournament name without year is not.

While comparing with the existing technique (Majumder and Saha, 2015), we found that the proposed technique identifies more number of sentences after pre- processing and post-processing steps. Omission of domain specific word and NER based rule mining restriction not only make the proposed system domain independent but also it outperforms the existing system in terms of selecting number of sentences.

Next we measure the performance of the overall MCQ system. After sentence selection, key selection and distractor generation are the major modules. We evaluate the performance of these modules using: key selection accuracy (whether the key is selected properly), distractor quality (whether the distractors are good). Again we employ the human evaluators to assess the system. The average evaluation accuracy of key selection is 83.03% (93 out of 112) and in distractor quality the accuracy is 91.07% (102 out of 112).

A few examples of the generated MCQs are given below:

1. *Which country won the 2014 ICC World Twenty20?*

   a) Australia b) India c) West Indies d) Sri Lanka

2. *Who was the man of the series of the 2011 ICC Cricket World Cup?*

   a) Sachin Tendulkar b) Tillakaratne Dilshan c) Yuvraj Singh d) Kumar Sangakkara

7 Conclusion

In this paper we have presented a novel technique for selecting informative sentences for multiple choice questions generation from an input corpus. The proposed technique selects informative sentences based on topic word and parse structure similarity. The system also uses a set of pre-processing steps like simplification of sentences, co-reference resolution etc. The selected sentences are used in the key selection and distractor generation modules to make a complete automatic MCQ system. We test the system in sports domain and use Wikipedia pages and news articles as input corpus. But we feel the system is generic and expected to work well in other domains also.

We have deeply studied the false identifications and observed that the accuracy of the system can be further improved by incorporating better pre-processing and post processing steps. A deeper co-reference resolution system can be used to remove a number of semi-informative sentences. Better identification of domain specific phrases or topics can also be helpful to handle a number of false detections. These observations may lead us to continue work in future.

Reference

Agarwal, M., and Mannem, P., 2011. Automatic gap-fill question generation from text books. In Proceedings of the 6th Workshop on Innovative Use of NLP for Building Educational Applications, pp. 56-64.

Agarwal, M., Shah, R., and Mannem, P., 2011. Automatic question generation using discourse cues. In Proceedings of the 6th Workshop on Innovative Use of NLP for Building Educational Applications, pp. 1-9.

Aldabe, I., Lopez de Lacalle, M., Maritxalar, M., Martinez, E., Uria, L., 2006. ArikIturri: An Automatic Question Generator Based on Corpora and NLP Techniques. In ITS. LNCS 4053, pp. 584-594.

Aldabe, I., Maritxalar, M., 2010. Automatic Distractor Generation for Domain Specific Texts. Proceedings of IceTAL, LNAI 6233. pp. 27-38.

Bernhard, D., 2010. Educational Applications of Natural Language Processing. In NATAL. pp. 1-123.

Bhatia, A. S., Kirti, M., and Saha, S. K., 2013. Automatic Generation of Multiple Choice Questions Using Wikipedia. In Proceedings of Pattern Recognition and Machine Intelligence, Springer Berlin Heidelberg, pp. 733-738.

Brown, J. C., Frishkoff, G. A., and Eskenazi, M., 2005. Automatic question generation for vocabulary assessment. In Proceedings of the conference on Human Language Technology and Empirical Methods in Natural Language Processing, Association for Computational Linguistics, pp. 819-826.

Coniam, D., 1997. A preliminary inquiry into using corpus word frequency data in the automatic generation of English language cloze tests. Calico Journal, 14(2-4), pp. 15-33.

Correia, R., Baptista, J., Eskenazi, M., and Mamede, N., 2012. Automatic generation of cloze question stems. In Computational Processing of the Portuguese Language, Springer Berlin Heidelberg, pp. 168-178.

De Marneffe, M. C., and Manning, C. D., 2008. The Stanford typed dependencies representation. In Coling 2008: Proceedings of the workshop on Cross-Framework and Cross-Domain Parser Evaluation, Association for Computational Linguistics, pp. 1-8.

Karamanis, N., Ha, L. A., and Mitkov, R., 2006. Generating multiple-choice test items from medical text: A pilot study. In Proceedings of the Fourth International Natural Language Generation Conference, Association for Computational Linguistics, pp. 111-113.

Kurtasov, A., 2013. A System for Generating Cloze Test Items from Texts in Russian. In Proceedings of the Student Research Workshop associated with RANLP 2013, pp. 107–112.

Majumder, M., Saha, S. K., 2014. Development of NER System for Wikipedia without using Wikipedia text as training data: Sports (Cricket) a case study. In Proceedings in EIIC-The 3rd Electronic International Interdisciplinary Conference (No. 1).

Majumder, M., Saha, S. K., 2015. Automatic selection of informative sentences: The sentences that can generate multiple choice questions. Knowledge Management & E-Learning: An International Journal (KM&EL), 6(4), 377-391.

Mazur, E., 1997. Peer instruction. Upper Saddle River, NJ: Prentice Hall. pp. 9-18.

Mitkov, R., Ha, L.A., 2003. Computer-aided generation of multiple-choice tests. Proceedings of the HLT/NAACL Workshop on Building educational applications using Natural Language Processing, pp. 17–22.

Mitkov, R., Ha, L. A., and Karamanis, N., 2006. A computer-aided environment for generating multiple-choice test items. Natural Language Engineering, Vol. 12(2), pp. 177-194.

Narendra, A., Agarwal, M. and Shah, R., 2013. Automatic Cloze-Questions Generation. In Proceedings of Recent Advances in Natural Language Processing, Hissar, Bulgaria, pp. 511–515.

Nicol, D., 2007. E-assessment by design: using multiple-choice tests to good effect. Journal of Further and Higher Education, Vol. 31(1), pp. 53-64.

Papasalouros, A., Kanaris, K., and Kotis, K., 2008. Automatic Generation Of Multiple Choice Questions From Domain Ontologies. In e-Learning, pp. 427-434.

Pino, J., Heilman, M., and Eskenazi, M., 2008. A selection strategy to improve cloze question quality. In Proceedings of the Workshop on Intelligent Tutoring Systems for Ill-Defined Domains. 9th International Conference on Intelligent Tutoring Systems, Montreal, Canada, pp. 22-32.

Santorini. B., 1990. Part-of-Speech Tagging Guideline for Penn Treebank Project (3rd Revision, 2nd Printing).

The "News Web Easy" news service as a resource for teaching and learning Japanese: An assessment of the comprehension difficulty of Japanese sentence-end expressions

Hideki Tanaka, Tadashi Kumano and Isao Goto
Science and Technology Research Labs. of NHK
1-10-11, Kinuta, Setagaya, Tokyo, Japan
{tanaka.h-ja,kumano.t-eq,goto.i-es}@nhk.or.jp

Abstract

Japan's public broadcasting corporation, NHK, launched "News Web Easy" in April 2012 [1]. It provides users with five simplified news scripts (easy Japanese news) on a daily basis. This web service provides users with five daily simplified news scripts of "easy" Japanese news. Since its inception, this service has been favorably received both in Japan and overseas. Users particularly appreciate its value as a Japanese learning and teaching resource. In this paper, we discuss this service and its possible contribution to language education. We focus on difficulty levels of sentence-end expressions, compiled from the news, that create ambiguity and problems when rewriting news items. These are analyzed and compared within regular news and News Web Easy, and their difficulty is assessed based on Japanese learners' reading comprehension levels. Our results revealed that current rewriting of sentence-end expressions in News Web Easy is appropriate. We further identified features of these expressions that contribute to difficulty in comprehension.

1 Introduction

The convergence of TV and internet has enabled the creation of new services that allow users to overcome various temporal and spatial constraints (Hamada, 2013; Fu et al., 2006). It may even prove possible to effectively re-purpose content across different media. In this paper, we describe one such example: the application of TV news scripts for language teaching and learning on the internet.

Japan's public broadcaster, NHK, launched the News Web Easy web service in April 2012 (Tanaka et al., 2013). This site provides users with five daily simplified news scripts of easy Japanese news. Its purpose is to provide daily news to the foreign population in Japan, which has steadily increased to currently over two million. It would, of course, be preferable to provide news to these residents in their native languages. However, Japan's foreign population is so diverse that it would be virtually impossible to provide broadcasts in all of the expatriates' languages. NHK decided to tackle this issue by providing broadcasting services in simplified Japanese tailored to the language comprehension levels of foreign residents. Surveys among foreign residents have confirmed that a demand exists for broadcasts in easy Japanese (Yonekura, 2012).

News Web Easy's targeted audience in Japan comprises foreign residents learning Japanese as a second language [2] who are already fairly fluent in conversational Japanese, but who want to learn to read news articles and newspapers. Their Japanese is thus at a pre-intermediate level.

The easy Japanese news comprises regular news that is jointly rewritten by a Japanese language instructor, with special training in easy Japanese, and a reporter. They closely adhere to the basic vocabulary and sentence patterns listed in the test guidelines of the Japanese-Language Proficiency Test (JLPT) (The Japan Foundation and Japan Educational Exchange and Services, 2002).

The test measures learners' Japanese proficiency at four levels ranging from level 4 (elementary) to level 1 (the most advanced) [3]. The vocabulary lists and sentence patterns in the test guidelines are graded, and the instructors can consult

[1] http://www3.nhk.or.jp/news/easy

[2] For the sake of brevity, in this paper we use the terms "foreigners" or "foreign residents" to signify foreign residents learning Japanese as a second language.

[3] The test has now been revised to cover five levels ranging from N5 (elementary) to N1 (the most advanced).

Proceedings of The 2nd Workshop on Natural Language Processing Techniques for Educational Applications, pages 73–81,
Beijing, China, July 31, 2015.

these to verify the level of difficulty. News Web Easy employs vocabularies and sentence patterns ranked at levels 3 and 4.

NHK has received favorable comments about News Web Easy from foreign residents in Japan as well as from people overseas who appreciate this service for learning Japanese. Japanese language instructors also regard News Web Easy as a valuable educational resource. We believe that this favorable reaction is the result of the language level being set to an educational standard appropriate for Japanese. Moreover, the News Web Easy interface is similar to that adopted in language tutoring systems.

In this paper, we outline the features of News Web Easy and discuss its impact on language learning and education. We focus analytically on sentence patterns (sentences-end expressions) in news scripts that are not adequately covered in the JLPT test guidelines. Our analysis was based on an extensive collection of these materials compiled from a corpus of regular news texts and easy Japanese texts. We present an assessment of the difficulty levels of these expressions according to foreigners' reading comprehension levels ascertained from online questionnaires. Last, we consider the possibility of extending News Web Easy as a learning and teaching resource for native-level Japanese used within regular news scripts.

2 News Web Easy and language teaching and learning

In this section, we explain the features of News Web Easy and discuss its impacts on Japanese teaching and learning.

2.1 Features of Japanese in News Web Easy

Target level

We were involved in the production of News Web Easy content. Our aim was to ensure that while the news texts were easy to understand, they were as natural as possible. After many trials conducted by NHK the pre-intermediate level was found to be the lowest level necessary for achieving these aims. This level was consequently set by NHK as the target for Japanese rewriting. It approximately corresponds to the proficiency level ranked between levels 3 and 2 of the old JLPT, and between levels N3 and N2 of the new JLPT.

Rewriters

For the production of News Web Easy, five regular news texts are chosen daily and rewritten by a news reporter and a Japanese instructor who perform different tasks. While the reporter streamlines the news texts and retains only the core information, the instructor simplifies difficult expressions.

Rewriting policies

When rewriting news articles, reporters and Japanese instructors confine themselves as much as possible to elementary vocabulary and sentence patterns. As noted above, rewriters use the JLPT test guidelines to check words and sentence patterns. An editor is specially assigned for this purpose to News Web Easy.

It is noteworthy that reporters and instructors also use terms that are not listed. These include technical terms, proper nouns, and terms that frequently appear in news articles but are difficult to simplify.

2.2 Features of News Web Easy interface

In addition to the above-mentioned measures used to simplify Japanese, News Web Easy has several reading support functions, described below and shown in Figure 1.

Furigana (ruby) characters

Japanese text is a combination of Chinese characters (*kanji*), two types of Japanese phonetic symbols (*hiragan*a and *katakana*), Latin characters (*romaji*), and numbers.

Kanji characters are notoriously difficult to master because there are so many of them and also because the same characters can be read in different ways depending on the context. Foreign residents often find themselves unable to understand the meaning of words written in *kanji*.

To assist them, very small *hiragana* characters, called *furigana*, are offered above all *kanji* characters in News Web Easy to indicate the pronunciation. This enhances the ability of foreign readers to understand the meanings of Japanese words, even if they are unable to read *kanji*.

Glossaries

The basic approach adopted by News Web Easy is to write simple Japanese using elementary vocabulary. However, it is not possible to simplify the vocabulary of all difficult terms.

Figure 1: Screen shot of News Web Easy

News Web Easy resolves this issue by providing glossaries to explain difficult terminology. On the News Web Easy site, a glossary entry can be accessed by simply positioning the cursor over a word. A pop-up explaining the term is then displayed. A dictionary for Japanese elementary school students was used to provide the glossary entries.

Proper nouns

Proper nouns, not included within preexisting glossaries, inevitably appear in news articles. On the News Web Easy pages, different kinds of proper nouns are highlighted in different colors to capture the readers' attention. The reader may not know exactly what the terms mean, but at least this feature enables them to differentiate between the names of people, places, and organizations.

Text to speech

Some foreigners have difficulty reading Japanese, but are perfectly capable of understanding the text if it is read out to them. News Web Easy features a text-to-synthesized voice function to facilitate this mode of understanding.

Links to original news

Because News Web Easy reporters usually condense information from the original news item, full details are available through a link provided to the source web page.

2.3 Teaching and learning

The content produced by broadcasters is quite often used for language learning and teaching. Accordingly, it is important that News Web Easy contributes to this educational purpose as long as the main goal of providing news to foreign residents is not hampered. In this section, we discuss News Web Easy's contribution to Japanese teaching and learning.

Contribution of Japanese texts

News Web Easy essentially delivers "authentic" documents at a pre-intermediate level in natural Japanese. These texts are incorporated within automatic tutoring (learning) systems such as Reader-Specific Lexical Practice for Improved Reading Comprehension (REAP) (Brown and Eskenazi, 2004). Such documents attract keen interest among educators, although texts in languages other than English and French are rare (Uitdenbogerd, 2014). Thus, the simplified texts featured in News Web Easy are all the more valuable.

Contribution of the interface

The interface of News Web Easy offers reading support, as elaborated in section 2.2. Reading support is often used in language tutoring systems. For example, the Automatic Text Adaptation Tool (Burstein et al., 2007) automatically adds vocabulary support, automatic text reading by a speech synthesizer, summary text, and a translation of the original text as "marginal notes." The reading support functions in News Web Easy can, therefore, be invaluable by providing simplified texts for pre-intermediate level Japanese learners.

The interface could also facilitate understanding of regular news for foreigners. As noted above, News Web Easy provides links to the original news stories so readers can compare both versions of the text. The scaffolding effect of providing simplified text for reading original text is widely recognized (Burstein et al., 2007; Eskenazi et al., 2013; Petersen and Ostendorf, 2007). Thus, this comparative reading should contribute to the comprehension of regular news.

2.4 Language-level issues

As noted in section 2.1, the News Web Easy rewriters currently use the JLPT test guidelines to check the language levels of words and sentence patterns in news items.

Because Japanese lessons typically start with the use of daily conversations, words and sentence patterns specific to news texts are often lacking in the JLPT test guidelines.

The rewriters have to judge for themselves the difficulty levels of words and phrases that are missing from the list. This could result in inconsistency in the language level of the simplified texts. Therefore, the content of the JLPT guidelines needs to be extended. As a first step toward this, we decided to focus on sentence patterns that were not included in the guidelines.

3 Analysis of sentence-end expressions

The sentence patterns in the JLPT test guidelines takes the form of a word sequence in the final positions of a sentence. We refer to this as sentence-end expressions. In the next section, we will define these and explain the features.

3.1 Features of Japanese sentence-end expressions

Japanese is a subject-object-verb (SOV) type of language in which predicates are positioned at the end position of a sentence. Japanese predicates usually contain one content word followed by some function words. Content words are typically verbs, nouns, and adjectives, and function words are auxiliary verbs, particles, formal nouns, and delexical (formal) verbs.

In this paper, we use the term sentence-end expressions (SEEs) to signify the function word sequence. SEEs add tense, polarity, voice, and modality to a sentence which we refer to as functional information, or simply as function. Such functions play an important role in deciding the meaning of a sentence.

SEEs may have more than one function lined up at the sentence end positions. We refer to such lined up functions as the function sequence (FS). An SEE, therefore, has a FS whose length is at least one [4].

Because Japanese is an SOV type of language, SEEs may become quite long when the "O" is in an embedded sentence, as in S(SOV)V. Let us consider a sentence with a single function of probability:

> X 社は 来年の 利益を 3 倍に する かもしれない (probability).
> *Xsha wa rainen no rieki wo 3bai ni suru kamosirenai (probability).*
> (X Inc. may (probability) triple their profit next year.)

This may be embedded in a sentence that ends with ということです (toiukotodesu) (people say), which has a hearsay function, as in:

> X 社は 来年の 利益を 3 倍に する かもしれない (probability) ということです (hearsay).
> *Xsha wa rainen no rieki wo 3bai ni suru kamosirenai (probability) toiukotodesu (hearsay).*
> (People say (hearsay) that X Inc. may (probability) triple their profit next year.),

The English predicates in the above examples occupy different positions and do not have lined up functions. However, the Japanese predicates (SEEs) of both the main and subordinate clauses are linked to form a long SEE with the following FS: probability + hearsay (length 2). This complex structure is common in long Japanese SEEs and can be difficult for learners of the language to understand. We, therefore, consider SEE rewording to be essential for reducing the language difficulty level. We decided to extensively compile SEEs from regular news and News Web Easy to evaluate their difficulty for foreigners' comprehension.

[4] We consider the number of functions in FS as the length.

	Regular	Easy	Total
Sentence Count	3,937,214	20,616	-
SEEs	477	775	1,063
Meaningful SEEs	-	-	841

Table 1: Corpus size and SEE counts

3.2 Compilation of SEEs

We morphologically analyzed our corpus of regular news scripts covering a 16-year period and searched for SEEs. Our corpus contained about four million sentences. We only selected those that appeared over 100 times, resulting in a total of 466 SEE sentence types. Although our selection was restricted to the above frequency threshold, it still covered 98% of the total occurrence of all SEEs. Considering the corpus size, we found that SEE variation in the regular news was relatively limited.

We also extracted SEEs from our corpus of News Web Easy scripts, collected over a two-year period. This corpus contained about 20,000 sentences from which we obtained 755 SEE types. The total number of SEE types collected from both corpora was thus 1,063. We then excluded SEEs with a plain statement, that is, SEEs that did not contain any meaningful functional information. This yielded 841 SEE types. Table 1 shows the corpus size and SEE counts.

3.3 Functions specific to news scripts

Before assigning a FS to each of the 841 SEEs, we first checked the SEEs and functions in a leading Japanese grammar textbook (Nihongo Kizyutu Bunpô Kenkyûkai, 2010). We found that some SEEs did not appear in that textbook and thus represented new functions that we termed objectivity and perception groups.

Objectivity

Two expressions—*mono-da* and *koto-da*—fell within this category. The formal noun, *mono*, has little meaning and simply refers to things in general. Another formal noun, *koto*, refers to general events. These terms are often added to simple factual statements in news stories, as in *irei* (exceptional)-*no* <u>*koto-da*</u>. Although it is possible to simply say *irei-da*, the addition of *koto* adds formality to the sentence. We believe this reflects the journalistic tendency of describing events as objectively as possible. We, therefore, termed this an objectivity function.

Perception group

Verbs such as *mieru* (seem), *kiku* (hear), and *omou* (think) entail the modality of how the speaker recognizes an statement's proposition. We thus referred to this modality as perception. We identified several SEEs that varied in objectivity and contained perceptions of third parties. Table 2 presents a list of SEEs with the perception group function.

The first expression, *to-miteiru*, comprises the content verb *miru* (see). The second expression, *to-mirareteiru*, is the passive version. Because, Japanese passive forms are often used without an agent (subject in a positive sentence), the person who does the seeing is not specified in this case. This lack of specification increases the level of abstraction of the sentence and adds objectivity.

The third expression, *to-shiteiru*, entails a delexical verb, *suru* (do) that ambiguously refers to *miru* (see), *iu* (say), and *omou* (think). This ambiguity further increases the level of abstraction and objectivity of the sentence.

The last expression, *to-sareteiru*, is the passivized version of *to-shiteiru* that we consider to have the highest level of ambiguity and objectivity.

Table 3 shows a list of all the functions used in this study. These are divided into functions of syntax, common modalities, and regular news specific modalities.

3.4 FS assignment to SEEs

To assign a FS to each of the 841 SEEs (described in section 3.2), we first compiled a set of regular expressions that linked function words to units bearing a single function. We then applied these regular expressions to the 841 SEEs and assigned a FS to each SEE.

Each SEE with a FS had a number of occurrence counts for each news type: regular and News Web Easy. We used these numbers to determine the association between FS and news type. An odds ratio was used to estimate the association:

$$O = \frac{p}{1-p}\frac{1-q}{q}, \qquad (1)$$

where p is the relative frequency of a given FS in normal news and q is the relative frequency of the FS in News Web Easy. A FS whose odds ratio was greater than or equal to 1 was considered to have

SEE	Function	Explanation	Objectivity
to miteiru	percept.	see	low
to mirareteiru	pas.-percept.	be seen	middle
to shiteiru	amb.-percept.	do (see, say or think)	middle
to sareteiru	pas.-amb-percept.	be done (seen, said, or thought)	high

amb. = ambiguous, pas. = passive, percept. = perception

Table 2: SEEs bearing perception group function

Syntax	causative	passive	aspect	give-get	change
	example	parallel	nominalization	noun	
Modality	hope	need	order	question	will
(Common)	selection	prohibition	invitation	guess	probability
	reason	explanation	change-guess		
(News specific)	percept.group	objectivity	hearsay		

Table 3: Functions assigned to SEEs

Length	1	2	3	4
Regular	9(0.14)	35 (0.54)	21 (0.32)	0 (0)
Easy	13 (0.16)	43 (0.51)	22 (0.27)	3 (0.04)

Table 4: The distribution of FS types

an association with normal news; otherwise it had an association with News Web Easy [5] .

Table 4 shows the number and relative frequency of FS types categorized by length and news type. The numbers for both news types peaked with the FS length of 2 and showed a similar distribution.

We calculated the relative frequency distribution of FSs using the same categories as in Table4. The results are shown in Figure 2.

Because FS may have occurrence counts in both news types, we calculated the average relative frequency for each one. We found that FSs assciated with News Web Easy had a high frequency concentration at length 1, while FSs associated with regular news peaked at length 2. We therefore concluded that SEEs with a single function were preferred in easy Japanese news.

Next, we compared the unique single functions that appeared specifically in each news type . We collected these functions from FSs of length 1 and the final functions in FSs of length 3 (see Table 4). Table5 summarizes these results. A sharp contrast is evident between the two types. Those functions

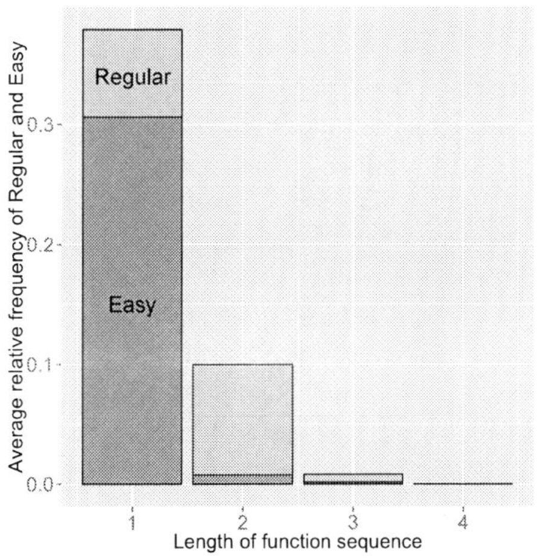

Figure 2: Average relative Frequency

used exclusively in regular news were all functions in the perception group. Those used exclusively in News Web Easy were syntactic types and modalities commonly used in daily conversation.

4 Evaluation of SEE difficulty for foreigners

4.1 Measure of difficulty

The difficulty levels of SEEs for foreign students were determined based on Japanese proficiency levels. This was measured according to the new JLPT version, using the lowest grade required to read and understand SEEs. Since the new JLPT has five grades, ranging from N1 (the most advanced) to N5 (elementary), we attached numbers

[5]We, therefore, considered the function sequence to be associated with regular news if p was greater than or equal to q; otherwise, it was considered to be associated with News Web Easy.

Length	Easy	Regular
1	give-get order probability prohibition	amb.-percept. pas.-percept. pas.-amb.-percept.
3 (final)	order explanation reason	amb.-percept. pas.-percept.

Table 5: Single functions unique to each news type

Grade	Number	Grade	Number
N5	1	N2	4
N4	2	N1	5
N3	3	above N1	6

Table 6: JLPT levels and numbers for selection

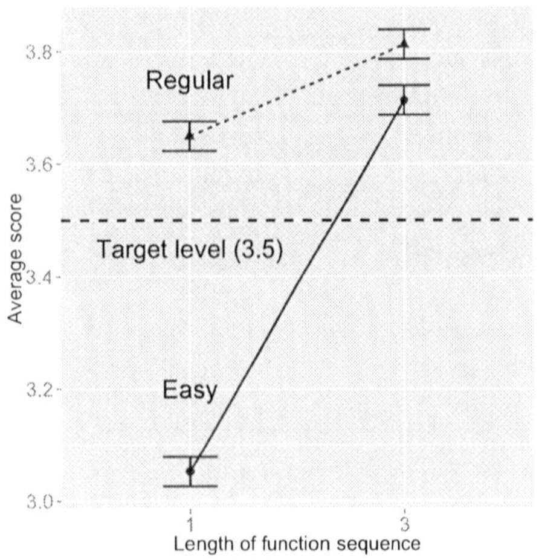

Figure 3: Score difference for the SEEs

ranging from 1 to 5 to them, with 5 indicating the most difficult SEEs and 1 the easiest. The number 6 was designated to SEEs that were difficult, even for N1-grade students. Table 6 presents the JLPT grades and numbers for the selection.

4.2 Selection of SEEs

We aimed to evaluate the difficulty levels of the 841 SEEs for foreign students learning Japanese and to analyze the factors governing these difficulty levels. The total number of SEEs (841) was too high to evaluate individually. Moreover, the word types for building SEEs were too diverse for the extraction of just a few factors.

We, therefore, decided to first sample FSs and then select SEEs bearing the sampled FSs. The number of FS types was 146 (Table 4) and that of function types was only 28 (Table 3) which would result in a highly tractable analysis of FSs. Accordingly, we selected SEEs based on the following assumptions and procedures.

(A1) Any FS belonging to the same cell in Table 4 would have the same difficulty level [6].
Based on this assumption, we randomly sampled 13 FSs from the four cells in Table 4 of length 1 and 3, and for both news types. This resulted in a sample of 52 FSs.

(A2) Any SEE belonging to the same FS had the same difficulty level. Based on this assumption, we selected the most frequently occurring SEEs from each of the 52 FSs sampled in (A1) which also yielded 52 SEEs.

[6] In other words, the difficulty level of FS only depends on the news type and the length of FS.

Because the regular news cell with a length of 1 had nine functions, we sampled 13 SEEs, allowing for FS duplication. It should be noted that the difficulty level of each sampled SEE and its FS was considered to be equal, because FS and SEE corresponded on a one-to-one basis.

4.3 Subjects and questions

We believed that foreign students—especially at the elementary level—would find it very difficult to respond to questions about their comprehension levels of SEE as they would need an in depth understanding of the functions to do so. We, therefore, asked Japanese instructors, and not the students, directly, to evaluate the difficulty levels of the SEEs.

Each questionnaire for the 52 SEEs consisted of the following parts: the SEE in question; functional features; and examples of usage in sentences. We sent questionnaires to 500 Japanese instructors through Internet. They specified the difficulty number in Table 6 for each of the 52 SEEs. In total, 390 effective responses were returned to us.

4.4 Results and discussion

Based on the responses of the 390 instructors, Figure 3 shows the average numbers (scores) calculated for the difficulty of SEEs and FSs obtained for the four cells (see Table4). The x-axis shows the FS length and the y-axis shows the average

Function	News type	Score
pas.-percept.	regular	3.800
pas.-amb.-percept.	regular	3.791
percept.	regular	3.736
noun	regular	3.731
amb.-percept.	regular	3.701
objectivity	regular	3.513
hearsay	regular	3.485
causative	regular	3.369
passive	regular	3.354
probability	easy	3.346

Table 7: The top 10 single functions according to difficulty levels

scores. The solid line indicates score changes for News Web Easy and the dotted line shows those for regular news. It should be noted that we set our target level of Japanese between N3 and N2 of the current JLPT. The target threshold score was 3.5.

The graph shows that the difficulty level of SEEs with a FS length of 1 from the News Web Easy cell was under the target threshold, while those in other cells were above this level.

Effect of news type and FS length

From that graph, it is evident that for both the lengths, SEEs obtained from News Web Easy were easier to comprehend than those obtained for regular news. We may conclude that the rewriting of the SEEs evidently reduced difficulty in understanding.

SEEs of a FS length of 3 were more difficult than those of a length of 1 for both types of news. As can be seen from the difference in the lines' gradients, the increase in difficulty associated with an increase in FS length was more apparent for SEEs from News Web Easy [7]. Although single functions used in News Web Easy evidenced low difficulty levels, these levels rose rapidly when they were lined up. Length of SEE is obviously one of the factors that affect the difficulty level.

Effect of functions

To confirm individual differences in FSs found in regular news and News Web Easy, we focused on the FSs with a length of 1 and arranged them, score-wise, in descending order (Table 7).

It is evident from Table 7 that the nine single functions that appeared in regular news (see Table 4) occupied the top nine positions. In particular, the perception group functions were considered the most difficult. These were the ones that only appeared in regular news (c.f. Table 5). We can, therefore, conclude that many Japanese instructors consider the elimination of these functions in easy Japanese news to be an appropriate approach for maintaining the difficulty level below the pre-intermediate level.

5 Conclusions and future work

We were involved in NHK's web service initiative, News Web Easy. This initiative aims to deliver news in simplified Japanese to foreign residents learning Japanese as a second language. As we reported, the service has been welcomed as a Japanese teaching and learning resource. For this study, we analyzed features of News Web Easy that contribute to learning the language.

We focused on SEEs occurring in news most of which are not listed in JLPT test guidelines. We compiled an extensive collection of SEEs from regular news texts and News Web Easy and identified differences in SEE usage within regular news and News Web Easy. Consequently, we found a sharp contrast in terms of grammatical functions. We then examined the difficulty levels of these expressions for foreign students learning Japanese based on a wide-scale evaluation by Japanese instructors. Our results revealed that the current rewriting of SEEs is appropriate. Moreover, we identified features of these expressions that contribute to the difficulty factor.

A future challenge entails extending News Web Easy to make it a useful resource for those who wish to follow regular news that is written in native-level Japanese. Because News Web Easy facilitates comparative reading of both normal and easy Japanese, it offers such an opportunity to some extent. To further enhance this function, we believe that the findings of the present study will be valuable. The difficult SEEs that we found were appropriately reworded into simpler expressions and became unnoticeable in the simplified texts. If we can explicitly provide feedback about such information to News Web Easy users, they will be able to learn native-level Japanese more efficiently. Creating such an interface is, therefore, part of our future plans.

[7] The two-way analysis of variance test revealed that the difference was statistically significant.

References

Jonathan Brown and Maxine Eskenazi. 2004. Retrieval of authentic documents for reader-specific lexical practice. In *Proceedings of InSTILL/ICALL Symposium*.

Jill Burstein, Jane Shore, John Sabatini, Yong-Won Lee, and Matthew Ventura. 2007. The automated text adaptation tool. In *Proceedings of Human Language Technologies: The Annual Conference of the North American Chapter of the Association for Computational Linguistics (NAACL-HLT)*, pages 3–4, April.

Maxine Eskenazi, Yibin Lin, and Oscar Saz. 2013. Tools for non-native readers: the case for translation and simplification. In *Proceedings of the Workshop on Natural Language Processing for Improving Textual Accessibility*, pages 20–28, June.

Hsin Chia Fu, Yeong Y. Xu, and C.L. Tseng. 2006. Generation of multimedia TV news contents for WWW. In *Proceedings of the 15th International Conference on World Wide Web*, pages 909–910. ACM, May.

Hiroyuki Hamada. 2013. Overview of the hybridcast system. *Broadcast Technology*, 51:1–8.

Nihongo Kizyutu Bunpô Kenkyûkai, editor. 2010. *Modern Japanese Syntax (Gendai Nihongo Bunpô) 1-7*. Kuroshio Shuppan. (in Japanese).

Sarah E. Petersen and Mari Ostendorf. 2007. Text simplification for language learners: A corpus analysis. In *Proceedings of ISCA SLaTE2007*, pages 69–72.

Hideki Tanaka, Hideya Mino, Shinji Ochi, and Motoya Shibata. 2013. News services in simplified Japanese and its production support systems. In *Proceedings of the International Broadcasting Convention 2013*.

The Japan Foundation and Japan Educational Exchange and Services, editors. 2002. *Japanese–Language Proficiency Test: Test Content Specifications (Revised Edition)*. Bonjinsha. (in Japanese).

Alexandra Uitdenbogerd. 2014. Tools for supporting language acquisition via extensive reading. In *Workshop Proceedings of the 22nd International Conference on Computers in Education*, pages 35–41.

Ritsu Yonekura. 2012. Information search and media access of foreign residents in Japan in disaster period—telephone interviews on four nationalities—. *The NHK Monthly Report on Broadcast Research*, pages 62–75, August. (in Japanese).

Grammatical Error Correction Considering Multi-word Expressions

Tomoya Mizumoto **Masato Mita** **Yuji Matsumoto**
Nara Institute of Science and Technology
8916-5 Takayama, Ikoma, Nara 630-0192, Japan

{tomoya-m, mita.masato.mz2, matsu}@is.naist.jp

Abstract

Multi-word expressions (MWEs) have been recognized as important linguistic information and much research has been conducted especially on their extraction and interpretation. On the other hand, they have hardly been used in real application areas.

While those who are learning English as a second language (ESL) use MWEs in their writings just like native speakers, MWEs haven't been taken into consideration in grammatical error correction tasks. In this paper, we investigate the grammatical error correction method using MWEs. Our method proposes a straightforward application of MWEs to grammatical error correction, but experimental results show that MWEs have a beneficial effect on grammatical error correction.

1 Introduction

Publicly usable services on the Web for assisting second language learning are growing recently. For example, there are language learning social networking services such as Lang-8[1] and English grammar checkers such as Ginger[2]. Research on assistance of second language learning also has received much attention, especially on grammatical error correction of essays written by learners of English as a second language (ESL) . In the past, three competitions for grammatical error correction have been held: Helping Our Own (Dale and Kilgarriff, 2011; Dale et al., 2012) and CoNLL Shared Task (Ng et al., 2013; Ng et al., 2014).

Most previous research on ESL learners' grammatical error correction is targeted on one or few restricted types of learners' errors. ESL learners make various kinds of grammatical errors (Mizumoto et al., 2012). For dealing with any types of errors, grammatical error correction methods using phrase-based statistical machine translation (SMT) are proposed (Brockett et al., 2006; Mizumoto et al., 2012). Phrase-based SMT carries out translation with phrases which are a sequence of words as translation units. However, since phrases are extracted in an unsupervised manner, an MWE like "a lot of" may not be treated as one phrase. In machine translation fields, phrase-based SMT considering MWEs achieved higher performance (Carpuat and Diab, 2010; Ren et al., 2009).

In this paper, we propose a grammatical error correction method considering MWEs. To be precise, we apply machine translation methods considering MWEs (Carpuat and Diab, 2010) to grammatical error correction. They turn MWEs into single units in the source side sentences (English). Unlike typical machine translation that translates between two languages, in the grammatical error correction task, source side sentences contain errors. Thus, we propose two methods; one is that MWEs are treated as one word in both source and target side sentences, the other is that MWEs are treated as one word in only the target side sentences.

2 Related work

Research on grammatical error correction has recently become very popular. Grammatical error correction methods are roughly divided into two types; (1) targeting few restricted types of errors (Rozovskaya and Roth, 2011; Rozovskaya and Roth, 2013; Tajiri et al., 2012) and (2) targeting

[1] http://lang-8.com
[2] http://www.gingersoftware.com

Proceedings of The 2nd Workshop on Natural Language Processing Techniques for Educational Applications, pages 82–86,
Beijing, China, July 31, 2015.

any types of errors (Mizumoto et al., 2012). In the first type of error correction, classifiers like Support Vector Machines have mainly been used. In the second type, statistical machine translation methods have been used. The only features for grammatical error correction that have been considered in many of previous works are token, POS and syntactic information of single words, and features considering two (or more) words as a whole such as MWEs have never been used.

There is the work dealing with collocations, a kind of MWEs, as target of error detection (Futagi et al., 2008). Our method is different in that we are aiming at correcting not MWEs but other expressions like articles, prepositions and noun numbers as targets considering MWEs.

A lot of research for identifying MWEs and constructing MWE resources have been conducted (Schneider et al., 2014; Shigeto et al., 2013). In addition, there is some research in natural language processing applications using MWEs; i.e., statistical machine translation (Carpuat and Diab, 2010; Ren et al., 2009), information retrieval (Newman et al., 2012) and opinion mining (Berend, 2011).

Our task is very similar to the research of SMT using MWEs (Carpuat and Diab, 2010; Ren et al., 2009). However we are in different situation where incorrect words may be included in source sentence side, thus identifying MWEs in source side may make mistakes.

3 Multi-word expressions

MWEs are defined as expressions having "idiosyncratic interpretations that cross word boundaries (or spaces)" (Sag et al., 2002). In this paper, we mainly deal with fixed expressions that function either as adverbs, conjunctions, determiners, prepositions, prepositional phrases or pronouns.

3.1 Multi-word expressions in native corpora and learner corpora

ESL learners also use a lot of MWEs in their writings just like native speakers. For comparing MWEs usages of ESL learners and native speakers, we prepare a native corpus and a learner corpus. We use the MWE data set from (Shigeto et al., 2013), MWE-annotated Penn Treebank sections of OntoNotes Release 4.0[3] as the native corpus. We use Lang-8 Learner Corpora[4] as the learner corpus[5].

Table 1: The rate of overlap of multi-word expressions from Penn Treebank section of OntoNotes and Lang-8 Learner Corpora

top number	rate of overlap
10	30.0%
20	45.0%
30	46.7%
40	57.5%
50	54.0%
70	57.1%
120	66.7%
170	66.5%

Table 1 shows the rate of overlap of multi-word expressions from Penn Treebank section of OntoNotes and Lang-8 Learner Corpora in taking top *N*. Although they are in different domains, MWEs used by learners overlap about 60% with those used by native speakers.

The occurrence frequency of MWEs obeys the Zipf's law. In the learner corpus, top 70 MWEs cover about 50%, top 120 MWEs cover about 80% and top 170 MWEs cover 90% of all the MWEs in the corpus by token count.

3.2 Advantage of using Multi-word Expressions for Grammatical Error Correction

There are two advantages to use MWEs in grammatical error correction. The first advantage is that it prevents translation of correct parts of MWEs to other words. To illustrate this, let us consider the following example:

He ate sweets, for example ice and cake.

This sentence does not have grammatical errors, thus error correction systems does not need to correct it. However, the system might correct the word "example", into the following:

He ate sweets, for examples ice and cake.

This is because the system has no knowledge of MWEs.

[3]https://catalog.ldc.upenn.edu/LDC2011T03

[4]http://cl.naist.jp/nldata/lang-8/

[5]MWEs are automatically tagged by tools which explained in 5.1.

The second advantage is that the system becomes capable of considering longer contexts when using MWEs. To illustrate this, let us consider the following example:

I have a lot of red apple.

Without considering MWEs, the system takes "I have a", "have a lot", "a lot of", "lot of red", "of red apple"as word 3-grams, unable to consider the relationship between "a lot of" and "apple".

4 Grammatical error correction methods using multi-word expressions

In this section, we describe our error correction method with MWEs. We use statistical machine translation approaches for grammatical error correction. We apply MWEs to the phrase-based SMT.

4.1 Error correction with phrase-based SMT

The error correction method with phrase-based SMT was proposed for the first time by (Brockett et al., 2006). Although they used phrase-based SMT for grammatical error correction, they only handled one error type, *noun number*. Mizumoto et al. (2012) also used phrase-based SMT, however they targeted all error types. In this paper, we use phrase-based SMT which many previous research used for grammatical error correction.

4.2 Error correction methods considering multi-word expressions

We propose two methods for grammatical error correction considering MWEs. Previous research of machine translation using MWEs (Carpuat and Diab, 2010) handled MWEs in source side sentences by simply turning MWEs into single units (by conjoining the constituent words with underscores). We essentially apply their method to grammatical error correction; however, in our case identifying MWEs might fail because source side sentences contain grammatical errors. Therefore, we propose and compare the following two methods.

Using MWEs in both source side and target side In this method, MWEs are considered in both source side and target side. We show an example in the following:

Source: I have a_lot_of pen.
Target: I have a_lot_of pens.

Table 2: Results of grammatical error correction

		P	R	F
Baseline (without MWEs)		30.1	32.9	31.4
Source: w/ MWE, Target: w/ MWE	70 (50%)	27.3	37.8	31.7
	120 (80%)	30.0	34.9	32.2
	170 (90%)	27.9	38.2	32.3
	All	29.2	32.8	30.9
Source: w/o MWE, Target: w/ MWE	70 (50%)	30.1	35.1	32.4
	120 (80%)	29.3	36.9	32.7
	170 (90%)	29.8	36.7	**32.9**
	All	31.3	29.4	30.4

Using MWEs in target side In this method, MWEs are considered only in target side. We show an example in the following:

Source: I have a lot of pen.
Target: I have a_lot_of pens.

We train both language model and translation model using texts of considering MWEs.

5 Experiments of grammatical error correction using multi-word expressions

5.1 Experimental settings

We used cicada 0.3.0[6] for the machine translation tool. This includes a decoder and a word aligner. As the language modeling tool we used expgram 0.2.0[7]. We used ZMERT[8] as the parameter tuning tool.

For automatic identifying MWEs, we use AMALGr 1.0[9] (Schneider et al., 2014). The MWE identification tool is re-trained using the MWE data set tagged by (Shigeto et al., 2013) on the Penn Treebank sections of OntoNotes Release 4.0. This is because their annotation was more convenient for our purpose.

The translation model was trained on the Lang-8 Learner Corpora v2.0. We extracted English essays which were written by ESL learners whose native language is Japanese from the corpora and cleaned the noise with the method proposed in (Mizumoto et al., 2011). As the results, we got 629,787 sentence pairs. We used a 5-gram

[6] http://www2.nict.go.jp/univ-com/multi_trans/cicada/
[7] http://www2.nict.go.jp/univ-com/multi_trans/expgram/
[8] http://cs.jhu.edu/~ozaidan/zmert/
[9] https://github.com/nschneid/pysupersensetagger

Table 3: Examples of system outputs

Learner	Last month, she gave me a lot of rice and onion.
Baseline	Last month, she gave me a lot of rice and onion.
with MWE	Last month, she gave me a lot of rice and onions.

language model built on corrected sentences of the learner corpora. Konan-JIEM Learner Corpus[10] (Nagata et al., 2011) are used for evaluation and development data. We use 2,411 sentences for evaluation, and 300 sentences for development.

5.2 Experimental Result

As evaluation metrics, we use precision, recall and F-score. We compare phrase-based SMT without using MWEs (baseline) with the two methods explained in 4.2. In addition, we varied the number of MWEs used for training the translation model and the language model. This is because MWEs that appear few times may introduce noises. We use top 70 (50%), 120 (80%) and 170 (90%) MWEs described in 3.1.

Table 2 shows the experimental results. The methods considering MWEs achieved higher F-score than baseline except for the case that uses All MWEs. In addition, using more MWEs increases the F-score.

5.3 Discussion

Using all MWEs shows worse results because infrequent MWEs become noise in training and testing.

We got better results when we use MWEs only in the target side. This is likely because learners tend to fail to write MWEs correctly, only writing them in partial forms. One cause of deterioration of precision is that a single word like "many" is wrongly corrected into an MWE like "a lot of", although it is actually not incorrect.

There are two reasons why the performance improved considering MWEs. The first reason is that the system becomes capable of considering the relationship between MWEs which are made up of a sequence of two or more lexemes and words lie adjacent to MWEs. We show an example of system results in Table 3. Although the baseline system did not correct the example, the system considering MWEs was able to correct this error. This is because the system was able to consider the MWE "a lot of".

[10]http://www.gsk.or.jp/en/catalog/gsk2015-a/

The second reason is that the probabilities of translation model and language model are improved by handling MWEs as single units. Let us consider the two sentences, "There are a lot of pens" and "There is a pen." as examples of language model. Without considering MWEs, the word 3-grams, "There are a" and "There is a", have high probability. With considering MWEs, however, the former trigram becomes to "There are a_lot_of pens" and then the probabilities of trigrams that should not be given high probability like "There are a" come to low. The correction performance of articles and prepositions that are likely to become a component word of MWEs is considered to improve by this revision. The number of true positive for article as compared with baseline and MWE (170) of only target side are 190 and 227, respectively. Likewise, the number of true positive for preposition as compared with them are 108 and 121, respectively.

6 Conclusion

We proposed a grammatical error correction method using multi-word expressions. Our method proposes a straightforward application of MWEs to grammatical error correction, but experimental results show that MWEs have quite good effects on grammatical error correction. Experimental results show that the methods considering MWEs achieved higher F-score than baseline except for the case that uses all MWEs. We plan to use more multi-word expressions which we did not handle in this paper, such as phrasal verbs. Moreover, we plan to conduct grammatical error correction considering MWEs which contain gaps that are dealt with (Schneider et al., 2014).

References

Gábor Berend. 2011. Opinion Expression Mining by Exploiting Keyphrase Extraction. In *Proceedings of IJCNLP*, pages 1162–1170.

Chris Brockett, William B. Dolan, and Michael Gamon. 2006. Correcting ESL Errors Using Phrasal SMT Techniques. In *Proceedings of COLING-ACL*, pages 249–256.

Marine Carpuat and Mona Diab. 2010. Task-based Evaluation of Multiword Expressions: a Pilot Study in Statistical Machine Translation. In *Proceedings of HLT-NAACL*, pages 242–245.

Robert Dale and Adam Kilgarriff. 2011. Helping Our Own: The HOO 2011 Pilot Shared Task. In *Proceedings of ENLG*, pages 242–249.

Robert Dale, Ilya Anisimoff, and George Narroway. 2012. HOO 2012: A Report on the Preposition and Determiner Error Correction Shared Task. In *Proceedings of BEA*, pages 54–62.

Yoko Futagi, Paul Deane, Martin Chodorow, and Joel Tetreault. 2008. A Computational Approach to Detecting Collocation Errors in the Writing of Non-Native Speakers of English. *Computer Assisted Language Learning*, 21(4):353–367.

Tomoya Mizumoto, Mamoru Komachi, Masaaki Nagata, and Yuji Matsumoto. 2011. Mining Revision Log of Language Learning SNS for Automated Japanese Error Correction of Second Language Learners. In *Proceedings of IJCNLP*, pages 147–155.

Tomoya Mizumoto, Yuta Hayashibe, Mamoru Komachi, Masaaki Nagata, and Yuji Matsumoto. 2012. The Effect of Learner Corpus Size in Grammatical Error Correction of ESL Writings. In *Proceedings of COLING*, pages 863–872.

Ryo Nagata, Edward Whittaker, and Vera Sheinman. 2011. Creating a Manually Error-tagged and Shallow-parsed Learner corpus. In *Proceedings of ACL-HLT*, pages 1210–1219.

David Newman, Nagendra Koilada, Jey Han Lau, and Timothy Baldwin. 2012. Bayesian Text Segmentation for Index Term Identification and Keyphrase Extraction. In *Proceedings of COLING*, pages 2077–2092.

Hwee Tou Ng, Siew Mei Wu, Yuanbin Wu, Christian Hadiwinoto, and Joel Tetreault. 2013. The CoNLL-2013 Shared Task on Grammatical Error Correction. In *Proceedings of CoNLL Shared Task*, pages 1–12.

Hwee Tou Ng, Siew Mei Wu, Ted Briscoe, Christian Hadiwinoto, Raymond Hendy Susanto, and Christopher Bryant. 2014. The CoNLL-2014 Shared Task on Grammatical Error Correction. In *Proceedings of CoNLL Shared Task*, pages 1–14.

Zhixiang Ren, Yajuan Lü, Jie Cao, Qun Liu, and Yun Huang. 2009. Improving Statistical Machine Translation Using Domain Bilingual Multiword Expressions. In *Proceedings of Workshop on MWE*, pages 47–54.

Alla Rozovskaya and Dan Roth. 2011. Algorithm Selection and Model Adaptation for ESL Correction Tasks. In *Proceedings of ACL-HLT*, pages 924–933.

Alla Rozovskaya and Dan Roth. 2013. Joint Learning and Inference for Grammatical Error Correction. In *Proceedings of EMNLP*, pages 791–802.

Ivan A. Sag, Timothy Baldwin, Francis Bond, Ann A. Copestake, and Dan Flickinger. 2002. Multiword Expressions: A Pain in the Neck for NLP. In *Proceedings of CICLing*, pages 1–15.

Nathan Schneider, Emily Danchik, Chris Dyer, and Noah A. Smith. 2014. Discriminative Lexical Semantic Segmentation with Gaps: Running the MWE Gamut. *Transactions of the Association for Computational Linguistics*, 2:193–206.

Yutaro Shigeto, Ai Azuma, Sorami Hisamoto, Shuhei Kondo, Tomoya Kouse, Keisuke Sakaguchi, Akifumi Yoshimoto, Frances Yung, and Yuji Matsumoto. 2013. Construction of English MWE Dictionary and its Application to POS Tagging. In *Proceedings of Workshop on MWE*, pages 139–144.

Toshikazu Tajiri, Mamoru Komachi, and Yuji Matsumoto. 2012. Tense and Aspect Error Correction for ESL Learners Using Global Context. In *Proceedings of ACL*, pages 198–202.

Salinlahi III: An Intelligent Tutoring System for Filipino Language Learning

Ralph Vincent Regalado , Michael Louie Boñon, Nadine Chua, Rene Rose Piñera, Shannen Rose Dela Cruz
Center for Language Technologies
De La Salle University, Manila
ralph.regalado@delasalle.ph,
{michael.bonon, chuanadine}@gmail.com,
{renepinera, shannenrose.delacruz}@yahoo.com

Abstract

Heritage language learners are learners of the primary language of their parents which they might have been exposed to but have not learned it as a language they can fluently use to communicate with other people. Salinlahi, an Interactive Learning Environment, was developed to teach these young Filipino heritage learners about basic Filipino vocabulary while Salinlahi II included a support for collaborative learning. With the aim of teaching learners with basic knowledge in Filipino we developed Salinlahi III to teach higher level lessons focusing on Filipino grammar and sentence construction. An internal evaluation of the system has shown that the user interface and feedback of the tutor was appropriate. Moreover, in an external evaluation of the system, experimental and controlled field tests were done and results showed that there is a positive learning gain after using the system.

1 Introduction

The idea behind Intelligent Tutoring Systems is letting a computer simulate a sophisticated human tutor and be able to use a teaching strategy appropriate for each student (Murray, 1999) (Massey, Psotka, & Mutter, 1988). According to (Kassim, Kazi, & Ranganath, 2004), there are four important elements that must be present in instructional systems. These four are the tutor, the student, the domain knowledge to be learned by the student, and lastly, the computer itself. These four elements were the basis of the functional model of an ITS according to (Kassim, Kazi, & Ranganath, 2004) which consists of the following: expert module, tutoring module, student model and user interface module. This functional model is accepted as a standard in building the system architecture of ITSs (Polson & Richardson, 1988). Many ITSs have been built for different fields (such as cardiovascular physiology, algebra, language learning, electronics troubleshooting etc). Some of these ITSs are AutoTutor and ELM-ART. AutoTutor, developed by (Graesser et al., 2004), features tutoring done in natural language dialogue while ELM-ART, developed by (Brusilovsky, Schwarz, & Weber, 1996), pioneered ITSs in the World Wide Web.

Intelligent Tutoring Systems served as the inspiration in developing Salinlahi III. Unlike the two previous iterations of Salinlahi which are purely Interactive Learning Environments, Salinlahi III was designed from the ITS perspective. In the previous systems, students have the freedom to choose which lessons to take while in Salinlahi III, students are directed toward a sequential progress of lessons by a tutor which is the system itself. The lessons in this system are structured in terms of content and skill complexity, starting from basic concepts to lessons dealing with construction of basic Filipino sentences. The tutor decides when to advance to the next lesson based on the student's performance in the exercises given in every lesson. These exercises are namely Translation Exercise and Creation Exercise. The exercises were designed as a dialogue type of exercise between the tutor and the student. However, it is only in the Translation Exercise where the tutor will guide the student to attain the correct answer by giving feedback on his or her current answers. The feedback given by the tutor is done in natural language inspired by AutoTutor. This is made possible through the use of template-based Natural Language Generation (NLG), a technique used in generating content in natural language.

Proceedings of The 2nd Workshop on Natural Language Processing Techniques for Educational Applications, pages 87–93,
Beijing, China, July 31, 2015.

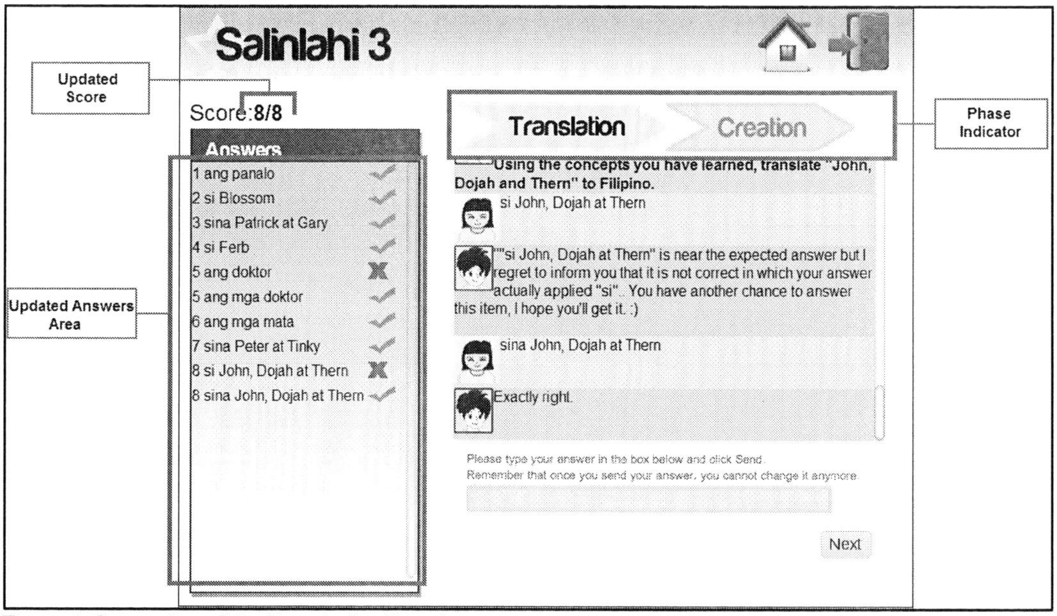

Figure 1. Screenshot of the Translation Exercise

Salinlahi III focuses on teaching basic Filipino grammar whereas the two previous iterations focus on Filipino vocabulary. This change in the domain of knowledge is a solution to accommodate learning needs of older students with a basic knowledge of Filipino vocabulary. These students are assumed to be at the range of fourteen (14) to seventeen (17) years old.

2 System Architecture

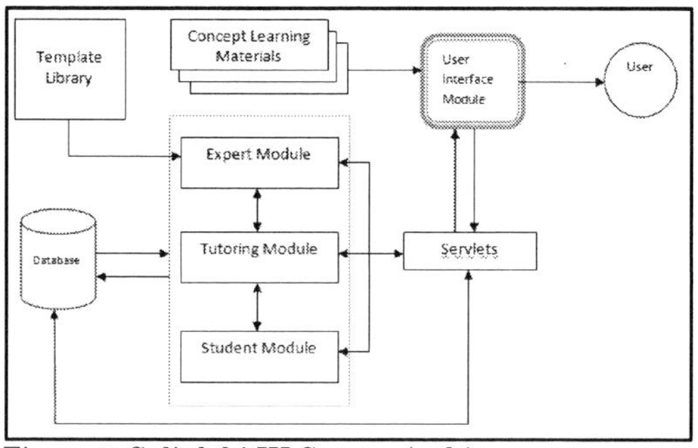

Figure 2. Salinlahi III System Architecture

The system architecture of Salinlahi III follows the functional model of an ITS by (Kassim, Kazi, & Ranganath, 2004). Based from this model, Salinlahi III has been designed with four main modules namely, User Interface Module, Expert Module, Tutoring Module, and Student Module.

2.1 User Interface Module

The User Interface Module provides lesson and exercises to the user. It is also responsible for passing the user input to the different system modules.

2.2 Expert Module

The Expert Module does the analysis of the user's input. This module contains two different analyzers for the exercises. The first input analyzer is for the Translation Exercise. This analyzer checks the translation of the student with the corresponding expected translation by the tutor. After analysis, the tutor will come up with its assessment. The second analyzer is for the Creation Exercise. This analyzer's main job is to parse the student's input and check if the student has successfully applied in his or her answer what is being discussed in the current lesson. This module also does different functions such as the computation of the Levenshtein distance, tokenization of strings and the Realiser which prepares the tutor's feedback.

2.3 Tutoring Module

The Tutoring Module handles the processes of the exercises. For the Translation Exercise, the tutor's move is managed. This move, as discussed earlier in Section 2.3, is based from the assessment of the tutor on the student's answer. The assessment is produced in the Expert Module. This module includes (but is not limited to) keeping track of the chances of the student, managing the number of items given, updating the student model, managing the turns between the student and the tutor, communicating with the Expert Module for analysis, management of the student model, and the production of evaluation after the exercises.

2.4 Student Module

The Student Module contains student model. It is in this module that the tree for the student model is handled. This module is accessed by the Tutoring Module to update the student model based on the student's performance in the exercises. It is also accessed when the evaluation for the student is needed. The evaluation is generated based from the data in the nodes of the student model.

3 System Exercises

In every lesson, students are given exercises to test their learning on the current lesson they are studying which are Translation Exercise and Creation Exercise. This phase where students answer exercises corresponds to the "Response" stage in the Initial- Response-Evaluation (IRE) model mentioned by (Murray, 1999). According to the IRE model, the Response stage is where students are expected to have gained knowledge or skills after being exposed to instructions. Furthermore, in this stage, students are expected to have learned how to translate new knowledge or skills into practice (Murray, 1999).

3.1 Translation Exercise

Students go through Translation Exercise first before the Creation Exercise. In Translation Exercise, the learner is given a certain number of phrases or sentences he or she needs to translate to Filipino in the context of the lesson where it belongs. The exercise begins with the tutor giving instructions to learners followed by giving the first problem. For each problem, the learner is given at most three chances to answer correctly. In case the learner does not get it right at the last chance, the score will be based on his or her last answer. As the learner tries to answer the problem, the tutor in turn gives the appropriate feedback in order to facilitate learning as seen in Figure 1.

After the student enters his or her answer, the tutor immediately reflects and gives feedback based from the student's answer. It can be seen in Figure 3 that the tutor immediately tries to make its move after the student's input. The moves of the tutor are not random. It makes its move based from its assessment on the student's answer. Figure 3 shows the flow on how the tutor's feedback is formed.

Figure 3. Flow on how the tutor comes up with a feedback

3.1.1 The Assessment of Student's Answer

$$Difference\ Value = \frac{LevenshteinDistance}{LengthOfExpectedAnswer}$$

Equation 1. Difference Value

In the Translation Exercise, there are four possible assessments for the student's answer. These are "Correct", "Near the Answer", "Incorrect" and "Cannot be understood". "Correct" is the assessment that the tutor would come up with when the student gave an answer that exactly matches the expected answer of the tutor. "Near the Answer" is assessed by the tutor if it sees that the answer is wrong but have analyzed that the student possibly applied a misconception in his or her answer. "Near the Answer" could also be assessed by the tutor if the computed difference value of the student's answer against the expected answer is less than or equal to .30. The formula of the difference value is shown on Equation 1. In Equation 1, "LengthOfExpectedAnswer" corresponds to the number of characters the string, which is the student's answer, has. The "LevenshteinDistance" corresponds to the Levenshtein distance. It is a string metric used to measure how many insertions, substitutions and deletions are required to transform a given string to a target string (Nielsen, 1994).

"Incorrect" on the other hand is assessed by the tutor if the answer is also wrong. However, it only becomes the assessment when the student applied a misconception and the computed difference value exceeds the threshold which is .30. "Cannot be understood" is the assessment given by the tutor when it sees that the student's answer is wrong, no misconception was applied and the computed difference value exceeds the threshold.

3.1.2 The Move of the Tutor

The move that the tutor should make is based from the assessment of the student's answer. The four moves of the tutor are *Explain*, *Warn, State* and *Produce*. All of these moves have different types of feedback. *Explain* will be the move used when the learner's input is "Incorrect" or "Near the Answer." *Warn* will be the move used when the learner's input is "Cannot be Understood". This would tell the user to enter a more sensible input. *State* will be the move used when the learner's input is "Correct". *Produce* will be the move to be used to give an exercise to the learner.

3.1.3 The Feedback of the Tutor

The feedback of the tutor is based from the move that the tutor has to make. The feedbacks are produced using template-based NLG. Under each of the four moves are different templates for the feedback of the tutor. The type of feedback to be given by the tutor also takes into account the number of chances left in the current item. An example of a feedback can be seen on Figure 1. In that scenario (see Figure 1) the tutor used an *Explain* move. The type of feedback under this move to be used by the tutor would be based from the assessment and the number of chances left. The tutor's feedback which is '*"si John, Dojah at Thern" is near the answer but I regret to inform you that it is not the correct answer in which your answer actually applied "si". You have another chance to answer this item, I hope you'll get it. :)* '. Notice in this scenario, the tutor informed the student his or her answer is wrong but is near to the expected answer. The tutor also tried to show why the answer was wrong by pointing out the misconception applied by the student. Also, since it is the student's first time to get a wrong answer in that item, the last part of the message indicates that the tutor tries to give the student a positive feedback to boost up his or her confidence.

3.2 Creation Exercise

In the Creation Exercise, the student is asked by the tutor to construct or create his or her own Filipino phrases or sentences. The phrases or sentences that need to be created would be based from the lessons or sub lessons discussed in the concept learning materials. The tutor would randomly pick a sub lesson and ask the user. Unlike the Translation Exercise, in the Creation Exercise, the tutor does not give immediate feedback on the student's input. The student would only see an overall evaluation after the exercise.

3.2.1 Reflection in Action

The Translation Exercise was designed based on "reflection in action" by (Schön, 1987). According to (Schön, 1987) "reflection in action" is a case where people "reflect in the midst of action". It shows here that it is during the task that the person reflects on what he or she is doing. In accordance to this, the Translation Exercise was designed to help the student to reflect in his or her performance while taking the exercise. The tutor gives feedback to guide the student and make him or her rethink about his or her answer while there is still a chance. There is an immediate feedback whose goal is to let the student immediately reflect and react.

3.2.2 Reflection on Action

The Creation Exercise was designed with basis on "reflection on action" by (Schön, 1987). (Schön, 1987) stated that "We may reflect on action, thinking back on what we have done in order to discover how our knowing-in-action may have contributed to an unexpected outcome." The Creation Exercise is designed to be taken after the Translation Exercise. This is to allow the student to think on his or her previous actions previously committed during the Translation Exercise. In the Creation Exercise, the student can think back on his or her actions and reflect on it based from the feedback of the tutor at that time. Compared to the Translation Exercise, the tutor during the Creation Exercise does not give an immediate feedback to the student's input. This is to promote self-reflection on the student's part and have a recall about the tutor's feedback earlier (in the Translation Exercise). Whatever phrase or sentence the student has created, this could most likely show how much he or she really knows, without the help of the tutor.

4 System Evaluation

Tests were done to determine whether the system was able to achieve its main objective, which is to teach Filipino grammar to secondary level heritage language learners. Experts evaluated the system to determine whether the feedback and user interface is appropriate for the target users. Experts also evaluated the system to determine whether it can be considered as a potential educational software. Students also tested the first lesson of the system to know whether there was an increase or decrease in their learning. The increase or decrease in learning may also determine the potential of Salinlahi III as an educational software.

4.1 Internal Evaluation

The internal evaluation focused on seeing the system as a potential educational software. The experts who evaluated the system came from different fields – User Interface (UI), development of teaching tools, second/foreign language teaching (experts from this field teaches languages not only Filipino), education, Filipino teaching. The experts evaluated the system based on UI design, feedback, and as a potential educational software

Two experts evaluated the system based on the UI design. They did a test over the system and were later given a questionnaire. The questionnaire is based from the general principles of interface design that was developed by (Nielsen, 1994). The experts gave an average grade of 4.17, which is between excellent and good. Since they evaluated based on general principles in designing the user interface, this means that it is acceptable for all types of target users. However, these experts gave the following recommendations: (1) it would be helpful if there will be a status that would show that the page is loading or that the tutor is typing a message. (2) Instructions should be provided for first time users. (3) The number of chances during the exercise should be made known to the users. In addition, (4) the system should provide a way to retrieve the password once the user forgets it.

An interview was conducted with an expert who evaluated the system based on the tutor's feedback. The results of the interview with the expert show that the tutor's feedback is appropriate for the learners. The expert verified that the messages are gender-neutral and appropriate for the age range of the target users. In addition, the approaches of the tutor are acceptable and overall the tutor sounds human. However, the expert stated that if the answer falls for the assessment "Cannot be Understood", the tutor must inform the student to refer back to the lesson (e.g. "*Your answer is not within the framework of the discussion. Please refer to the review lessons*").

Three experts evaluated the system as a potential educational software. They were also given a questionnaire after testing the system. These experts gave an over-all average rating of 4.3, which is between excellent and good. With this grade and the average grade under all the criteria given, the system is believed to have passed or has a potential to be an educational software. However, few recommendations was made: (1) the numbers given in the exercises should be in Filipino and not in Spanish, (2) the learning materials should be in Filipino (e.g. using "*saging*" instead of "*banana*"), and (3) add more Filipino words to the system. One of the system's limitation is having a small collection of words. Because of this, the system may have a wrong assessment of the learner's answer only because the Filipino word used by the learner is not found in the system's collection of words.

4.2 External Evaluation

The external evaluation was done in order to assess how the system affected the learner specifically in determining its performance in teaching students. During the said evaluation, a total of twenty-seven students (27), six coming from the De La Salle University and twenty-one (21) came from MIT International School, went through a series of tests illustrated in Figure 2. Students who have not finished the series of tests were excluded from the analysis.

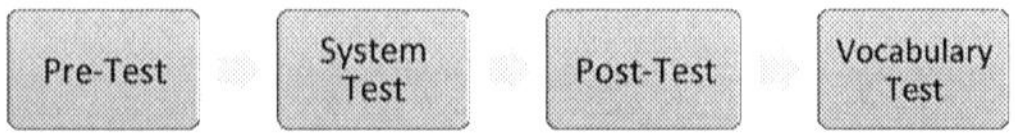

Figure 2. Flow of External Evaluation

Students were grouped into two: experimental and controlled end-user testing. Students who went through experimental end-user testing were allowed to interact with the system and use it on their own while those who went through controlled end-user testing were supervised. Results from both groups were compared to observe whether supervising the students while they use the system affects their scores in the post-test. This was important since previous iterations of Salinlahi did controlled end-user test only. The addition of the uncontrolled group gives a more realistic scenario where most likely there would be no one to supervise the users aside from the system itself and some accompanying documents.

In pre-test, post-test, and vocabulary test, students were asked to translate English words and phrases into Filipino. The scores in pre-tests and post-tests were used to determine whether students' performance increased after using the system, or in other terms, they had a positive learning gain. Thereby learning gains can be measured using the paired t-test. According to (Shier, 2004), "a paired t-test is used to compare two population means where you have two samples in which observations in one sample can be paired with observations in the other sample".

Table 1 shows the scores of the students for the pre-test and post-test under the experimental group. As seen in Table 1, scores of twelve (12 – approximately 67%) students increased, five of them did not show any increase at all and the score of one student decreased. Using paired t-test on these values, results have shown that there is a significant increase in the scores as determined by the value of p which is 0.003. The values obtained in the paired t-test are shown in Table 2.

Student No.	Pre-Test Score (X)	Post-Test Score (Y)	Difference (Y-X)
1	0	4	4
2	1	4	3
3	5	7	2
4	4	8	4
5	3	6	3
6	2	4	2
7	2	2	0
8	6	8	2
9	0	0	0
10	2	4	2
11	0	2	2
12	3	7	4
13	1	2	1
14	2	2	0
15	2	2	0
16	4	3	-1
17	0	2	2
18	0	0	0

Table 1. Students' pre-test and post-test scores for experimental end-user testing

Label	Value (X)
n	18
Mean Difference	1.666667
Standard Deviation	1.57181
Standard Error of the Mean	0.370479287
t	4.498677054
Degrees of Freedom	17
p-value	0.003

Table 2. Paired t-test values for experimental end-user testing

On the other hand, Table 3 shows the scores of the students for the pre-test and post-test under the controlled group. As seen in Table 3, scores of twelve (6 – approximately 67%) students increased, two of them did not show any increase at all and the score of one student decreased. Using paired t-test on these values, results have shown that there is a significant increase in the scores as determined by the value of p which is 0.0325. The values obtained in the paired t-test done for this group are shown in Table 4.

Student No.	Pre-Test Score (X)	Post-Test Score (Y)	Difference (Y-X)
1	0	2	2
2	0	4	4
3	6	7	1
4	6	8	2
5	0	5	5
6	6	8	2
7	7	6	-1
8	8	8	0
9	7	7	0

Table 3. Students' pre-test and post-test scores for controlled end-user testing

Label	Value (X)
n	9
Mean Difference	1.666666667
Standard Deviation	1.936491673
Standard Error of the Mean	0.645497224
t	2.581988897
Degrees of Freedom	8
p-value	0.0325

Table 4. Paired t-test values for controlled end-user testing

5 Conclusions and Recommendations

Salinlahi III is the third iteration in a series of systems that were developed to teach the Filipino language to heritage language learners. These learners are those who grew up oversees, but did not learn Filipino formally, but may be exposed to it through their Filipino parent(s).

Based on the internal and external evaluations, Salinlahi III has a potential to be an educational software. It got a high average score on the expert evaluations based on UI design, feedback, and as an educational software. The students who used the system got a positive learning gain, which means that the system was able to achieve its objective. However, since these students are residing in the Philippines, different results may arise once the system is tested on its actual target users.

Salinlahi III's future works may include having a conversational tutor that would be able to understand other user's input. This can be done by adding Natural Language Understanding techniques and tools to the current system. Another would be to include sound into the system. Currently, the system does not support voice recognition as it is also not able to produce the tutor's response through sound. Having the system support voice recognition will aid in making the tutor more conversational especially during the exercises.

References

Brusilovsky, P., Schwarz, E., &Weber, G. (1996). Elm-art: An intelligent tutoring system on world wide web. In (pp. 261–269). Springer Verlag.

Graesser, A., Lu, S., Jackson, G., Mitchell, H., Ventura, M., Olney, A., et al. (2004). Autotutor: A tutor with dialogue in natural language. Behavior Research Methods, 36, 180-192. Available from http://dx.doi.org/10.3758/BF03195563 (10.3758/BF03195563)

Kassim, A. A., Kazi, S. A., & Ranganath, S. (2004). A web-based intelligent learning environment for digital systems. International Journal of Engineering Education, 20, 13-23.

Lê, Q., & Lê, T. (2007) Evaluation of educational software: theory into practice. In: Technology and Teaching. Nova Science Publishers, New York, UK. ISBN 978-1-60021-699-2

Levenshtein, V. I. (1966). Binary codes capable of correcting deletions, insertions, and reversals. , 10 . Available from http://sascha.geekheim.de/wp-content/uploads/2006/04/levenshtein.pdfnumber=journal=Soviet Physics Doklady, publisher=American Institute of Physics., pages=707--710

Massey, L. D., Psotka, J., & Mutter, S. A. (1988). Intelligent tutoring systems : lessons learned / edited by joseph psotka, l. dan massey, sharon a. mutter, advisory editor, john seely brown [Book]. L. Erlbaum Associates, Hillsdale, N.J. :.

Murray, T. (1999). Authoring Intelligent Tutoring Systems: An Analysis of the State of the Art. International Journal of Artificial Intelligence in Education, 10, 98-129.

Nielsen, J. "Heuristic Evaluation". In J. Nielsen and R.L. Mack, editors, Usability Inspection Methods, John Wiley, 1994.

Polson, M. C., & Richardson, J. J. (Eds.). (1988). Foundations of intelligent tutoring systems. Hillsdale, NJ, USA: L. Erlbaum Associates Inc.

Regalado, R. V. , Antay, M. R., Fernandez, L., Cheng, C., & Jumarang, L. (2010). Building web-based Filipino language learning tool for heritage learners. Philippine Information Technology Journal, Vol. 2, Issue No. 2, pp 54-57.

Shier, R. (2004). Statistics: Paired t-tests. Retrieved from http://mlsc.lboro.ac.uk/resources/statistics/Paireddttest.pdf

Schön, D. A. (1987). Educating the reflective practitioner (Vol. 58) (No. 4). Jossey-Bass.

Using Finite State Transducers for Helping Foreign Language Learning

Hasan Kaya
Istanbul Technical University
Department of Computer Engineering
Istanbul, 34469, Turkey
kayahasa@itu.edu.tr

Gülşen Eryiğit
Istanbul Technical University
Department of Computer Engineering
Istanbul, 34469, Turkey
gulsenc@itu.edu.tr

Abstract

The interest and demand to foreign language learning are increased tremendously along with the globalization and freedom of movement in the world. Today, the technological developments allow the creation of supportive materials for foreign language learners. However, the language acquisition between languages with high typological differences still poses challenges for this area and the learning task it self. This paper introduces our preliminary study for building an educational application to help foreign language learning between Turkish and English. The paper presents the use of finite state technology for building a Turkish word synthesis system (which allows to choose word-related features among predefined grammatical affix categories such as tense, modality and polarity etc...) and a word-level translation system between the languages in focus. The developed system is observed to outperform the popular online translation systems for word-level translation in terms of grammatically correct outputs.

1 Introduction

The influence of mother tongue on foreign language learning is discussed in many linguistic and psychological studies (Hakuta et al., 2000; Hakuta, 1999; Durgunoglu and Hancin-Bhatt, 1992; Ringbom, 1987; Swan, 1997; Corder, 1983) in the literature. The typological differences between the mother tongue and the second language have an important role on the duration of learning process. In these studies, it is emphasized that one of the causes of frequently made mistakes in the second language is the rules learned from the first language. English and Turkish being languages from totally different language families compose a very representative and interesting language pair for this phenomena.

Turkish is an agglutinative language with a very rich morphological structure. Most of the syntactic information on the English side become morphological properties of a word on the Turkish side. In some cases, a single Turkish word may correspond to a full English sentence. This situation results in difficulties during language learning between this language pair and also in statistical machine translation (MT) systems. In daily life in Turkey, it is very common to come across with foreigners making mistakes in constructing Turkish words with invalid grammatical constructions (i.e. having difficulty to produce the correct morpheme order to form a valid Turkish word). Bisazza and Federico (2009), Yeniterzi and Oflazer (2010), El-Kahlout and Oflazer (2010) and Eyigöz et al. (2013) show the influence of using morphological clues in increasing the MT quality.

Finite state technology is proven to increase the efficiency in many rule-based NLP related tasks (Mohri, 1997; Roche and Schabes, 1997). Today, the availability of finite state transducer (FST) frameworks such as OpenFST (Allauzen et al., 2007), HFST (Lindén et al., 2009) and XFST (Beesley and Karttunen, 2003) makes possible to create FST applications very efficiently. In this paper, we present the results of our elementary studies on using finite state transducers to build supportive tools for foreign language learning; namely Turkish for English native speakers and English for Turkish native speakers. We compare our results with four popularly online translation systems: 1. Google[1], 2. Yandex[2], 3. Bing[3] and 4. Tureng[4]. The paper is organized as follows: Section 2 introduces the Turkish morphology, Section 3 the system architecture, Section 4 the learning use cases and Section 5 the conclusion and future work.

2 Turkish Morphology

As mentioned in the previous section, agglutinative language morphology has a high impact on the performance

[1]https://translate.google.com/
[2]https://ceviri.yandex.com.tr/
[3]http://www.bing.com/translator/
[4]http://tureng.com/search/translate

Proceedings of The 2nd Workshop on Natural Language Processing Techniques for Educational Applications, pages 94–98,
Beijing, China, July 31, 2015.

of translation process of a word. Turkish has a complex morphology and because of this reason, the usage of suffix concatenations at the end of a word lemma may cause the word to denote different meanings. Table 1 gives some translation examples from Turkish to English to show that the usage of dictionary/lexicon look-up systems are not suitable for word translation between Turkish and English due to unpredictable dictionary size. Foreign language learners have even difficulty to search for the meaning of a Turkish word from a Turkish dictionary since this task requires to firstly determine the lemma of that word. To give an example for this problem, word stem for "git" (*go*) can be written in different conjugated word forms such as: "gidiyorum", "gideceğim", "gidecek" etc. (up to nearly 50 variations) which refer to very different translations in the English side although the lemma of these words are the same. As a result, a Turkish word may be expressed as a single English word or a phrase or even a sentence as shown in Table 1.

Turkish	English
git	Go
gidiyorum	I am going
gideceğim	I'll go
gidecek	He will go
gittim	I went
gidebiliyor	He is able to go
gidebilmişlerdi	They had been able to go

Table 1: Translation of Turkish words

3 System Architecture

Eryiğit (2014) introduces a web service for morphological analysis and generation of Turkish. The provided analyzer is an updated version of the work presented in Şahin et al. (2013) and uses finite state technology for the analysis and generation purposes. In the provided interface the *surface word form* "gidiyorum" (*I'm going*) is analyzed as the *lexical form* "git+Verb+Pos+Prog1+A1sg" where "git" (*to go*) is the lemma of the word and the following tags hold for main parts-of-speech tag and additional inflectional features: "+Pos" for the positive marker, "Prog1" for the progressive tense, "A1sg" for the 1st singular person. Similarly the same analysis given to the morphological generator produces the same input word. Inspired from this work, we develop a new finite state transducer transfer model and an English analyzer/generator which take the produced morphological analysis as input and produces its English counterpart. The system also works in reverse direction so that once an English input is given to the system, it transfers it to a Turkish lexical form and then uses the morphological generator to produce a valid Turkish word. Figure 1 draws the main flow of our system which we call "ITU Morphological Transfer module for English-Turkish language pairs"; ITUMorphTrans4ET in short from now on. The figure provides the intermediate stages for two given examples: "gidiyorum" (*I'm going*) and "gittim" (I went).

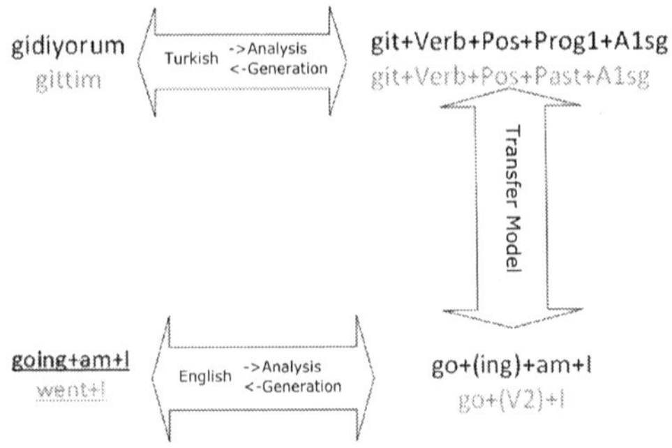

Figure 1: ITUMorphTrans4ET System Architechture

The transfer model is very similar to an FST morphological analyzer but instead of producing the relevant morphological tags for a given surface form, it produces a new lexical form (the English counterpart) of the input Turkish lexical form. To this end, it contains a bilingual lexicon for word lemmas and the transfer rules. An example from the transfer model FST is given below where each morphological tag (i.e. a suffix in the word surface form) representing person agreements are coded to produce two English words.

```
LEXICON Fin-ED-PC
+A1sg:+am+I #;
+A2sg:+are+you #;
+A3sg:+is+he/she/it #;
+A1pl:+are+we #;
+A2pl:+are+you #;
+A3pl:+are+they #;
```

The English output of the transfer model may be either some words or some tags to be further processed by the lexical post-processor. It is not necessary that all the Turkish tags produce an output; some of them are only required for determining the possible paths on the FST. This may be observed on the lexical forms of Turkish words in Figure 1. While the "+Prog1" tag is changed to an "+ing" tag, the "+Past" tag is changed to a "+V2" tag and the "+A2sg" tag is changed to the word "+he/she/it" in the transfer model's output, the "+Verb" or "+Noun" tags are only used for forwarding the process to possible FST paths in the coded rules.

The English analysis and generation FST converts between lexical and surface forms of English inputs. One should keep in mind that the English analyzer differing from the Turkish one also accepts inputs with multiple

Turkish	ITUMorphTrans4ET	Google	Bing	Tureng	Yandex
gidebilirse	**if he can go** ✓	can go	if he can go ✓	go	he could leave
gidecek	**he will go** ✓	will go	will go	be destined for	go
gitmelilerdi	**they should have gone** ✓	they should go	they need to get it	go	they have to go
gitmişlerse	**if they had gone**✓	they have gone	if they went	go	if they're gone
gidebilecekse	**if he will be able to go**✓	go abilecekse	can go	go	if you can go
yapmalılarsa	**if they should do** ✓	sign mAIlIArsA	if they're making	go	do they
masalarımızla	**with our tables** ✓	our table	our table	table	our desks
English	ITUMorphTrans4ET	Google	Bing		Yandex
if he can go	**gidebilirse**✓	O gidebilirsiniz	Eğer gidebilir		eğer gidip o
he will go	**gidecek** ✓	O gidecek ✓	o-ecek gitmek		gidecek ✓
they should have gone	**gitmelilerdi**✓ **gitmelilermiş**✓	Onlar gitmiş olmalı	Onlar gitmiş olmalı		gitmelilerdi ✓
if they had gone	**gitmişlerse**✓ **gitmişseler**✓	onlar gitmişti eğer	Onlar ne gitseydin		eğer gitmiş olsalardı
if he will be able to go	**gidebilecekse**✓	O gitmek mümkün olacak eğer	Eğer o-ecek var olmak güçlü-e doğru gitmek için		eğer gitmek mümkün olacak
if they should do	**yapmalılarsa**✓ **etmelilerse**✓	Onlar yapmalıyım	onlar yoksa		eğer yapmalıyım eğer
with our tables	**listelerimizle**✓ **tablolarımızla**✓	Bizim tablolarla ✓	Bizim tablolarla ✓		bizim tablolar ile ✓

Table 2: Comparison of ITUMorphTrans4ET with other popular systems

words. This doesn't mean that the input may be any English utterance but rather English phrases or sentences which maps to single words in the Turkish side or some compound verb forms such as "telefon etmek" (*to phone*). This FST also contains the list of irregular words for correct transformations: e.g. "to go" with lexical form "go+V2+I" will be converted to "went+I" as the surface form whereas a regular verb "play+V2+I" will be converted to "played+I". There are some additional rules for specific cases such as "clap+ing" which be transferred to "clapping" requiring a character repetition of the letter "p". Finally after obtaining the last surface form such as "playing+am+I", we output this in reverse order[5] by the use of a script.

Table 2 gives the comparison of our proposed system with popular online translation systems of namely Google, Yandex, Bing and Tureng. Since the Tureng MT system is only available from Turkish to English, its results are not provided in the second half of the table. The acceptable translations for each case are marked with check marks in the table. As can be noticed, the proposed system produces better results at word-level translation.

4 Learning Use Cases

Learning a foreign language which belongs to a different language family than the native one as in the case of Turkish and English is a problematic task. Since, there are no stable working translators which may be used as a reference, learning becomes a challenging process for new learners. Most commonly used machine translators get use of statistical methods and do not always produce grammatically correct results. In our study, we focus on obtaining a better learning language system which translates words between Turkish and English in two-way effi-

[5]The order of the words are rearranged so that the resulting sentence is grammatical.

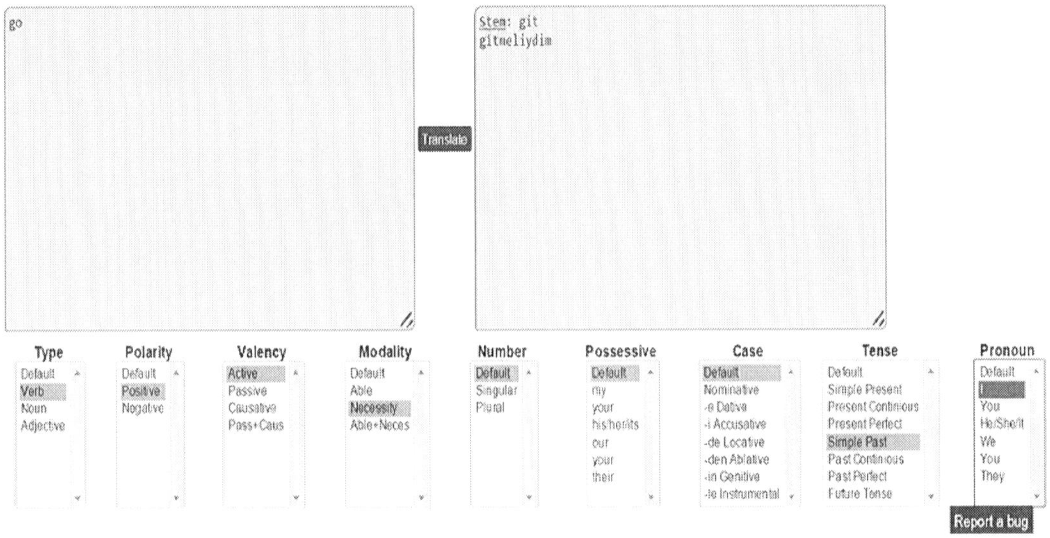

Figure 2: An example output from ITUMorphTrans4ET (from English to Turkish)

ciently by providing a user friendly interface for learners.

4.1 Turkish Learning

Learning Turkish is very tough process especially for learners whose mother tongue is not agglutinative due to the fixed order of suffix concatenations to the end of the words which may become dizzy for the new language learners. To give an example for this problem, instead of saying "gitmişlerdi" (*they had been gone*) one may say "gittilermiş" which is not a valid word in terms of suffix order. In the future, ITUMorphTrans4ET system may detect these mistakes (by the help of additional spelling suggesters) and make produce correct translations. In other term, after having a valid analysis and necessary lexical rules, our system can translate any written Turkish word to English language or vice-versa. We believe that same approach may be used for other agglutinative languages by constructing necessary transfer rules.

Figure 2 shows the preliminary interface of ITUMorphTrans4ET where one may type an English lemma and then select morphological properties by using list boxes below. For this example, the word "go" is typed and its properties are selected as "Verb" for the word type, "Positive" for the polarity and so on. Using these information, our system easily translates the word to "gitmeliydim" (*I should have gone*). We believe by improving our system with a more user-friendly interface, the effect of suffixes in Turkish may be efficiently realized and learned by the users.

4.2 English Learning

As explained in previous sections, learning English is as hard as learning Turkish for native Turkish speakers and has same challenging problems. There exists no translation system that works well from Turkish to English at word level. As a consequence, these translators can not be efficient for language learning purposes. However, ITUMorphTrans4ET presents a very strong translation mechanism for two way Turkish-English word translation. It uses morphological model of words in order to translate words. Using the advantage of the morphological structure, even very complex words can be simplified into meaningful tags and then translated to English. Figure 3 gives an example screen for English learners: The word "gitmeliydim" is translated into "I should have gone".

5 Conclusion & Future Work

In this study, we presented our elementary system to develop an educational application for foreign language learners from Turkish and English language pair. Our system uses finite state transducer technology to help the language learning to learn the morphologically complex structure of an agglutinative language and may be applied to other similar languages by developing a transfer model. Although we couldn't test with on large data sets due to the unavailability of APIs of the used MT systems, our preliminary experiments revealed the better performance of ITUMorphTrans4ET. ITUMorphTrans4ET

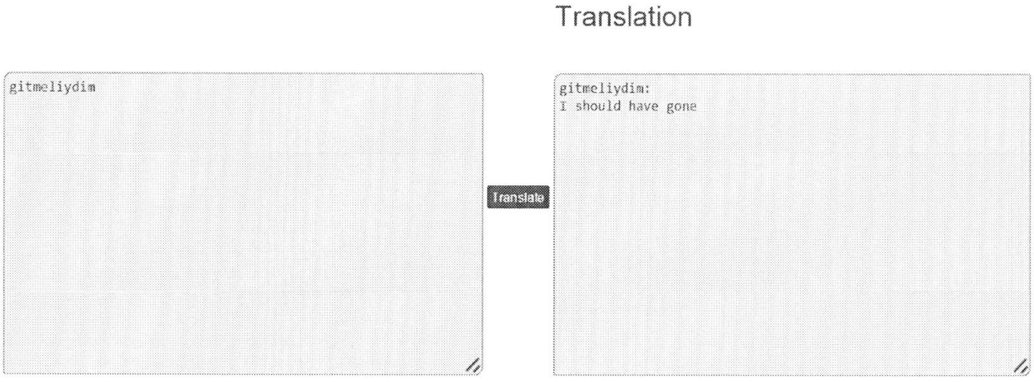

Figure 3: An example output from ITUMorphTrans4ET (from Turkish to English)

may be used in many platforms such as smart boards in classrooms, mobile applications etc. To this end, for future work we plan to focus on improving our system by 1) Developing an user-friendly interactive application for foreign Turkish learners, 2) Developing a mobile application for accessing the interface more easily, and 3) Stepping up to sentence level instead of word level translation by using statistical machine learning approaches. The implementation of ITUMorphTrans4ET is available through a web service found at http://tools.nlp.itu.edu.tr/ (Eryiğit, 2014).

Acknowledgments

The authors want to thank Dilara Torunoğlu Selamet for her valuable contributions to this work.

References

Cyril Allauzen, Michael Riley, Johan Schalkwyk, Wojciech Skut, and Mehryar Mohri. 2007. Openfst: A general and efficient weighted finite-state transducer library. In *Implementation and Application of Automata*, pages 11–23. Springer.

Kenneth R Beesley and Lauri Karttunen. 2003. Finite-state morphology: Xerox tools and techniques. *CSLI, Stanford.*

Arianna Bisazza and Marcello Federico. 2009. Morphological pre-processing for Turkish to English statistical machine translation. In *IWSLT*, pages 129–135.

Stephen Pit Corder. 1983. A role for the mother tongue. *Language transfer in language learning*, pages 85–97.

Aydin Y. Durgunoglu and Barbara J. Hancin-Bhatt. 1992. The role of first language in the second-language reading process. Technical report, University Illinois at Urbana-Champaign.

Ilknur Durgar El-Kahlout and Kemal Oflazer. 2010. Exploiting morphology and local word reordering in English-to-Turkish phrase-based statistical machine translation. *Audio, Speech, and Language Processing, IEEE Transactions on*, 18(6):1313–1322.

Gülşen Eryiğit. 2014. ITU Turkish NLP web service. In *Proceedings of the Demonstrations at the 14th Conference of the EACL*, Gothenburg, Sweden, April. Association for Computational Linguistics.

Elif Eyigöz, Daniel Gildea, and Kemal Oflazer. 2013. Simultaneous word-morpheme alignment for statistical machine translation. In *Proceedings of NAACL-HLT*, pages 32–40.

Kenji Hakuta, Yuko Goto Butler, and Daria Witt. 2000. How long does it take English learners to attain proficiency? *University of California Linguistic Minority Research Institute.*

Kenji Hakuta. 1999. A critical period for second language acquisition? a status review. *National Center for Early Development of Learning. Chapel Hill, NC: University of North Carolina.*

Krister Lindén, Miikka Silfverberg, and Tommi Pirinen. 2009. Hfst tools for morphology–an efficient open-source package for construction of morphological analyzers. In *State of the Art in Computational Morphology*, pages 28–47. Springer.

Mehryar Mohri. 1997. Finite-state transducers in language and speech processing. *Computational linguistics*, 23(2):269–311.

Håkan Ringbom. 1987. *The role of the first language in foreign language learning*, volume 34. Multilingual Matters Ltd.

Emmanuel Roche and Yves Schabes. 1997. *Finite-state language processing*. MIT press.

Muhammet Şahin, Umut Sulubacak, and Gülşen Eryiğit. 2013. Redefinition of Turkish morphology using flag diacritics. In *Proceedings of The Tenth Symposium on Natural Language Processing (SNLP-2013)*, Phuket, Thailand, October.

Michael Swan. 1997. The influence of the mother tongue on second language vocabulary acquisition and use. *Vocabulary: Description, acquisition and pedagogy*, pages 156–180.

Reyyan Yeniterzi and Kemal Oflazer. 2010. Syntax-to-morphology mapping in factored phrase-based statistical machine translation from English to Turkish. In *Proceedings of the 48th Annual Meeting of ACL*, pages 454–464. Association for Computational Linguistics.

Chinese Grammatical Error Diagnosis Using Ensemble Learning

Yang Xiang, Xiaolong Wang†, Wenying Han, and Qinghua Hong
Intelligent Computing Research Center,
Harbin Institute of Technology Shenzhen Graduate School, China
{xiangyang.hitsz, hanwenying09, hongqh65}@gmail.com,
†wangxl@insun.hit.edu.cn

Abstract

Automatic grammatical error detection for Chinese has been a big challenge for NLP researchers for a long time, mostly due to the flexible and irregular ways in the expressing of this language. Strictly speaking, there is no evidence of a series of formal and strict grammar rules for Chinese, especially for the spoken Chinese, making it hard for foreigners to master this language. The CFL shared task provides a platform for the researchers to develop automatic engines to detect grammatical errors based on a number of manually annotated Chinese spoken sentences. This paper introduces HITSZ's system for this year's Chinese grammatical error diagnosis (CGED) task. Similar to the last year's task, we put our emphasis mostly on the error detection level and error type identification level but did little for the position level. For all our models, we simply use supervised machine learning methods constrained to the given training corpus, with neither any heuristic rules nor any other referenced materials (except for the last years' data). Among the three runs of results we submitted, the one using the ensemble classifier Random Feature Subspace (HITSZ_Run1) gained the best performance, with an optimal F1 of 0.6648 for the detection level and 0.2675 for the identification level.

1 Introduction

Automatic grammatical error detection for Chinese has been a big challenge for NLP researchers for a long time, mostly due to the flexible and irregular ways in the expressing of this language. Different from English which follows grammatical rules strictly (i.e. subject-verb agreement, or strict tenses and modals), the Chinese language has no verb tenses or numbers and endures heavily for the incompleteness of grammatical elements in a sentence (i.e. the zero subject or verb or object). Some examples are shown below in Table 1.

	Examples
1.	四月/最/熱。 April is the hottest.
2.	我/一/看到/你/**就**/覺得/非常/開心。 I feel very happy as soon as I see you.
3.	他們**很**高興。 They are very happy

Table 1. Some typical examples for special grammatical usage in Chinese.

In the above table, the first sentence contains no verb elements in the Chinese version. In the Chinese language, the adjectives will not co-occur with copulas in many cases. So if we add a *be* (*是*) into the sentence (四月/是/最/熱), it will be grammatically incorrect. In the second sentence, the conjunction *就* has nothing to do with the meaning of the whole sentence, but it is a necessary grammatical component when collocate with the word 一 to express the meaning of *as soon as*. The adverb *很* is an essential element for the third sentence which corresponds to the word *very* in the English version. However, we can simply remove *very* but cannot remove *很* due to some implicit grammatical rules. Overall, the expression of the Chinese language is flexible and the grammar of Chinese is complicated and sometimes hard to summarize, so that it is very difficult for foreign language learners to learn Chinese as the second language.

The CFL14 and 15 shared tasks provide a platform for learners and researchers to observe various cases of grammatical errors and think deep-

Proceedings of The 2nd Workshop on Natural Language Processing Techniques for Educational Applications, pages 99–104,
Beijing, China, July 31, 2015. ©2015 Association for Computational Linguistics and Asian Federation of Natural Language Processing

er about the intrinsic of these errors. The goal of the shared task is to develop computer-assisted tools to help detect four types of grammatical errors in the written Chinese. The error types include *Missing, Redundant, Disorder* and *Selection*. And in last years shared task, several groups submitted their report, employing different supervised learning methods in which some groups obtained good results in detection and classification (Yu et al., 2014). Similar to the last year's task, we put our emphasis mostly on the error detection level and error type identification level but did little for the position level although this year's task includes the evaluation on this level.

In this paper, we use supervised learning methods to solve the error detection and identification sub tasks. Different from most of previous work, we didn't use any external language materials except for the dataset for the year 2014's shared task. What we adopt include feature extraction, data construction and ensemble learning. We also report some of our observations towards the errors and summarize some conceivable rules, which might be useful for future developers. At last, we analyze the limitation of our work and propose several directions for improvement.

The following of this paper is organized as: Section 2 briefly introduces the literature in this community. Section 3 shows some observations towards the data provided. Section 4 introduces the feature extraction and learning methods we used for the shared task. Section 5 includes experiments and result analysis. And future work and conclusion are arranged at last.

2 Related Work

In the community of grammatical error correction, more work focused on the language of English such as those researches during the CoNLL2013 and 2014 shared tasks (Ng et al., 2013; Ng et al., 2014). A number of English language materials and annotated corpus can be used such that the research on this language went deeper. However, the resource for Chinese is far from enough, and very few previous works are related to Chinese grammatical error correction. Typical ones are the CFL 2014 shared task (Yu et al., 2014) ant the task held in this year. Following, we briefly introduce some previous work related to Chinese grammatical error diagnosis.

Wu et al. proposed two types of language models to detect the error types of word order, omission and redundant, corresponding to three of the types in the shared task. Chang et al. (2012) proposed a probabilistic first-order inductive learning algorithm for error classification and outperformed some basic classifiers. Lee et al. (2014) introduced a sentence level judgment system which integrated several predefined rules and N-gram based statistical features. Cheng et al. (2014) shown several methods including CRF and SVM, together with frequency learning from a large N-gram corpus, to detect and correct word ordering errors.

In the last year's shared task, there are also some novel ideas and results for the error diagnosis. Chang et al. (2014)'s work included manually constructed rules and rules that automatically generated, the latter of which are something like frequent patterns from the training corpus. Zhao et al. (2014)'s employed a parallel corpus from the web, which is a language exchange website called Lang-8, and used this corpus to training a statistical machine translator. Zampieri and Tan (2014) used a journalistic corpus as the reference corpus and took advantage of the frequent N-grams to detect the errors in the data provided by the shared task. NTOU's submission for the shared task was a traditional supervised one, which extracted word N-grams and POS N-grams as features and trained using SVM (Lin et al., 2014). In their work, they also employed a reference corpus as the source of N-gram frequencies.

Our submission was similar to NTOU's work whereas we didn't use any large scale textural corpus as references. Our target was to see to what extent can the supervised learner learn only from the limited resource and what types of classifiers perform better in this task.

3 Data Analysis

We show some of our observations towards the training data in this section. What we observed are some frequent cases among the error types *Missing* and *Redundant*.

For the error type *Missing*, we noticed that errors often occur in some certain cases. For example, the auxiliary word 的 (of/'s) accounts for 11.35% in all the *Missing* sentences (and 7.93% sentences contain 的 in the training data are incorrect). One of the most frequent missing cases is the missing between an adjective (~est for short) and a noun. For instance, 最好(的) 電影院 (the best cinema), 附近(的) 飯店(a near restaurant), and 我(的)日常生活(my daily life). From the English translation we see that there is no 's or of in the phrase such as *the girl's dress* (女孩

的衣服) or *a friend of mine* (我的一個朋友), but in the grammar of Chinese, a 的 is inserted due to the incompleteness of the expressions.

For the error type *Redundant*, the word 了 (an auxiliary word related to a perfect tense) accounts for 10.88% in all the *Redundant* sentences (and 21.78% sentences contain 了 are incorrect). The word is redundant when the sentence contains nothing related to a perfect tense. For instance, 我第一次去(了) 英國留學。 (I studied abroad in Britain for the first time.) and 當時他不老(了)。(He wasn't old at that time.). So we can judge whether the word is redundant according to the tense of the sentence.

Words that are grammatical incorrect are almost function words, which behave differently in the grammars for Chinese and English (or other languages). Typical examples are 是 (is), 都 (auxiliary), 有 (be), 會(will), 在 (in/at), 要(will), etc. However, we didn't do much towards specific words in our research but only recognize there should be some frequent rules that we can follow. And we will further discuss some proposals later.

4 Supervised Learning

In this work, neither did we use any external corpora except for the dataset for the year 2014's shared task, nor are any language specific heuristic rules or frequent patterns included. We were going to see what kind of features and what type of supervised learners can benefit this problem most. As declared previously, we did little for the position level extraction, so we introduce mostly on feature extraction, model selection and the construction of the training data.

4.1 Feature Extraction

For this task, we tried several kinds of features such words, POS (part-of-speech), as well as syntactic parse trees and dependency trees. Finally, we find that POS Tri-gram features perform stably and generate the best results. Therefore, we define the POS Tri-gram for sentential classification at first.

For each word in a sentence, we extract the following triple as the Tri-gram for this word: <POS-1, POS, POS+1>. And for the beginning and the ending of a sentence, we add two indicators to make up the column vectors. For example, in the sentence這/一天/很/有意思。(This day is very interesting.), the sentence-level POS features are (r, m, zg, l) the features for the word這 (This) are <start, r, m>[1].

In addition, we extract the relative frequency (probability) for each triple based on the CLP 14 and 15 dataset as *P(<POS-1, POS, POS+1>)*. In the experiment, we noticed that the frequency features are also good indicators to detect candidates for grammatical errors.

To summarize, we extract two types of POS Tri-gram features: the binary Tri-gram and the probabilistic Tri-gram. The binary Tri-gram demands that if the sentence contains this Tri-gram (i.e. <start, r, m>), the corresponding position in the gram vector (the union set of all possible Tri-grams after removing those with very low frequencies) is set to be 1. For probabilistic Tri-gram, the position is set to be the relative frequency (the proportion for the Tri-gram).

4.2 Supervised Learning

After feature extraction, we put the features into several supervised learners. We use a series of single classifiers such as Naïve Bayes (NB), Decision Tree (DT), Support Vector Machines (SVM) and Maximum Entropy (ME), and ensemble learners Adaboost (AB), Random Forest (RF) and Random Feature Subspace (RFS). RF is an ensemble of several DTs, each of which samples training instances with replacement and samples features without replacement. RFS is an ensemble classifier based on feature sampling which takes results trained on different feature subspace as majority voters. The classifiers are from Weka (Hall et al., 2009).

We take those training sentences with annotated errors as positive instances and subsample the correct sentences as negative ones. Through tuning towards the proportion of negative instances, we discovered that the number of negative instances also affected the final results.

5 Experiment and Analysis

In the experiment, we use the training data from this year's and last year's shared tasks. Table 2 lists the number of sentences for each type in the training data. Since the scale of this year's data is really small, we add last year's corpus into the training data and do cross validations in the training steps. Table 2 lists the number of sentences for each error type in these two years' dataset.

Our experiments cover training data construction, feature selection and supervised learning.

[1] The POS tags are generated by LTP (Liu et al., 2011)

Method	Detection Level				Identification Level			
	Accuracy	Precision	Recall	F1	Accuracy	Precision	Recall	F1
ME	0.4985	0.3235	0.0028	0.0055	0.4975	0.1154	0.00075	0.0015
SVM	0.5144	0.6091	0.0803	0.1418	0.4969	0.4677	0.0453	0.0825
NB	0.5146	0.5562	0.1448	0.2297	0.4771	0.3765	0.0698	0.1177
DT	0.6255	0.6285	0.6140	**0.6211**	0.5249	0.5321	0.4128	0.4649
RFS	0.6284	**0.7479**	0.3873	0.5103	0.6064	**0.7245**	0.3433	0.4658
RF	0.6510	0.7173	0.4985	0.5882	**0.6121**	0.6817	0.4208	0.5203
AB	**0.6654**	0.7177	**0.5453**	0.6197	0.6105	0.6700	**0.4355**	**0.5279**

Table 3. CV results based on POS Tri-gram features

Method	Detection Level				Identification Level			
	Accuracy	Precision	Recall	F1	Accuracy	Precision	Recall	F1
ME	0.4985	0.3235	0.0028	0.0055	0.4975	0.1154	0.00075	0.0015
SVM	0.5144	0.6091	0.0803	0.1418	0.4969	0.4677	0.0453	0.0825
NB	0.5145	0.5443	0.1783	0.2686	0.4661	0.3532	0.0815	0.1324
DT	0.6306	0.6354	**0.6130**	0.6230	0.5285	0.5375	0.4087	0.4644
RFS	0.6574	0.7338	0.4940	0.5905	0.6200	0.7005	0.4193	0.5246
RF	0.6588	**0.7554**	0.4695	0.5791	**0.6300**	**0.7305**	0.4120	0.5269
AB	**0.6618**	0.6899	0.5878	**0.6347**	0.5951	0.6323	**0.4545**	**0.5289**

Table 4. CV results based on POS Tri-gram and probability features

Error type	No. in 15	No. in 14
Correct	2205	5541
Disorder	306	710
Redundant	430	1803
Missing	620	2201
Selection	849	827

Table 2. Error type distribution for the two years' shared tasks.

We tried several groups of training data, different combinations of features and a variety of classifiers in the training phase.

5.1 Training Data Construction

As mentioned previously, the sentences that contain no grammatical errors behave as the negative instances for training. To avoid imbalance between the positive and negative instances, negative ones were randomly selected to construct the training set. At last, we divided the training data into 8 parts and used 8-fold cross validation (CV) for the classifiers. We found that, when we selected 4000 negative instances, the system achieved the best results.

5.2 Feature Selection

As mentioned in §4.1, we investigate the features POS Tri-gram and POS Tri-gram + POS Tri-gram probability. We report the CV results generated by four single classifiers and three ensemble classifiers in Table 3 and Table 4 for the two set of features, respectively. The results have been optimized through tuning the parameter settings for each classifier.

From the results, we find that the ensemble classifiers generally perform better than the single ones, and AB achieves the best results for detection and identification.

5.3 Final Results

Among the three runs of results we submitted, the first run is the best. We show the results in Table 5 and compare them with the CV results.

Accuracy	Precision	Recall	F1
Detection Level			
0.509	0.5047	0.974	0.6648
Identification Level			
0.173	0.2401	0.302	0.2675

Table 5. The final results

This submission is generated by the ensemble classifier RFS by using POS Tri-gram and probability features. We see that the performance of the identification level greatly falls behind that in the cross validation. One of the possible reasons for this gap, we consider is the setting of instances, which may be quite distinct between the training and the testing data. And another possible reason is the reasonability of the probability features.

5.4 Analysis

Compare the results generated by the two feature sets (Table 1), it can be seen that the second fea-

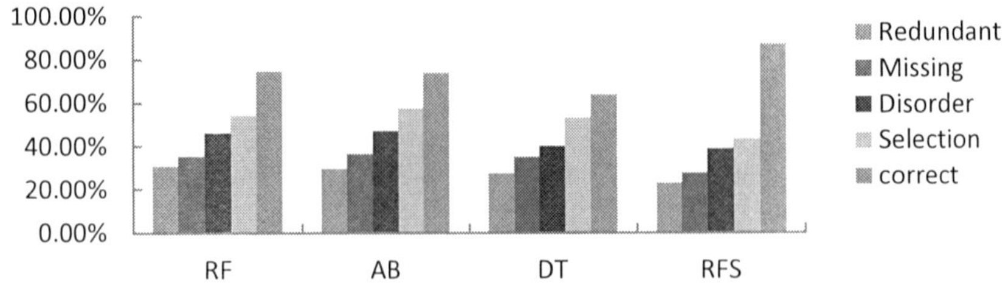

Figure 1. Accuracy of the four error types and the correct type on four classifiers that perform best.

ture set outperforms the first, on both the detection level and the identification level. To some extent, it indicates that the patterns for the grammatical phrases may frequently occur in the datasets.

Further, we pick up the last four classifiers which perform relatively better on the task data, including DT and three ensemble classifiers, and do statistical analysis on the true positive rates during cross validation (Figure 1). The results reveal that the difficulty on judging decreases from Redundant, Missing to Disorder and Selection. In addition, the accuracy for the correct label is not quite high, leading to a number of false negative sentences.

Through observation, we found several cases might affect the predicting results. A typical case is that a grammatically wrong sentence can be corrected through several ways, corresponding to more than one error types. For example, the sentence 他馬上準備上學 (He is preparing for school.) can be classified to any of the four types:

	Correct Sentence	Type
1.	他(馬上)準備上學	Redundant
2.	他(準備)(馬上)上學	Disorder
3.	他(很快地)準備上學	Selection
4.	他馬上要準備上學(了)	Missing

Table 6. Example on multiple ways for correction.

All the four directions are reasonable but the dataset only provide the third one. Therefore, these data may create confusion for classification and should be considered in the future work. In addition, some annotation maybe not so cleat, for instance in the sentence 但是這幾天我發現(到)你有一些生活上不好的習慣 (But these days I noticed some bad habits on you in your daily life). The given annotation is *selection*, but we think *redundant* is much more reasonable.

6 Future Work

According to the observations towards the training data, we think the following direct proposal is learning from the position level, just as the shared task demands. On this level, we can extract more pointed features, integrating both syntactic and semantic ones. Besides, for the sentential level classification, the deep neural network based methods (i.e. Convolutional Neural Networks) are expected, with traditional features or embeddings, to detect more structured rules. In addition, we deem that dependency tree features may be useful and should be further developed. And improvement may also be achieved by mining the confusion in annotation (i.e. the difference between *selection* and *redundant*).

7 Conclusion

In this paper, we introduce the ensemble learning based method used in the CFL shared task for Chinese grammatical error diagnosis. We report some of our observations towards the training data, features and learners we used in our experiments. Different from most previous work, we didn't use any other external language corpus for reference and we didn't use any rules either. The results show that the ensemble methods perform better than the single classifiers based on our simple features. From the results, we see space for further development.

Acknowledgement

This work was supported in part by the National Natural Science Foundation of China (61272383, 61173075 and 61203378), and the Strategic Emerging Industry Development Special Funds of Shenzhen (JCYJ20120613151940045).

Reference

Ru-Yng Chang, Chung-Hsien Wu, and Philips Kokoh Prasetyo. 2012. Error Diagnosis of Chinese Sentences using Inductive Learning Algorithm and Decomposition-based Testing Mechanism. ACM Trans. Asian Language Information Processing.

Tao-Hsing Chang, Yao-Ting Sung, Jia-Fei Hong and Jen-I Chang. 2014.KNGED:a Tool for Grammatical Error Diagnosis of Chinese Sentences. In Proceedings of the 1st Workshop on Natural Language Processing Techniques for Educational Applications (NLPTEA'14), Nara, Japan, 30 November, 2014, pp. 48-55.

Shuk-Man Cheng, Chi-Hsin Yu, and Hsin-Hsi Chen. 2014. Chinese Word Ordering Errors Detection and Correction for Non-Native Chinese Language Learners. In Proceedings of COLING 2014, pp. 279-289.

Mark Hall, Eibe Frank, Geoffrey Holmes, Bernhard Pfahringer, Peter Reutemann, Ian H. Witten. 2009. The WEKA Data Mining Software: An Update; SIGKDD Explorations, Volume 11, Issue 1.

Lung-Hao Lee, Liang-Chih Yu, Kuei-Ching Lee, et al. 2014. A Sentence Judgment System for Grammatical Error Detecgtion. In Proceedings of COLING 2014: System Demonstrations, 67–70.

Chuan-Jie Lin and Shao-Heng Chan. 2014. Description of NTOU Chinese Grammar Checker in CFL 2014. In Proceedings of the 1st Workshop on Natural Language Processing Techniques for Educational Applications (NLPTEA'14), Nara, Japan, 30 November, 2014, pp. 75-78.

Ting Liu, Wanxiang Che, Zhenghua Li. 2011. Language Technology Platform. Journal of Chinese Information Processing. 25(6), pp. 53-62.

Hwee Tou Ng, Siew Mei, Yuanbin Wu, Christian Hadiwinoto and Joel Tetreault. 2013. The CoNLL-2013 Shared Task on Grammatical Error Correction. In Proceedings of the Seventeenth Conference on Computational Natural Language Learning: Shared Task (CoNLL-2013 Shared Task). Sofia, Bulgaria.

Hwee Tou Ng, Siew Mei Wu, Ted Briscoe, Christian Hadiwinoto, Raymond Hendy Susanto and Christopher Bryant. 2014. The CoNLL-2014 Shared Task on Grammatical Error Correction. In Proceedings of the Eighteenth Conference on Computational Natural Language Learning: Shared Task (CoNLL-2014 Shared Task). Baltimore, Maryland.

Chung-Hsien Wu, Chao-Hong Liu, Harris Matthew and Liang-Chih Yu. 2010. Sentence Correction Incorporating Relative Position and Parse Template Language Models, IEEE Trans. on Audio, Speech and Language Processing, vol. 18, no. 6, pp. 1170-1181.

Liang-Chih Yu, Lung-Hao Lee, and Li-Ping Chang (2014). Overview of Grammatical Error Diagnosis for Learning Chinese as a Foreign Language. In Proceedings of the 1st Workshop on Natural Language Processing Techniques for Educational Applications (NLPTEA'14), Nara, Japan, 30 November, 2014, pp. 42-47.

Marcos Zampieri and Liling Tan. 2014. Grammatical Error Detection with Limited Training Data: The Case of Chinese. In Proceedings of the 1st Workshop on Natural Language Processing Techniques for Educational Applications (NLPTEA'14), Nara, Japan, 30 November, 2014, pp. 69-74.

Yinchen Zhao, Mamoru Komachi and Hiroshi Ishikawa. 2014. Extracting a Chinese Learner Corpus from the Web: Grammatical Error Correction for Learning Chinese as a Foreign Language with Statistical Machine Translation. In Proceedings of the 1st Workshop on Natural Language Processing Techniques for Educational Applications (NLPTEA'14), Nara, Japan, 30 November, 2014, pp. 56-61.

Condition Random Fields-based Grammatical Error Detection for Chinese as Second Language

Jui-Feng Yeh, Chan-Kun Yeh, Kai-Hsiang Yu, Ya-Ting Li, Wan-Ling Tsai
Department of Computer Science and Information Engineering, National Chiayi University
No.300 Syuefu Rd., Chiayi City 60004, Taiwan (R.O.C.)
{ralph, s1030484, s1030495, s1013037, s1013048 }@mail.ncyu.edu.tw

Abstract

The foreign learners are not easy to learn Chinese as a second language. Because there are many special rules different from other languages in Chinese. When the people learn Chinese as a foreign language usually make some grammatical errors, such as missing, redundant, selection and disorder. In this paper, we proposed the conditional random fields (CRFs) to detect the grammatical errors. The features based on statistical word and part-of-speech (POS) pattern were adopted here. The relationships between words by part-of-speech are helpful for Chinese grammatical error detection. Finally, we according to CRF determined which error types in sentences. According to the observation of experimental results, the performance of the proposed model is acceptable in precision and recall rates.

1 Introduction

As the world globalize, travel around the world is quicker than before. With the growth of Chinese market and more and more china town. There are more than 1.3 billion people who speak Chinese. That means there is one speak Chinese out of every five people. Chinese is the most spoken language in the world. Sell products to the Chinese people, study and travel around Asia is much easier than before. To speak with foreigners and trade with foreigners we have to understand their language first. So we believe that learning Chinese is important now.

To learn Chinese as second language we have to know not only pronunciations and glyph of the word, but also grammar and the part of speech of Chinese. For example, there are eight parts of speech (nouns, pronouns, adjectives, verbs, adverbs, prepositions, conjunctions, and interjections) in English. But in Chinese there are ten parts of speech (nouns, adjectives, verbs, adverbs, pronouns, interjections, prepositions, conjunctions, auxiliary words, and quantifiers). Nouns indicate the names of people or things, they can be further divided into four sub sorts, proper nouns, common nouns, abstract nouns, time nouns, place nouns. Adjective show the quality or forms of people or things, or the state of action or behavior. Verbs indicate the behaviors, actions or changes of people or things. They have several subsidiary categories: modal verbs, tendency verbs and deciding verb. Adverb is used in front of verbs or adjectives to show degree, extent, time or negation. Pronoun is replace nouns or numerals. Preposition introduces nouns, pronouns or other linguistic units to verbs or adjectives and show the relationship between time, space, objects or methods. Conjunction connects words, phrases or sentences.

With Chinese become more popular. But it is not an easy language to learn, you will make a fool of yourself even if just one word mistake. More and more people pay their attention to Chinese grammar error. We may not write the right Chinese sentence all the time. Sometimes we make some mistakes such as, overuse preposition, overuse of "a/an", semantic overlap and quantifier error. In the past, the way to detect the grammar mistakes is extremely inefficient. People usually correct grammar mistakes by manual work.

In recent year, there are many researches about Chinese grammar. There are few papers help us as reference. Li et al. (2012) proposed a hierarchical structure of dependency relations based on CDG for Chinese, in which the constraints have been partitioned into three hierarchies: in-the-phrase, between-the-phrase and between-the simple-sentence. And Li, Z., Zhang et al (2014) proposed to integrate the POS (part-of-speech) tagging and parsing can reduce the complexity and improve the accuracy of parsing. Jiang et al. (2012) divided

Proceedings of The 2nd Workshop on Natural Language Processing Techniques for Educational Applications, pages 105–110,
Beijing, China, July 31, 2015.

Table 1. Example of error types.

Error Types	Error Sentence	Correct Sentence
Missing Error	我(Nh) 送(VD) 你(Nh) 那裡(D)	我(Nh) 送(VD) 你(Nh) ***到(VCL)*** 那裡(Ncd)
Redundant Error	他(Nh) 是(SHI) 我(Nh) ***的(DE)*** 以前(Nd) 的(DE) 室友(Na)	他(Nh) 是(SHI) 我(Nh) 以前(Nd) 的(DE) 室友(Na)
Selection Error	吳(Nb) 先生(Na) 是(SHI) 修理(VC) 腳踏車(Na) 的(DE) ***拿手(Nv)***	吳(Nb) 先生(Na) 是(SHI) 修理(VC) 腳踏車(Na) 的(DE) ***好手(Na)***
Disorder Error	所以(Cbb) 我(Nh) 不會(D) 讓(VL) ***失望(VH) 她(Nh)***	所以(Cbb) 我(Nh) 不會(D) 讓(VL) ***她(Nh) 失望(VH)***

Chinese grammar into three groups: morphology of content words, morphology of empty words and syntax. And each group is subdivided. Jiang et al. (2012) proposed the effectiveness of the XML and the goodness of XML structure these two parts compose XML syntax check. They improved local tree grammar of the XML document type definition, and then do XML validity checking in the grammatical structure based on the document type definition. Rozovskaya et al. (2012) presented a linguistically-motivated, holistic framework for correcting grammatical verb mistakes. Describe and evaluate several methods of selecting verb candidates, an algorithm for determining the verb type, and a type-driven verb error correction system. And they gloss a subset of the FCE dataset with gold verb candidates and gold verb type. Lee et al. (2014) develops a sentence judgment system using both rule-based and n-gram statistical methods to detect grammatical errors in sentences written by CFL learners. Users can input Chinese sentences into the proposed system to check for possible grammatical errors. Wu et al. (2012) through examining the collected English-to-Chinese corpus composed of error sentences, in contrast to the errors commonly made by learners of ESL such as the use of articles and prepositions, we found that learners of Chinese whose L1 is English tend to produce sentences with word order, lexical choice, redundancy, and omission errors. And they present an approach using the proposed Relative Position Language Model (RP) and Parse Template Language Model (PT) to deal with the error correction problem, which is especially suitable for the correction of word order errors that comprise about one third of the errors made by learners of Chinese as a Second Language. The four error types considered for correction in their paper are errors of Lexical Choice, Redundancy, Omission, and Word Order. In this paper, we show the four error types in Table 1. Islam et al. (2010) use the Google n-gram data set in a back-off fashion. And it increases the performance of the method. Their method can be applied to other languages for which Google n-grams are available. Sun, X., & Nan, X. (2010) defined the phrase's format to "Modifier + head + complement".

In our method, we tag some labels such as POS and binary variables in the sentences. In the section II, we described the models how to train the corpus by CRF. And show the experiment in the section III.

2 Method

In this section, the architecture of our system is illustrated in Figure 1. Then we will describe the grammatical error detection using CRF in the section 2.2. And the procedures distinguish into two parts: training phase and test phase.

Table 2. Punctuation tagged by CKIP Autotag.

COLONCATEGORY	(：)
COMMACATEGORY	(，)
DASHCATEGORY	(－)
ETCCATEGORY	(…)
EXCLAMATIONCATEGORY	(！)
PARENTHESISCATEGORY	(（）)
PAUSECATEGORY	(、)
PERIODCATEGORY	(。)
QUESTIONCATEGORY	(？)
SEMICOLONCATEGORY	(；)
SPCHANGECATEGORY	(‖)

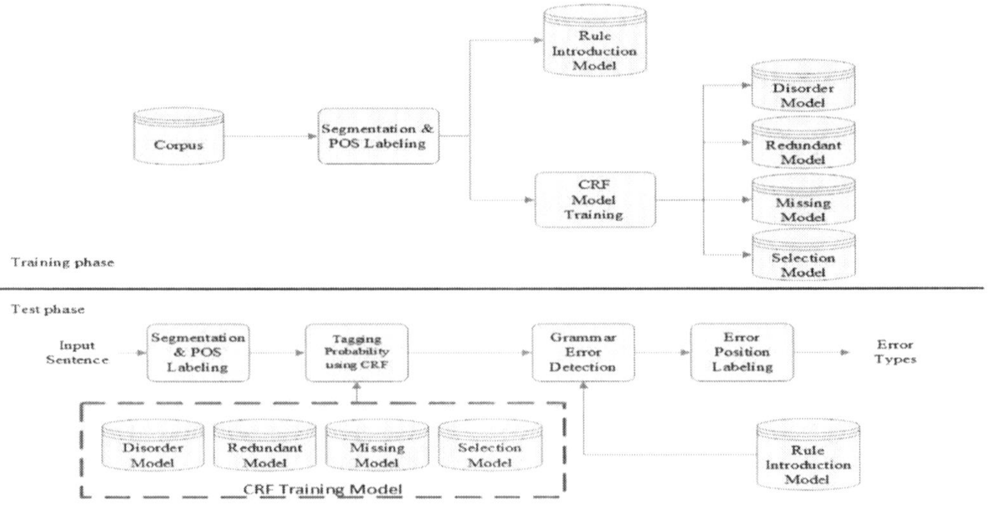

Figure 1. The Architecture of Our System

2.1 Data Preprocessing

CKIP Autotag is a word segment system which made by Taiwan Academia Sinica. CKIP Autotag can segment a long Chinese sentence into Chinese word. And then tag the punctuation (punctuation are listed in Table 2) and the POS to the word. This system classifies Chinese word into 47 different POS.

We use this system to chunking words and tagging the POS on the sentence. We survey the grammar of Chinese sentence by CKIP Autotag. And observe the relation between the words by the POS.

2.2 Condition Random Fields

Conditional random fields (CRFs) is a class of statistical modelling method that is generally applied in machine learning and pattern recognition, where they are used for structured prediction. It was an extension of both Maximum Entropy Model (MEMs) and Hidden Markov Models (HMMs) that was firstly introduced by Lafferty et al., 2001.Whereas an ordinary classifier predicts a label for a single sample without regard to adjacent samples. A CRF can take context into account. It's a discriminative of undirected probabilistic graphical model. It is used to encode known relationships between observations and construct consistent interpretations. Conditional random field defined conditional probability distribution P(Y|X) of given sequence given input sentence. Y is the "class label" sequence and X denotes as the observation word sequence.

A common used special case of CRFs is linear chain, which has a distribution of:

$$P_{\Lambda}(y|x) = \frac{\exp(\sum_{t=1}^{T}\sum_{k}\lambda_k f_k(y_{t-1},y_t,x,t))}{Z_x} \quad (1)$$

Where $f_k(y_{t-1}, y_t, x, t)$ is usually an indicator function. λ_k is the learned weight of the feature and Z_x is the normalization factor that sum the probability of all state sequences. The feature functions can measure any aspect of a state transition, y_{t-1} to y_t and the entire observation sequence, x, centered at the current time step, t.

Here we use three conditional random field models to calculate the conditional probability of the missing sentences, redundant sentences, disorder sentences and error selection sentences.

In training phase, we give the matrix {Word, POS, TAG} to denote the sentence of the words in the train set. Such as {去, VCL, T} or {去, D, F}, the word "去(go)" has many part-of-speech in different sentences. The tag "T" means correct word in current sentence and tag "F" means error word in current sentence. Then we use this training data to generate the model by Conditional random fields.

In testing phase, we segment and tag POS labeling by CKIP Autotag. Then we also use the matrix {Word, POS} to denote the words. After preprocessing, we can get the tag's probability of testing words by our training models using CRF++.

For example, input the sentence of "但是(but) 駕駛(driver) 都(neither) 裝作(pretend) 沒(not)

看到(see) 或者(or) 聽到(hear) 我(me) 了(interjection)". There are some probabilities from different models, "Missing 0.872773, Redundant 0.465524, Selection 0.832839" and judge it is a redundant error. So we found every word's probability in this sentence. The probability of words are show in Table 3. And we found the error word is "了".

Table 3. Probability of Words in the Sentence.

Word	POS	Probability
但是	Cbb	T/0.963663
駕駛	VC	T/0.986188
都	D	T/0.975163
裝作	VF	T/0.970347
沒	D	T/0.962676
看到	VE	T/0.984734
或者	Caa	T/0.953170
聽到	VE	T/0.988986
我	Nh	T/0.997955
了	T	*F/0.579991*

According the probability of tagging, we can determine what type's error and speculate the position in the sentence.

2.3 Rule Induction

There are many special cases of selection error types in Chinese. Such as quantifier is one case of all. In English, we usually use "a" or "an" to denote quantifier.

But Chinese needs more different quantifiers then the other language. In many cases, Chinese use '個' as a quantifier. There are more times we do not use '個' as a quantifier. About quantifier of human we should use '位' or '個'. About quantifier of animals we should use '隻', '匹', '頭', or '條'. About quantifier of things we should use '件'. About quantifier of buildings we should use '座' or '棟'. About quantifier of transportations we should use '臺', '輛', '架' or '艘' etc.

We also focused on finding the ordering type of the wrong words. There are some rules which we follow to finding ordering error.

- Behind the words "把 (let)" is connected the POS 'Nh' or 'Na' or 'Nep'.
- Behind the POS 'VA' is connected the word "跟(with)", and the POS 'Nh' or 'Na' also is connected behind the words "跟(with)".
- Behind the words "應該(maybe)" or "好像(like)" or "到底(at last)" is connected the POS 'Nh' or 'Na'.
- Behind the word "已經(already)" is connected the POS 'Neqa' or 'Neu', and the POS 'P' or 'Na' or 'VA' is connected behind the POS 'Neqa' or 'Neu'.

Above those rules, we can enhance our method during the detection grammatical errors.

3 Result

To evaluate the performance of our system, we used three parameters: precision, recall and f-score.

Precision is the fraction of retrieved documents that are relevant to the query.

$$\text{Precision} = \frac{tp}{tp + fp}$$

Recall is the fraction of the documents that are relevant to the query that are successfully retrieved.

$$\text{Recall} = \frac{tp}{tp + fn}$$

F1-Score is a measure of a test's accuracy. It considers both the precision and the recall of the test to compute the score.

$$\text{F1} - \text{score} = 2 * \frac{Presision * Recall}{Presision + Recall}$$

The comparative study of all the three cases has done. And a result of these cases are given in the Table 4 and Table 5 with the NLP-TEA 2014 dataset.

In this paper, we collect 2,212 sentences in training dataset. And it contains 622 sentences of missing, 435 sentences of redundant, 849 sentences of selection and 306 sentences of disorder. Then we use two dataset 1,750 sentences from NLP-TEA 2014 and 1,000 sentences from NLP-TEA 2015.

We can find only use CRF it can't find many error but its precision is better. Then add the rule induction can promote the recall means we can find more error from test data. Although its precision is reduced.

Table 4. Detection level

Method	Precision	Recall	F1
CRF	0.6863	0.2000	0.3097
CRF + Rule Induction	0.5257	0.4674	0.4949

Table 5. Identification level

Method	Precision	Recall	F1-Score
CRF	0.5897	0.1314	0.2150
CRF + Rule Induction	0.3549	0.2320	0.2806

Table 6, Table 7, and Table 8 are the performance with the NLP-TEA 2015 dataset and compare the other team

Table 6. Detection level

	Accuracy	Precision	Recall	F1
NCYU	**0.607**	0.6112	0.588	0.5994
CYUT	0.579	0.7453	0.240	0.3631
NTOU	0.531	0.5164	0.976	0.6754

Table 7. Identification level

	Accuracy	Precision	Recall	F1
NCYU	0.463	0.4451	0.300	**0.3584**
CYUT	0.525	0.6168	0.132	0.2175
NTOU	0.225	0.2848	0.364	0.3196

Table 8. Position level

	Accuracy	Precision	Recall	F1
NCYU	0.374	0.2460	0.122	0.1631
CYUT	0.505	0.5287	0.092	0.1567
NTOU	0.123	0.1490	0.160	0.1543

In detection level (see the Table 6.), our recall is better than CYUT's method. It means we can find more error in dataset. And our precision is better than NTOU's method. It means our find correct error rate is better, although we find error quantity less than NTOU.

In identification level (Table 7.), it show who can find most error and error type is correct. In our method, our recall is nearly NTOU's method, it means we find more correct error type than CYUT's method. But our precision is better than NTOU's method. And our F1-Score is the best in this level.

In position level (Table 8.), our method's precision and recall are between the CYUT's method and NTOU's method. It means our method is not illustrious in this level. We consider the reasons are our correction is not enough standard.

4 Conclusion

In this paper, we present a method using conditional random field model for predicting the grammatical error diagnosis for learning Chinese.

After observe the experiment results, our method is acceptable in NLP-TEA 2015. We believe this system is feasible. This system is useful for a foreign who learn Chinese as a second language. Even the people who use Chinese as a first language might use the wrong grammars.

There are some issues should be revise. First, the CRF models can be improved in some ways, such as words tagging or using the parsing tree. Second, increase the ranking mechanism to find the optimal words to correct the sentence.

In the future, we will pay attention to improve the precision and recall rates in this system. And let it can automatic correct the error if the people input the sentences.

Reference

Islam, A., & Inkpen, D. (2010, August). An unsupervised approach to preposition error correction. In Natural Language Processing and Knowledge Engineering (NLP-KE), 2010 International Conference on (pp. 1-4). IEEE.

Jiang, Y., Wang, T., Lin, T., Wang, F., Cheng, W., Liu, X., ... & Zhang, W. (2012, June). A rule based Chinese spelling and grammar detection system utility. In System Science and Engineering (ICSSE), 2012 International Conference on (pp. 437-440). IEEE.

Jiang, Y., Zhou, Z., Wan, L., Li, M., Zhao, W., Jing, M., & Liu, X. (2012, October). Cross sentence oriented complicated Chinese grammar proofreading method and practice. In Information Management, Innovation Management and Industrial Engineering (ICIII), 2012 International Conference on (Vol. 3, pp. 254-258). IEEE.

Lafferty, J., McCallum, A., and Pereira, F. 2001. Conditional Random Field: Probabilistic models for segmenting and labeling sequence data. In Proceedings of the International Conference on Machine Learning.

Lance A. Ramshaw and Mitchell P. Marcus. 1995. Text chunking using transformation-based learning. In Proceedings of the 3rd Workshop on Very Large

Corpora, pages 82-94. Nocedal, J., and Wright, S. 1999. Numerical optimization. Springer.

Lee, L. H., Yu, L. C., Lee, K. C., Tseng, Y. H., Chang, L. P., & Chen, H. H. (2014). A Sentence Judgment System for Grammatical Error Detection. COLING 2014, 67.

Liang-Chih Yu, Lung-Hao Lee, and Li-Ping Chang (2014). Overview of Grammatical Error Diagnosis for Learning Chinese as a Foreign Language. Proceedings of the 1st Workshop on Natural Language Processing Techniques for Educational Applications (NLPTEA'14), Nara, Japan, 30 November, 2014, pp. 42-47.

Li, P., Liao, L., & Li, X. (2012, July). A hierarchy-based constraint dependency grammar parsing for Chinese. In Audio, Language and Image Processing (ICALIP), 2012 International Conference on (pp. 328-332). IEEE.

Li, Z., Zhang, M., Che, W., Liu, T., & Chen, W. (2014). Joint Optimization for Chinese POS Tagging and Dependency Parsing. Audio, Speech, and Language Processing, IEEE/ACM Transactions on, 22(1), 274-286.

Rozovskaya, A., Roth, D., & Srikumar, V. (2014, April). Correcting grammatical verb errors. In Proceedings of EACL.

Chang, R. Y., Wu, C. H., & Prasetyo, P. K. (2012). Error diagnosis of Chinese sentences using inductive learning algorithm and decomposition-based testing mechanism. ACM Transactions on Asian Language Information Processing (TALIP), 11(1), 3.

Sun, X., & Nan, X. (2010, August). Chinese base phrases chunking based on latent semi-CRF model. In Natural Language Processing and Knowledge Engineering (NLP-KE), 2010 International Conference on (pp. 1-7). IEEE.

Wu, C. H., Liu, C. H., Harris, M., & Yu, L. C. (2010). Sentence correction incorporating relative position and parse template language models. Audio, Speech, and Language Processing, IEEE Transactions on, 18(6), 1170-1181.

Yu, C. H., & Chen, H. H. (2012). Detecting Word Ordering Errors in Chinese Sentences for Learning Chinese as a Foreign Language. In COLING (pp. 3003-3018).

Academia Sinica CKIP. http://ckipsvr.iis.sinica.edu.tw/

CRF++: Yet Another CRF toolkit http://taku910.github.io/crfpp/

Improving Chinese Grammatical Error Correction using Corpus Augmentation and Hierarchical Phrase-based Statistical Machine Translation

Yinchen Zhao **Mamoru Komachi** **Hiroshi Ishikawa**
Graduate School of System Design, Tokyo Metropolitan University, Japan
chou.innchenn@gmail.com
komachi@tmu.ac.jp
ishikawa-hiroshi@tmu.ac.jp

Abstract

In this study, we describe our system submitted to the 2nd Workshop on Natural Language Processing Techniques for Educational Applications (NLP-TEA-2) shared task on Chinese grammatical error diagnosis (CGED). We use a statistical machine translation method already applied to several similar tasks (Brockett et al., 2006; Chiu et al., 2013; Zhao et al., 2014). In this research, we examine corpus-augmentation and explore alternative translation models including syntax-based and hierarchical phrase-based models. Finally, we show variations using different combinations of these factors.

1 Introduction

The concept of "translating" an error sentence into a correct one was first researched by Brockett et al. (2006). They proposed a statistical machine translation (SMT) system with noisy channel model to correct automatically erroneous sentences for learners of English as a Second Language (ESL).

It seems that a statistical machine translation toolkit has become increasingly popular for grammatical error correction. In the CoNLL-2014 shared task on English grammatical error correction (Ng et al., 2014), four teams of 13 participants each used a phrase-based SMT system. Grammatical error correction using a phrase-based SMT system can be improved by tuning using evaluation metrics such as $F_{0.5}$ (Kunchukuttan et al., 2014; Wang et al., 2014) or even a combination of different tuning algorithms (Junczys-Dowmunt and Grundkiewicz, 2014). In addition, SMT can be merged with other methods. For example, the language model-based and rule-based methods can be integrated into a single sophisticated but effective system (Felice et al., 2014).

For Chinese, SMT has also been used to correct spelling errors (Chiu et al., 2013). Furthermore, as is shown in NLP-TEA-1, an SMT system can be applied to Chinese grammatical error correction if we can employ a large-scale learner corpus (Zhao et al., 2014).

In this study, we extend our previous system (Zhao et al., 2014) to the NLP-TEA-2 shared task on Chinese grammatical error diagnosis, which is based on SMT. The main contribution of this study is as follows:

- We investigate the hierarchical phrase-based model (Chiang et al., 2005) and determine that it yields higher recall and thus F score than does the phrase-based model, but is less accurate.
- We increase our Chinese learner corpus by web scraping (Yu et al., 2012; Cheng et al., 2014) and show that the greater the size of the learner corpus, the better the performance.
- We perform minimum error-rate training (Och, 2003) using several evaluation metrics and demonstrate that tuning improves the final F score.

2 Hierarchical phrase-based model

A hierarchical phase-based model for SMT was first suggested by Chiang et al. (2005). The system first achieves proper word alignment, and instead of extracting phrase alignment, the sys-

Proceedings of The 2nd Workshop on Natural Language Processing Techniques for Educational Applications, pages 111–116,
Beijing, China, July 31, 2015.

tem extracts rules in the form of synchronous context-free grammar (SCFG) rules. In a Chinese error correction task, such error-correction rules are extracted as follows:

X → (X_1 一 好消息 X_2, X_1 一个 好消息 X_2)
(a piece of good news)
X → (我 有, 我 有)
(I have)
X → (告诉 你, 告诉 你)
(to tell you)

The symbols X and X_i here are non-terminal and represent all possible phrases. In addition, glue rules are used to combine a sequence of Xs to form an S.

The glue rules are given as:

S → (X_1, X_1)

S → (S_1X_2, S_1X_2)

A complete derivation of this simple example can then be written:

S → (X_1, X_2)
→ (X_3 一 好消息 X_4, X_3 一个 好消息 X_4)
→ (我 有 一 好消息 X_4, 我 有 一个 好消息 X_4)
→ (我 有 一 好消息 告诉 你, 我 有 一个 好消息 告诉 你)
(I have a piece of good news to tell you)

To determine a weight of a derivation, this model utilizes features such as generation probability, lexical weights, and phrase penalty. In addition, to avoid too many distinct yet similar translations, rules are constrained by certain filters that, for example, limit the length of the initial phrase the number of non-terminals per rule.

3 Chinese Learner Corpora

3.1 Lang-8 Learner Corpus

The Lang-8 Chinese Learner Corpus was built by extracting error-correct sentence pairs from the Internet (Mizumoto et al., 2011; Zhao et al., 2014). We use it as a training corpus for our SMT-based grammatical error diagnosis system in NLP-TEA-1.

However, after we analyzed edit distance (ED) between error-correct sentence pairs based on word level, we determined it may not be suitable for training our translation model. As Figugre 1 shows, NLP-TEA-2 training data has ED mostly from 1 to 3 whereas Lang-8 Chinese Corpus has many ED longer than 4.

This is reasonable because the NLP-TEA-2 training data are extracted from essays written by high-level Chinese learners and, in most cases, these learners produce only one- or two-word-mistakes. By contrast, Lang-8 is a language exchange social networking website where sentences are written by language learners of any level. If we use this corpus as it currently exists, sentences having too long ED may confuse the SMT system.

Therefore, we cleaned the Lang-8 Chinese Learner Corpus by randomly sampling sentence pairs whose ED is between 4 and 8 and deleting sentences pairs whose ED is longer than 8. This ensures it has a similar ED distribution to that of the NLP-TEA-2 training data. After cleaning, the number of sentences in the corpus decreased from 95,000 to approximately 58,000.

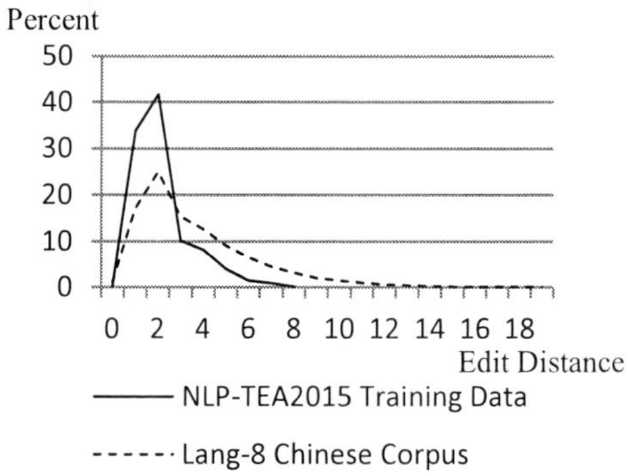

Figure 1: Distribution of ED in different data sets. The distribution of ED in the Lang-8 Chinese Learner Corpus shown here is prior to cleaning.

3.2 HSK Dynamic Essay Corpus

In this shared task, we augment the Chinese learner corpus with another learner corpus extracted from the Internet (Yu et al., 2012; Cheng et al., 2014). The HSK Dynamic Essay Corpus[1] is one such corpus built by Beijing Language and Culture University. In this corpus, approximately 11,000 essays are collected from HSK Chinese tests taken by foreign Chinese language learners, and error sentences are annotated with special marks.

For example:

这就{CQ 要}由有关部门和政策管理制度来控制。

[1] http://nlp.blcu.edu.cn/online-systems/hsk-language-lib-indexing-system.html

where {CQ 要} refers to a redundant word and is revised with the word that follows it.

可是这两个问题同时{CJX}要解决非常不容易。
where {CJX} refers to a reordering error.

However, detaching an erroneous sentence and a corresponded correction sentence from an annotated one as above is not easy because we don't know the position information of the reordering error. Moreover, such detachment is also difficult when dealing with some more complex errors, for example, a "ba (把)" error (a special preference of active voice in Chinese) or "bei (被)" error (a special preference of passive voice in Chinese), if we depend only on such marks.

Thus, we extracted sentences having only insertion, deletion, or replacement errors. We also cleaned the HSK corpus by deleting sentences pairs having too long ED as described. As a result, the corpus now contains approximately 59,000 sentences. The distribution of ED in the combined corpus is shown in Figure **2**.

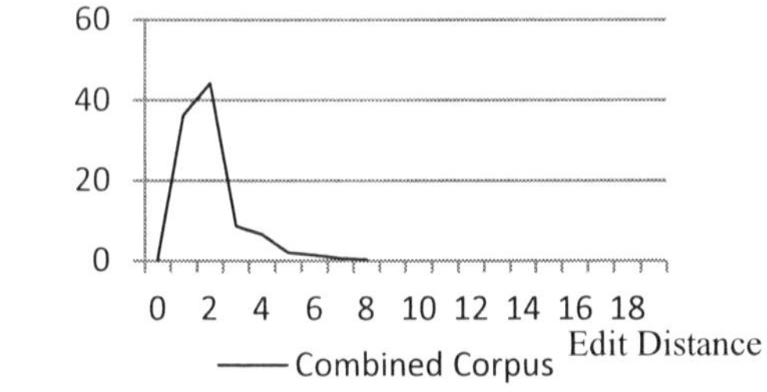

Figure 2: Distribution of ED in combined corpus.

4 Tuning

As previously described, an SMT system with tuning is proved to perform better than one without tuning. Because this shared task uses several evaluation metrics such as accuracy, F1 score, and FP rate, we tune our system using all these metrics with minimum error rate training (MERT) (Och, 2003) at identification level[1]. Our linear evaluation score is computed according to the following:

Score = α *Accuracy+ β * $F_{0.5}$+ γ *(1-FP_rate)
where $\alpha + \beta + \gamma = 1.0$.

We conducted a series of preliminary experiments to discover the most effective set of parameters. We followed Kunchukuttan et al. (2014) and Wang et al. (2014) in using $F_{0.5}$ instead of F1. In other words, we expected our system to have high accuracy because, as Ng et al. say in CoNLL-2014, "it is important for a grammar checker that its proposed corrections are highly accurate in order to gain user acceptance." However, we discovered that even when we used a parameter set of α =0.0, β =1.0, and γ =0.0, we still failed to reach a satisfactory correction rate.

Finally, we use α =0.5, β =0.0, and γ =0.5 as a final parameter set for phrase-based and hierarchical phrase-based systems because it produces the greatest number of corrections at identical level among our in-house experiments. In addition, our in-house experiments revealed that an improper parameter set could produce a reasonable but unacceptable result. We discuss this aspect with reference to an experiment regarding a syntax-based system in the next section.

5 Experiment and Results

5.1 Official Runs

We followed the WAT2015[2] baseline system to build phrase-based and hierarchical phrase-based SMT systems. This involves segmenting words using Stanford Word Segmenter version 2014-01-04, running GIZA++ v1.07 on training corpus in both directions, and parsing Chinese sentences with Berkeley parser (for java 1.7). We ran Moses v2.11 for decoding using the same parameters with the WAT2015 baseline. We trained two hierarchical phrase-based systems using different sized corpora according to whether the HSK corpus is included. For error classification, we followed Zhao et al. (2014) to identify error types and locate the positions of errors.

All three runs we submitted are shown in Table 1. In addition, the results of our runs at position level are shown in Table 2. RUN3 produced more corrections and obtained a higher F1 score at position level than did the other runs. However,

[1] Detection level: All error types will be regarded as incorrect. Identification level: All error types should be clearly identified, i.e., Redundant, Missing, Disorder, and Selection. Position level: The system results should be perfectly identical with the quadruples of gold standard.
We tried to tune in position level but we omit these results since this attempt mostly failed.

[2] http://orchid.kuee.kyoto-u.ac.jp/WAT/

it is inferior in terms of accuracy and FP rate compared to RUN2.

At position level, the phrase-based system generated only 15 correct predictions and among them only one Disorder and no Selection types appeared. By contrast, the hierarchical system performed much better, as it successfully predicted seven Disorder and five Selection types. In addition, it produced more correct predictions on Missing and Redundant types.

TMU-RUN1	Lang-8 + hierarchical
TMU-RUN2	Lang-8 + HSK + phrase-based
TMU-RUN3	Lang-8 + HSK + hierarchical

Table 1: Three RUNs submitted by TMU (Tokyo Metropolitan University) team.

	FP rate	Accuracy	Precision	Recall	F1
RUN1	0.478	0.270	0.0363	0.0180	0.0241
RUN2	0.134	0.449	0.1928	0.0320	0.0549
RUN3	0.350	0.362	0.1745	0.07400	0.1039

Table 2: Final test result of TMU RUNs at position level.

5.2 Hierarchical Phrase-based Model

We provide an example of the official test set to explain why hierarchical phrase-based systems appear to be more effective than those that are phrase-based. The following Chinese sentence is used:

B1-1033: 其中有一个人丢护照了。

(One of them lost his passport.)

In a hierarchical-phrase-based system and according to the synchronous CFG rule, the partial derivation of the phrase "丢 护照 了 (lost his passport)" is:

$(X, X) \rightarrow$(丢 X_1 , 丢 X_1)

$\rightarrow$(丢 X_2 了, 丢 了 X_2)

$\rightarrow$(丢 护照 了, 丢 了 护照)

where X denotes any phrase. Because "X 了" wrongly written as "了 X" is a typical Disorder error in Chinese sentences, the hierarchical phrase-based system extracts the rule X→(X 了, 了 X) and weighs it highly when training on the corpus. This means the model actually examined syntax errors in sentences. By contrast, the phrase-based system lacks the ability to identify syntax errors. Therefore, this translation model is less effective than the hierarchical phrase-based system, as it failed to select a correct translation such as "丢 了 X."

5.3 Corpus Augmentation

According to the results shown in Table 4, expanding the corpus has a beneficial effect. In RUN1, the F1 score of 0.024 means it nearly failed to produce any correction prediction. However, after we increased the corpus size, the F1 score increased to 0.10. The improved F1 score with corpus augmentation is illustrated in Figure 3. Among F1 scores, our RUN3 ranks exactly in the middle of 15 RUNS of all teams.

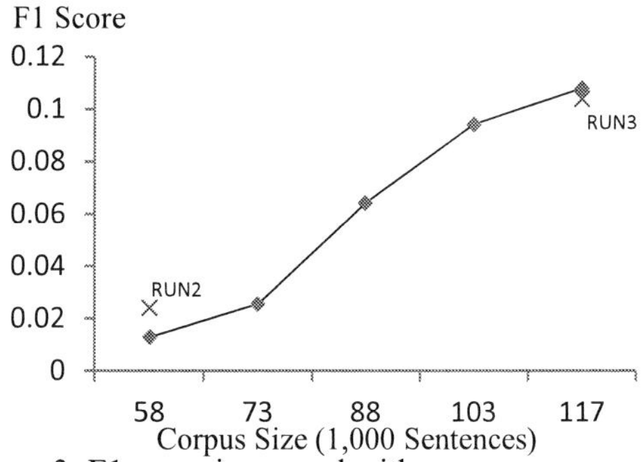

Figure 3: F1 score improved with corpus augmentation. The solid line represents results of our in-house test. The Xs represent results of this open task.

5.4 Tuning

To determine the effect of tuning for improving the two systems, we developed a test on the NLP-TEA-1 training set offered by organizers. Table 3 shows a contrast between tuned and untuned systems. As with the English grammatical error correction task, MERT clearly boosts the F1 score in this task. We tuned the system using the Z-MERT toolkit (Zaidan, 2009).

	F1 Score	
	Phrase-based	Hierarchical-phrase-based
Untuned	0.0513	0.0868
Tuned	0.0701	0.1080

Table 3: F1 score of SMT-based grammatical error correction system on NLP-TEA-1 dataset, with and without tuning.

To compare different syntax-based systems, we also developed a string-to-tree (s2t) SMT system. However, in our attempt to tune it, we failed to obtain a best set of parameters. We first tried a parameter set of (0.5, 0.0, 0.5), which performs most effectively with the phrase-based model. However, it failed to improve the F1 score, as is shown in Table 4.

	FP_Rate	Accuracy	Precision	Recall	F1
Untuned	0.3973	0.4087	0.1042	0.0787	0.0896
Tuned	0.1029	0.4747	0.0480	0.0057	0.0102

Table 4: Tuning result suitable to an evaluation score but unacceptable for its low precision and recall.

The system is clearly optimized to achieve the best performance in terms of FP rate and accuracy. However, this is because, as experiments showed, the system produces nearly all negative predictions, which causes low precision and recall, as increasing true negatives improves both the accuracy and FP rate. We determined that α =0.5, β =0.0, γ =0.5 may not be a "good" parameter set in this situation, even though it seemed acceptable for a preliminary experiment. Unfortunately, we did not identify any parameter sets that can generate more acceptable results than can the s2t system without tuning.

6 Conclusion

We have described a Chinese grammatical error correction system based on SMT for the TMU-NLP team. First, we examined hierarchical phrase-based and string-to-tree translation models of SMT on CGED. Second, we constructed an error-correction parallel corpus based on the HSK Dynamic Essay Corpus, which is nearly equal in size to the Lang-8 Chinese Learner Corpus. We then cleaned and combined the two into a single expanded corpus. Third, we tuned the system with a linear combination of evaluation metrics using MERT. Finally, we showed that the augmented corpus considerably improved performance. In addition, the hierarchical phrase-based translation model generated a higher F1 score than did the phrase-based model.

For future research, we will attempt to expand the corpus further. A possible direction in building a large-scale parallel corpus is to introduce errors artificially to correct sentences. This has already been applied in an English error correction task of Yuan and Felice (2013). In addition, we confirmed that our system produces correct predictions in generated N-best output. However, oracle predictions were not selected during decoding. To solve this, we will employ a much more powerful language model such as the Google n-gram model as well as a re-ranking approach on the N-best output.

Acknowledgments

We would like to thank Xi Yangyang for granting use of extracted texts from Lang-8.

Reference

Chris Brockett, William Dolan, Michael Gamon. (2006). Correcting ESL Errors Using Phrasal SMT Techniques. *Proceedings of the 21st International Conference on Computational Linguistics and the 44th Annual Meeting of the Association for Computational Linguistics*, pages 249–256. Sydney, Australia.

Shuk-Man Cheng, Chi-Hsin Yu, Hsin-Hsi Chen. (2014). Chinese Word Ordering Errors Detection and Correction for Non-Native Chinese Language Learners. *Proceedings of COLING 2014, the 25th International Conference on Computational Linguistics*: Technical Papers, pages 279–289, Dublin, Ireland.

David Chiang. (2005). A Hierarchical Phrase-Based Model for Statistical Machine Translation. *Proceedings of the 43rd Annual Meeting of the Association for Computational Linguistics (ACL'05)*, pages 263–270, Ann Arbor, Michigan.

Hsun-wen Chiu, Jian-cheng Wu, Jason S. Chang. (2013). Chinese Spelling Checker Based on Statistical Machine Translation. *Proceedings of the Seventh SIGHAN Workshop on Chinese Language Processing (SIGHAN-7)*, pages 49–53, Nagoya, Japan.

Mariano Felice, Zheng Yuan, Øistein E. Andersen, Helen Yannakoudakis, Ekaterina Kochmar. (2014). Grammatical Error Correction using Hybrid Systems and Type Filtering. *Proceedings of the Eighteenth Conference on Computational Natural Language Learning: Shared Task*, pages 15–24, Baltimore, Maryland.

Marcin Junczys-Dowmunt, Roman Grundkiewicz. (2014). The AMU System in the CoNLL-2014 Shared Task: Grammatical Error Correction by Data-Intensive and Feature-Rich Statistical Machine Translation. *Proceedings of the Eighteenth Conference on Computational Natural Language Learning: Shared Task*, pages 25–33, Baltimore, Maryland.

Anoop Kunchukuttan, Sriram Chaudhury, Pushpak Bhattacharyya. (2014). Tuning a Grammar Correction System for Increased Precision. *Proceedings of the Eighteenth Conference on Computational Natural Language Learning: Shared Task*, pages 60–64, Baltimore, Maryland.

Tomoya Mizumoto, Mamoru Komachi, Masaaki Nagata, Yuji Matsumoto. (2011). Mining Revision Logs of Language Learning SNS for Automated Japanese Error Correction of Second Language Learners. *Proceedings of the 5th International Joint Conference on Natural Language Processing*, pages 148–155, Chiang Mai, Thailand.

Hwee Tou Ng, Siew Mei Wu, Ted Briscoe, Christian Hadiwinoto, Raymond H. Susanto, Christopher Bryant. (2014). The CoNLL-2014 Shared Task on Grammatical Error Correction. *Proceedings of the Eighteenth Conference on Computational Natural Language Learning: Shared Task*, pages 1–14, Baltimore, Maryland.

Franz J. Och. (2003). Minimum Error Rate Training in Statistical Machine Translation. *Proceedings of the 41st Annual Meeting of the Association for Computational Linguistics*, pages 160–167. Sapporo, Japan.

Yiming Wang, Longyue Wang, Derek F. Wong, Lidia S. Chao, Xiaodong Zeng, Yi Lu. (2014). Factored Statistical Machine Translation for Grammatical Error Correction. *Proceedings of the Eighteenth Conference on Computational Natural Language Learning: Shared Task*, pages 1–14, Baltimore, Maryland.

Chi-Hsin Yu, Hsin-Hsi Chen. (2012). Detecting Word Ordering Errors in Chinese Sentences for Learning Chinese as a Foreign Language. *Proceedings of COLING 2012: Technical Papers*, pages 3003–3018, Mumbai, India.

Zheng Yuan, Mariano Felice. (2013). Constrained grammatical error correction using statistical machine translation. *Proceedings of the Seventeenth Conference on Computational Natural Language Learning: Shared Task*, pages 52–61, Sofia, Bulgaria.

Omar F. Zaidan. (2009). Z-MERT: A Fully Configurable Open Source Tool for Minimum Error Rate Training of Machine Translation Systems. *The Prague Bulletin of Mathematical Linguistics*, pages 79–88

Yinchen Zhao, Mamoru Komachi, Hiroshi Ishikawa. (2014). Extracting a Chinese Learner Corpus from the Web: Grammatical Error Correction for Learning Chinese as a Foreign Language with Statistical Machine Translation. *Proceedings of the 22nd International Conference on Computers in Education*, pages 56–61, Nara, Japan.

Chinese Grammatical Error Diagnosis System Based on Hybrid Model

Xiupeng Wu, Peijie Huang*, Jundong Wang, Qingwen Guo, Yuhong Xu, Chuping Chen
College of Mathematics and Informatics, South China Agricultural University,
Guangzhou 510642, Guangdong, China
zxc2012@gmail.com, pjhuang@scau.edu.cn, mo_xiao_wang@163.com,
tryven.guo@qq.com, 137610184@qq.com, 568093091@qq.com

Abstract

This paper describes our system in the Chinese Grammatical Error Diagnosis (CGED) task for learning Chinese as a Foreign Language (CFL). Our work adopts a hybrid model by integrating rule-based method and n-gram statistical method to detect Chinese grammatical errors, identify the error type and point out the position of error in the input sentences. Tri-gram is applied to disorder mistake. And the rest of mistakes are solved by the conservation rules sets. Empirical evaluation results demonstrate the utility of our CGED system.

1 Introduction

Chinese as a foreign language (CFL) is booming in recent decades. The number of (CFL) learners is expected to become larger for the years to come (Xiong et al., 2014). But the flexibility and complication in Chinese morphology, pronunciations and grammar make Chinese become one of the hardest languages to learn. If you cannot make good use of the grammatical rules, maybe the many different meaning or error meaning of the sentence will be get. Empirically, there were 2 errors per student essay on average in a learners' corpus (Chen et al.,2011).From some previous research on second language acquisition, it indicated that effective provision of corrective feedback can contribute to the development of grammatical competence in second language learners (Fathman and Whalley, 1990; Ashwell, 2000; Ferris and Robers, 2001; Chandler, 2003). Therefore developing a check tool which can automatically detect and correct Chinese grammatical errors is a very important and useful work for foreigners to learn Chinese. And it helps to detect the wrong grammar from a large number of documents.

Recently, there were a number of shared task of grammatical error correction for learners, including the CoNLL-2013 (Ng et al., 2013), the CoNLL-2014 (Ng et al., 2014), the ICCE-2014 (Yu et al., 2014), the Chinese Grammatical Error Diagnosis (CGED) task, etc. These tasks have been organized to provide a common platform for comparing and developing automatic Chinese grammatical error diagnosis system.

In NLP, grammar diagnosis is a difficult problem for sentence comprehension. In English, so much research is under way up to now and many learning assistance tools were developed by natural language processing technology to detect and correct the grammatical errors of EFL learners (Chodorow et al., 2012; Leacock et al, 2010). And the demand for automatic Chinese proofreading has driven an increase in study for this task in Chinese area. Cheng et al. (2014) and Yu and Chang (2012) designed word order error detection technology focused on the Chinese sentences in the HSK Dynamic Composition Corpus. Yuan and Felice (2013) proposed the use of phrase-based statistical machine translation to grammatical error correction. Chang et al. (2012) presented a rule-based learning algorithm combined with a log-likelihood function to identify error types in Chinese texts. In summary, all of these methods mainly focus on the statistical machine learning (SML) like n-gram language model (LM) and rule-based method, indicating that SML model and rule-based method still being useful and effective for Chinese grammatical correcting.

This paper propose a hybrid model for CGED

* Corresponding author

Proceedings of The 2nd Workshop on Natural Language Processing Techniques for Educational Applications, pages 117–125,
Beijing, China, July 31, 2015. ©2015 Association for Computational Linguistics and Asian Federation of Natural Language Processing

shared task by integrating rule-based methods and n-gram statistical methods to detect Chinese grammatical errors, identify the error type and point out the position of error in the input sentences. The rule-based method provides 405 handcrafted rules (Missing rule-30, Redundant rule-75, Selection rule-300) constructed from the training set provided by organizer to identify potential rule violations in input sentences and correct the error sentences. Tri-gram is applied to disorder mistake. After the above special processes, once the candidate sentence set does not have only one sentence, we adopt two strategies: first is a general process, in which the n-gram statistical method relies on the n-gram scores of both standard (correct) corpus and four non-standard (incorrect) training corpora is used to determine the correction and the error type in the input sentence, and second is just adjusting the priority among four special processes.

The remainder of this paper is structured as follows. Section 2 provides an overview of related work. Section 3 presents the rule we write and the tri-gram model we build. Section 4 presents our results. Section 5 is discussion of future work concludes the paper.

2 The Proposed System

2.1 System Overview

Figure 1 shows the flowchart of our CGED system. The system is mainly composed by two processes: preprocess and main process. In addition, main process contains two subprocesses: special process and general process.

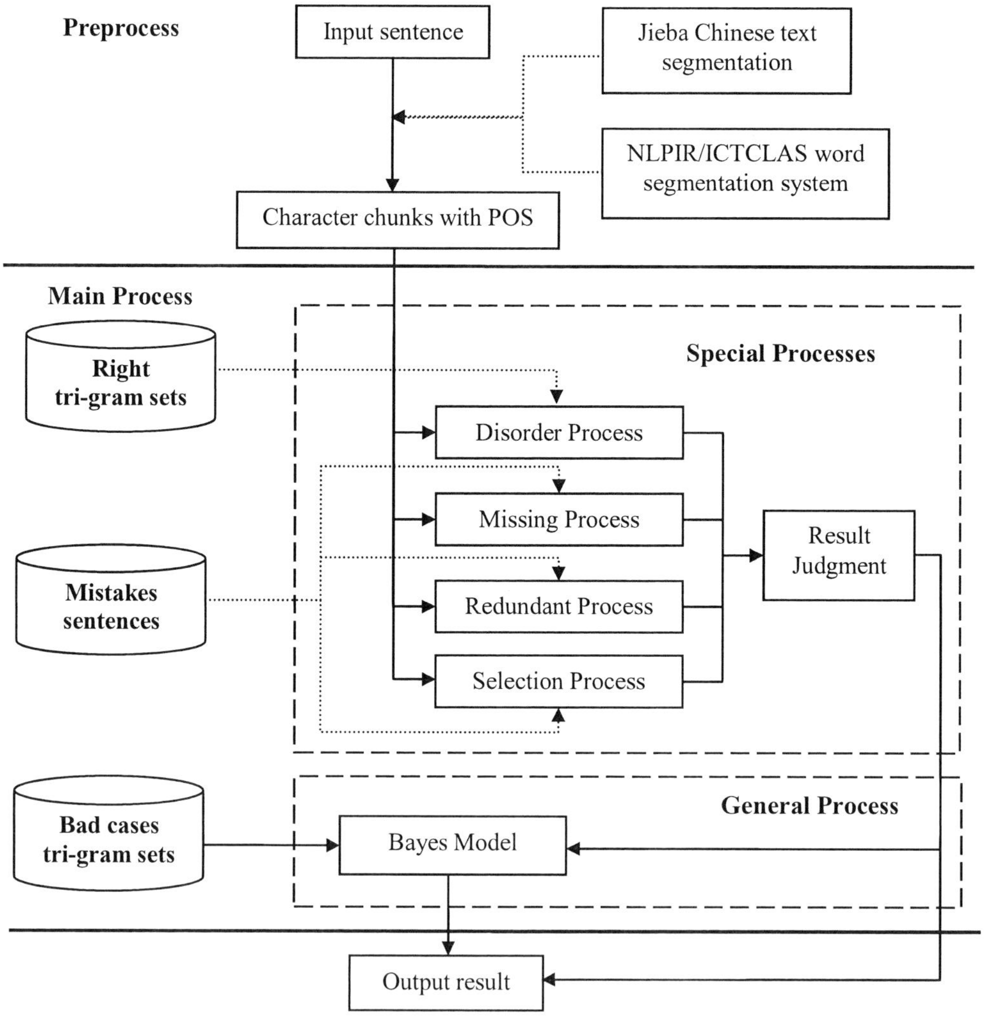

Figure 1. The flowchart of the hybrid CGED system.

It performs CGED in the following steps:

1. Given a test sentence, the CGED system gets the character chunks in the sentence with POS.

2. For each chunk in this sentence, the system will enumerate every rule in the missing, redundant and selection rules sets. In the meanwhile, we got the all permutations of the chunks. What's more we use tri-gram model (We use the corpus of CCL[1] to generate the frequency of tri-gram) to calculate the probabilities of each generated sentence in the all permutations and pop the highest one. We will get a candidate sentence set after this step.

3. If the candidate sentence set has only one sentence, the system will return related data based on the sentence. However, if the candidate sentence set does not have only one sentence, system will carry out the general process.

2.2 Preprocess

Preprocess in the system contains two modules: Chinese word segmentation and part-of-speech tagging. We uses "Jieba" Chinese text segmentation[2] and NLPIR/ ICTCLAS Chinese text segmentation[3] to achieve the goal. A set of chunks with POS will be generated after this process.

2.3 Main Process

Main process contains two subprocess: special process and general process. Special process has four different processes applied to detect and correct the sentence with correspondent grammatical error. General process decides sentences' error type through the Bayes model trained by data set from NTNU, if the sentence input has grammatical error. After that, we deal with the sentence according to its error type. If the candidate sentence set does not have only one sentence, system will carry out the general process.

3 Special processes and General process

3.1 Special processes

Disorder process

For the case of the missing syntax, we use the method as follow: System generates the all permutations of chunk set from preprocess. Then it calculates the probability of each sentence in the sentence set generated by method above through tri-gram. If the highest probability one differs from the origin one, system judges that the sentence has disorder error. Result generated by the tri-gram model used in this system has the lowest degree of confidence among the special processes. As a result, disorder process has the lowest priority level.

Figure 2 shows the process of disorder error detection and correction ("O" original, "M" modified).

O: 所以我不會讓失望她
Segmentation: 所以/c 我/r 不會/v 讓/v 失望/v 她/r
All Permutations:
1）所以我不會讓失望她
2）所以我不會讓她失望
(Highest probability in tri-gram)
3）所以我不會失望她讓
4）所以我讓失望她不會
5）所以不會讓失望她我
6）我不會讓失望她所以
7）所以我不會失望讓她
8）所以我讓失望不會她
9）所以不會讓失望我她
...
M: 所以我不會讓她失望

Figure 2. The process of disorder error detection and correction.

Missing process

For the case of the missing syntax, this paper uses rules to deal with them. Through the collection of the grammar deletion, extract the sentence features of the deletion of the grammar, and analyze the grammar and summarize the relevant rules.

We intend to extract common phrase structures from the training concentrate which has the missing syntax. The sentence structures containing the similar syntax are summed up, and the structural features of the sentence are summarized. For the missing part of syntax, we sum up about 30 rules consisting of the simplified structure of the sentence, and we give the corresponding correction rules. The common syntax missing sentence structures are similar to the rules: "m+n+v", "r+v+j+v+a+v", "c+r+d+v+m+a", we give the error correction rule that corresponds to it: "m+n+v+了", "r+v+j+v+a+的+v", "c+r+d+v+很+m+a". We

[1] ccl.pku.edu.cn:8080/ccl_corpus/index.jsp?dir=xiandai
[2] https://github.com/fxsjy/jieba
[3] http://ictclas.nlpir.org/

summed up the rules of missing detection to the training set contains 60% of the missing part of the grammar of the sentence, the investigation of the sentence probability is 40%, the sentence correct probability of 15%.

Figure 3 shows the process of missing error detection and correction ("O" original, "M" modified).

Case1:
O: 我高興我的老師是那位小姐
Segmentation: 我/r 高興/a 我/r 的/uj 老師/n 是/v 那位/r 小姐/nr
Detection rule: "r+b+r+uj+n+v+r+nr"
Correction rule: "r+很+b+r+uj+n+v+r+nr"
M: 我很高興我的老師是那位小姐

Case 2:
O: 他爬三個小時
Segmentation: 他/r 爬/v 三個/m 小/a 時/ng
Detection rule: "r+v+m+n"
Correction rule: "r+v+了+m+n"
M: 他爬了三個小時

Case 3:
O: 我是你小學朋友
Segmentation: 我/r 是/v 你/r 小學/n 朋友/n
Detection rule: "r+v+r+n+n"
Correction rule: "r+v+r+n+的+n"
M: 我是你小學的朋友

Figure 3. The process of missing error detection and correction.

Redundant process

Considering the redundant mistakes have strong syntax structure, this paper use rules to deal with the redundant mistakes. Previous work is done like the method of dealing with missing mistakes. Through the collection of the grammar redundant, extract the sentence features of the redundant of the grammar, and analyze the grammar and summarize the relevant rules. Then we intend to extract common phrase structures from the training concentrate which has redundant mistakes. The sentence structures containing the similar syntax are summed up, and the structural features of the sentence are summarized.

For the redundant part of syntax, we sum up about 75 rules. Rules are in form of the pattern as (wrong pattern, revised pattern, position mark) such as ("v+m+nr+ul", "v+m+nr", 4), ("v+ul +n", "v+n",2), ("v+n+c+d+uv+v", "v+n+d +uv+v", 3). The position mark takes an important part in the case of the wrong pattern has two same tags such as "v+v+r+uj+n" in ("v+v+r+uj+n", "v+r+uj+n", 1) .In this case, the position mark can prevent from deleting the second "v" which will turn the result into wrong direction.

We detection to the redundant part of the training set discovers that the rules has covered 118 sentences, accounting to 27.4%. In the covered cases, there are 71 sentences have been corrected rightly, accounting to 60.1% correct probability. Figure 4 shows the process of redundant error detection and correction ("O" original, "M" modified).

Case1:
O: 晚上五點半他們到了火車站去
Segmentation: 晚上/t 五點半/m 他們/r 到/v 了/ul 火車/n 站/v 去/v
Rule: ("v+ul+n", " v+n", 2)
M: 晚上五點半他們到火車站去

Case 2:
O: 她們一起看美國的電影
Segmentation: 她們/r 一起/m 看/v 美國/ns 的 /uj 電影/n
Rule: ("ns+uj+n", "ns+n", 2)
M:她們一起看美國電影

Case 3:
O: 我发现了你乱丢垃圾
Segmentation: 我/r 发现/v 了/ul 你/r 乱丢垃圾/n
Rule: ("v+ul+r", " v+r", 2)
M: 我发现你乱丢垃圾

Figure 4. The process of redundant error detection and correction.

Selection process

In linguistics, selection denotes the ability of specific words to determine the semantic contents of their arguments. It is a semantic concept, whereas subcategorization is a syntactic one. For the cases of selection syntax, this paper takes a more empirical approach to deal with them. We intended to summarize the relevant rules by observing the semantic relations of those specific words with parse tree and dependency tree. Unfortunately, we did not have enough time and resources to do it. We had to extract the sentence features of selection syntax, analyze the grammar and summarize the rules artificially.

Through the previous 50% of the training corpus, we can collect the specific words. Then we extract the collocation of those specific words to make the rules. In this paper, we use the NLPIR Chinese Word Segmentation to segment the sentences. The sentences containing the same specific words and similar syntax are summed up, and then we summarize the rule, a single generative equation for these sentences. Around 300 rules are made and we also give the corresponding correction rules. We find the way to be great because some rules have good generalization ability. Most common syntax selection sentence structures are similar to the rules like:“.[^部]/mq+電影”, “z+的+vn”, and we give the error correction rules that correspond to them: “.部/mq+電影”, “z+地+vn”. However, since we extract the rules by human beings, the rules are limited and even some of them are not very reasonable.

Figure 5 shows the process of selection error detection and correction (“O” original, “M” modified).

Case1:
O: 你決定那個電影
Segmentation:你/rr 決定/v 那個/rz 電影/n
Detection rule: .[^部]/mq+電影
Correction rule: .部/mq+電影
M: 你決定那部電影

Case 2:
O: 我要清清楚楚的說明
Segmentation:我/rr 要/v 清清楚楚/z 的 /ude1 说明/vn
Detection rule: z+的+vn
Correction rule: z+地+vn
M: 我要清楚地說明

Figure 5. The process of selection error detection and correction

3.2 General process

In this section, we describe an approach of general process to grammatical error diagnosis where the special process cannot well diagnose the error. Inspired by existing related work, we considered a frequency-based solution to approach the task. Therefore we use a frequency-based approach comparing n-gram frequency lists to both the standard corpus and the non-standard (error) corpus. The standard corpus above is made of correct sentences extracted from the training corpus provided by the shared task organizers and the error sentences consist of the non-standard corpus. The assumption behind this approach is that comparing a standard corpus to a non-standard corpus using frequency-based methods levels out non-standard features present in the non-standard corpus. These features are very likely to be, in the case of this corpus, grammatical errors.

As discussed above, we can acquire the keyword lists are produced by comparing two corpora (a standard corpus and a non-standard corpus) using association metrics such as log-likelihood, chi-square or mutual information. These keywords usually reflect salient features of the learner corpus. In the case of the present comparison, it is safe to assume that a reasonable amount of salient features from the learner corpus will be in frequent distributions of words which are very likely to be errors.

For proving our approach, we pre-processed the training corpus provided by organizers. As Chinese is a logographic language we treat every character in isolation in this process. Firstly, We separate the correct sentences and the error sentences from the training corpus to construct the standard corpus and non-standard corpora (for the task have four kind of errors so we will acquire four non-standard corpora, respectively the disorder corpus, the missing corpus, the redundant corpus, the selection corpus) and then extract the n-grams keywords from all corpora including the standard and the four non-standard corpora).By respectively comparing the four non-standard corpora to the standard corpus, we can extract the four kinds of a list of ungrammatical n-grams list corresponding to the four kinds of non-standard corpora and treat them as key expressions. This calculation returned us a list of 22071 ungrammatical n-grams (disorderset-5075, missingset-1035, redundantset-7810, selectionset-8151) not present in the standard corpus. In these experiments we just used the tri-gram set extracted from the corpus .With these n-gram lists, we trained a classifiers to identify the grammatical error type. An n-gram based Multinomial Naive Bayes (MNB) classifiers to identify grammatical error sentences using the formula below:

$$\mathrm{p}(s) = \prod_{i=1}^{l} p(w_i \mid w_{i-2} w_{i-1}) \qquad (1)$$

$$p(w_i \mid w_{i-2} w_{i-1}) = \frac{c(w_{i-2} w_{i-1} w_i)}{\sum_{w_i} c(w_{i-2} w_{i-1} w_i)} \qquad (2)$$

where p(s) is the probability of the sentence. We need to calculate the sentence’s probability in the four corpus and by comparing the probability of the four error type, we can select the error type having the maximum probability as the candidate. If all probability is less than the threshold x, we regard the sentences as the correct sentence. After a number of tests we found that the proper optimal value.

4 Empirical Evaluation

4.1 Task

The goal of this shared task, i.e. Chinese Grammatical Error Diagnosis (CGED) task for CFL is developing the computer-assisted tools to diagnose several kinds of grammatical errors, i.e., redundant word, missing word, word disorder, and word selection. The system should indicate which kind of error type is embedded in the given sentence and it's occurred positions. Passages of CFL (Chinese as a Foreign Language) learners' essays selected from the National Taiwan Normal University (NTNU) learner corpus are used for training purpose. The training data (consisting of 2212 grammatical errors) is provided as practice. The final test data set for the evaluation consists of 1000 passages cover different grammatical errors.

4.2 Metrics

The criteria for judging correctness are:

(1) Detection level: Binary classification of a given sentence, i.e., correct or incorrect should be completely identical with the gold standard. All error types will be regarded as incorrect.

(2) Identification level: This level could be considered as a multi-class categorization problem. In addition to correct instances, all error types should be clearly identified, i.e., redundant, missing, disorder, and selection.

(3) Position level: Besides identifying the error types, this level also judges the positions of erroneous range. That is, the system results should be perfectly identical with the quadruples of gold standard. The following metrics are measured in both levels with the help of the confusion matrix.

In CGED task of the NLP-TEA 2015 (The 2nd Workshop on Natural Language Processing Techniques for Educational Applications), 13 metrics are measured in both levels to score the performance of a CGED system. They are False Positive Rate (FPR), Detection Accuracy (DA), Detection Precision (DP), Detection Recall (DR), Detection F-score (DF), Identification Accuracy (IA), Identification Precision (IP), Identification Recall (IR), Identification F-score (IF), Position Accuracy (PA), Position Precision (PP), Position Recall (PR) and Position F-score (PF).

4.3 Evaluation Results

The CGED task of CFL attracted 13 research teams. Among 13 registered teams, 6 participants submitted their testing results. For formal testing, each participant can submit at most three runs that use different models or parameter settings. Finally, there are 18 runs submitted in total.

Validation

We use the 30% of NLP-TEA-1 CFL Datasets (Yu et al., 2014) as validation set to test the effect and performance of the four special processes and the MNB. Table 1 shows the validation results.

Test1 validates the four special processes and gives different type of rules the same privileges when the candidate sentence set does not have only one sentence after special process. The detective accuracy of the four special processes in this test, i.e. redundant, selection, missing, and disorder are 0.934, 0.967, 0.828, and 0.491 respectively.

Thus, we perform three tests which give lower priority to disorder process when the candidate sentence set does not have only one sentence after special process:

Test2 (Redundant = Selection = Missing > Disorder): This test gives different type of rules the same privileges, and gives the minimum priority to the disorder process.

	DP	DR	DF	IP	IR	IF	PP	PR	PF
Test1	0.486	0.508	0.496	0.171	0.111	0.135	0.038	0.021	0.027
Test2	0.494	0.643	0.559	0.192	0.156	0.172	0.056	0.039	0.046
Test3	0.494	0.643	0.559	0.198	0.162	0.178	0.060	0.042	0.049
Test4	0.522	0.285	0.369	0.281	0.102	0.150	0.103	0.030	0.047
Test5	0.504	0.976	0.665	0.160	0.183	0.171	0.021	0.021	0.021

Table 1. Validation results of NLP-TEA-1 CFL Datasets.

Test3 (Redundant = Selection > Missing > Disorder): This test decrease the priority of missing in order to adjust the collision rate of redundant rules and missing rules.

Test4 (Redundant = Selection = Missing && Disorder = 0): This test is the result using the method of Run1 without the disorder process in order to reduce the wrong judgment rate.

And we make another test, Test5, for using MNB when candidate sentence set does not have only one sentence after special process.

We found the approach using MNB (Test5) has mostly no advantage with that only using special process (Test2, Test3, and Test4). Therefore, the three runs of our system submitted to NLP-TEA-2 CLF final test are all based on the four special processes.

NLP-TEA-2 CLF final test

Table 2 shows the evaluation results of the NLP-TEA-2 CFL final test. Run1, Run2 and Run3 are the three runs of our system corresponding to Test2, Test3, Test4, respectively. The "Best" indicates the high score of each metric achieved in CGED task. The "Average" represents the average of the 18 runs. As we can see from Table 2, we achieve a result close to the average level. Some typical errors of our current system will be presented in the next subsection, and the corresponding improvements are summarized in the last section.

4.4 Error Analysis

Figure 6 shows some typical error examples of our system ("R" right sentence, "M" modified). This approach has several defects: if the segmentation results are wrong, and even wrong segmented place to the synthesis of the word having grammatical errors, it will lead later processing meaningless. And the tri-gram effect depends on the corpus. The Bad-case tri-gram extracted from the training corpus may not appear in the test set, which will affect the validity of the error correction. On the other hand, we use the extraction rules to correct the sentences that are syntax errors. First, training set cannot guarantee the existence of all syntax errors. Second, we extract the rules represents only a part of the grammar rules, and grammar mistakes in language is infinite, rules are not represented at all.

Case 1 (Redundant)
R: 我碰到一个小孩
Segmentation: 我/r 碰到/v 一个/m 小孩/n
Rule:("r+v+m", "r+m",2)
M: 我一个小孩

Case 2 (Missing)
R: 我看到一輛車的時候
Segmentation: 我/r 看到/v 一輛/m 車/n 的/uj 時候/n
Detection rule: "r+v+m+n"
Correction rule: "r+v+m+n+了"
M: 我看到一輛車了的時候

Case 3 (Disorder)
R: 最近很難找到工作
Segmentation: 最近/f 很/d 難/a 找到/v 工作 /vn
All Permutations:
1） 最近很難工作找到
2） 最近很工作難找到
3） 最近工作很難找到
4） 工作最近很難找到
5） 工作很难找到最近
(Highest probability in tri-gram)
…
M: 工作很难找到最近

Case 4 (Selection)
R: 我看到的是她很失望的臉
Segmentation: 我/r 看到/v 的/uj 是/v 她/r 很/d 失望/v 的/uj 臉/n
Detection rule: "看到 + r"
Correction rule: "看見 + r"
M: 我看見的是她很失望的臉

Figure 6. Error examples.

	FPR	DA	DP	DR	DF	IA	IP	IR	IF	PA	PP	PR	PF
Run1	**0.620**	**0.505**	**0.504**	**0.630**	**0.560**	**0.287**	**0.238**	**0.194**	**0.214**	**0.217**	**0.080**	**0.054**	**0.065**
Run2	0.636	0.503	0.502	0.642	0.564	0.279	0.234	0.194	0.212	0.209	0.078	0.054	0.064
Run3	0.266	0.503	0.506	0.272	0.354	0.416	0.269	0.098	0.144	0.385	0.119	0.036	0.055
Average	0.538	0.534	0.560	0.607	0.533	0.335	0.329	0.208	0.233	0.263	0.166	0.064	0.085
Best	0.082	0.607	0.7453	1.000	0.675	0.525	0.617	0.364	0.358	0.505	0.529	0.160	0.174

Table 2. Evaluation results of NLP-TEA-2 CFL final test.

In the first case about redundant, our rules (r+v+m) are in line with the sentence structure (我/r 碰到/v 一个/m), but the corrected sentence (r+m) is not correct. This sentence is a case of the missing, which has the same sentence structure of the redundant rule. The case should be due to the conflict between the redundant rules and the missing rules, which has match the same sentence structure.

In the second case about missing, we extracted the rule (r+v+m+n) from the sentence (我/r 沒有/v 很多/m 時間/n) in the corpus. The corrected rule for this type of sentence is: "r+v+m+n+了". However, this sentence is a case of the redundant, which has the same sentence structure of the missing rule. The case should be due to the conflict between the redundant rules and the missing rules, which has match the same sentence structure.

In the third case about disorder, the highest score in the tri-gram is not the result expected, because only using the POS and the sequence of words as a component of the rules has certain limitations. And tri-gram method could not distinguish long distance displacement.

In the fourth case about selection, there are two reasons for the wrong selection: incorrect usage of quantifiers and function words ("的"等虚词). Under this scenario, the artificial rules are hard to cover completely. Only using the POS and the sequence of words as the elements of the rules, it cannot resolve the problem of conflict of rules. As in the case, our rule (看到 + rr -> 看见 + rr) cannot be applied to the current test sentence, the corresponding rule to correct the sentence into a wrong sentence.

5 Conclusions and Future Work

This paper presents the development and preliminary evaluation of the system from team of South China Agricultural University (SCAU) that participated in the CGED shared task. We have developed hybrid model by integrating rule-based method and n-gram statistical method to detect Chinese grammatical errors, identify the error type and point out the position of error in the input sentences. Tri-gram is applied to disorder mistake. And the rest of mistakes are solved by the 405 handcrafted rules (Missing rule-30, Redundant rule-75, Selection rule-300).

It is our first attempt on Chinese grammatical error diagnosis, and our system achieves a result close to the average level. However, we still have a long way from the state-of-arts results. Due to limitation of time and resources in this task, we have to summarize the relevant rules by extracting the sentence features of selection syntax, analyzing the grammar and summarize the rules artificially instead of observing the semantic relations of those specific words with parse tree and dependency tree. Future work will use a more effective way to capture rules to further improve the CGED. Future work will not only aim at diagnosing grammatical errors, but also explore ways to correct grammatical errors.

Acknowledgments

This work was partially supported by National Natural Science Foundation of China under Grant No. 71472068, Science and Technology Planning Project of Guangdong Province, China under Grant No. 2013B020314013, and the Innovation Training Project for College Students of Guangdong Province under Grant No.201410564290.

References

Ashwell, T. (2000). Patterns of teacher response to student writing in a multi-draft composition classroom: Is content feedback followed by form feedback the best method? *Journal of Second Language Writing*, 9, 227–257.

Chandler, J. (2003). The efficacy of various kinds of error feedback for improvement in the accuracy and fluency of L2 student writing. *Journal of Second Language Writing*, 12, 267–296.

Chang, T. H., Sung, Y. T., & Lee, Y. T. (2012). A Chinese word segmentation and POS tagging system for readability research. *In Proceedings of the 42nd Annual Meeting of the Society for Computers in Psychology (SCiP 2012)*, Minneapolis, MN.

Yong-Zhi Chen, Shih-Hung Wu, Ping-che Yang, et al. (2011). Improve the detection of improperly used Chinese characters in students' essays with error model, *Int. J. Cont. Engineering Education and Life-Long Learning*, vol. 21, no. 1, pp.103-116.

Cheng, S. M., Yu, C. H., & Chen, H. H. (2014). Chinese Word Ordering Errors Detection and Correction for Non-Native Chinese Learners. *In Proceedings of the 25th International Conference on Computational Linguistics (COLING 2014)*, Dublin, Ireland, pp. 279-289.

Chodorow, M., Dickinson, M., Israel, R., & Tetreault, J. R. (2012). Problems in Evaluating Grammatical Error Detection Systems. *In Proceedings of the*

24th International Conference on Computational Linguistics (COLING 2012), Mumbai, India, pp. 611-628

Fathman, A. K., & Whalley, E. (1990). Teacher response to student writing: Focus on form versus content. In B. Kroll (Ed.), *Second language writing: Research insights for the classroom* Cambridge, UK: Cambridge University Press, pp. 178-190.

Ferris, D. & Roberts, B. (2001). Error feedback in L2 writing classes: How explicit does it need to be? *Journal of Second Language Writing*, 10, pp. 161–184.

Leacock, C., Chodorow, M., Gamon, M., et al. (2010). *Automated Grammatical Error Detection for Language Learners*. Morgan and Claypool Publishers.

Ng, H. T., Wu, S. M., Wu, Y., Hadiwinoto, C.,Tetreault, J. (2013). The CoNLL-2013 Shared Task on Grammatical Error Correction. *In Proceedings of the 17th Conference on Computational Natural Language Learning (CoNLL-2013): Shared Task.* Sofia, Bulgaria.9 August, pp. 1-12

Ng, H.T., Wu, S.M., Briscoe, T., et al. (2014). The CoNLL-2014 shared task on grammatical error correction. *In Proceedings of the 18th Conference on Computational Natural Language Learning (CoNLL-2014): Shared Task.* Baltimore, Maryland, USA, 26-27 June, pp. 1-14

Xiong J. H., Zhao Q., Hou J.P., et al. (2014). Extended HMM and Ranking Models for Chinese Spelling Correction. *In Proceedings of the Third CIPS-SIGHAN Joint Conference on Chinese Language Processing (CLP 2014)*, Wuhan, China, 20-21 Oct., pp. 133-138.

Yu, C.H., & Chen, H.H. (2012). Detecting word ordering errors in Chinese sentences for learning Chinese as a foreign language. *In Proceedings of the 24th International Conference on Computational Linguistics (COLING 2012)*, Bombay, India, pp. 3003-3018.

Yu L.C., Lee L.H., Chang L.P. (2014).Overview of Grammatical Error Diagnosis for Learning Chinese as a Foreign Language. *In Proceedings of the 22nd International Conference on Computers in Education(ICCE 2014)*,Nara, Japan,30 Nov. - 4 Dec., pp. 42-47

Yuan Z., Felice M. (2013). Constrained Grammatical Error Correction Using Statistical Machine Translation. *In Proceedings of the 17th Conference on Computational Natural Language Learning (CoNLL-2013): Shared Task.* Sofia, Bulgaria. 9 August, pp. 52-61.

Author Index

Association for Computational Linguistics
209 N. Eighth Street
Stroudsburg, Pennsylvania 18360

ISBN 978-1-5108-0951-2

9 781510 809512

CURRAN ASSOCIATES INC.
proceedings.com

TALAf 2014: Traitement Automatique des Langues Africaines

(TALAf 2014: African Language Processing)

TALN-RECITAL 2014 Workshop

Marseille, France
1 July 2014

ISBN: 978-1-63439-519-9